The Collected Works of
Marie-Louise von Franz

MLvF

Volume 9

General Editors
Steven Buser
Leonard Cruz

Marie-Louise von Franz
1915-1998

🌸 Volume 9 🌸

C.G. Jung

His Myth in Our Time

Marie–Louise von Franz

Adapted new English version
by Alison Kappes-Bates

CHIRON PUBLICATIONS • ASHEVILLE, NORTH CAROLINA

Logo of the Foundation of Jungian Psychology, Küsnacht Switzerland:
Fons mercurialis from Rosarium Philosophorum 1550 (Fountain of Life).

C. G. Jung - Sein Mythos in unserer Zeit,
Stiftung für Jung'sche Psychologie, ©2007
Previously published by Walter Verlag, ©1996

Adapted new English version by Alison Kappes-Bates
Cover Image by Martina Ott
Interior and cover design by Danijela Mijailovic

ISBN 978-1-68503-191-6 paperback
ISBN 978-1-68503-192-3 hardcover

◆

A Note on the Compilation of
The Collected Works of
Marie–Louise von Franz

Marie-Louise von Franz was blessed with a keen intellect and an outstanding memory. As a classical philologist with a doctorate in Latin and Greek, she was familiar with the writings of the ancient philosophers. She was exceptionally well read. Her private library alone contained over 8,000 books and writings. She was also both diligent and conscientious in her work. She met C.G. Jung in her youth and found him to be an excellent teacher and mentor. She went on to become a close confidant and collaborator, particularly in his work on alchemy. Jung's psychological observations and the conclusions and hypotheses he drew from them about the structures of the unconscious psyche increasingly coincided with her own observations. Marie-Louise von Franz was imbued with an inexhaustible creativity that inspired her well into her old age. She devoted her last lecture to the rehabilitation of the feeling function, a subject that was of great importance to her and to C.G. Jung. Her unconditional devotion to the manifestations of the unconscious psyche was exemplary for all who met her during her lifetime, and for many who came to know her from her writings or their own dreams.

Only a few of her works survived in the form of finished manuscripts. Many of her books derived from transcriptions of her lectures, some of which were delivered in German, though most were in English. The English transcriptions were later translated into her native German. Her primary focus was always on the psychological context and background of her books, and less on their linguistic delivery. Some publishers therefore took the liberty of adding or changing certain things in her texts to make it easier for the reader, as they thought. After realizing what they had done, Marie-Louise von Franz indignantly insisted on her original text being used, claiming that what she had written was what she had wanted to express. Since then, many of her works have been translated into 23 languages, with editions of varying quality being used as the basis for translations into local languages.

In addition to the publishing rights, Marie-Louise von Franz left to the Foundation for Jungian Psychology a handwritten list in which she noted which editions of her books she considered to be the best and most accurate. After her death in 1998, the members of the Foundation decided to republish all of her works in German in accordance with her list. We have respectfully endeavored to remain as close as possible to her original tone, to correct obvious audio or transcription errors, to add footnotes to facilitate understanding, and to supplement texts when written records or tape recordings of her lectures were available. In some instances, this has resulted in greatly altered and revised publications, which we consider to be the basis for all new translations.

For the publication of the Collected Works of Marie-Louise von Franz by Chiron Publications, the Stiftung commissioned Alison Kappes-Bates, Hirzel, a professional translator who knew Marie-Louise von Franz for over 30 years and was a close companion until her death, to translate into English the newly-revised texts in German. Mark Kyburz, Zürich, an experienced translator of Jungian texts, re-edited the first three English volumes of Archetypal Symbols in Fairytales, translated Volumes 4 and 5, and will translate further volumes. The Foundation for Jungian Psychology is responsible for the content and the design, the latter having been created in close consultation with Chiron Publication, Asheville.

On behalf of the Foundation for Jungian Psychology,
Küsnacht, April 24, 2023
PD Dr. Hansueli F. Etter

Foreword

After the death of C.G. Jung, three works were published about him that were authored by women who were particularly close to him. All three had been significant collaborators and had worked as independent analysts. Aniela Jaffé (1903-1991), who had been closely associated with Jung since 1937 and served as his private secretary from 1955 until his death, edited the book *Memories, Dreams, Reflections* by C.G. Jung, first published in German in 1962. In 1972, Marie-Louise von Franz published the German edition of *C.G. Jung, His Myth in Our Time*. And finally, in 1974, Barbara Hannah (1891-1986) published the original English edition of her book *C.G. Jung, His Life and Work*, which drew upon her memories of her long affiliation with Jung.

Marie-Louise von Franz (1915-1998), who began her analysis with Jung as a student, became his most important collaborator on alchemy, and the publication of her *Collected Works* in revised form by Chiron, Asheville, attest to the continued interest in her publications. This book on the myth behind Jung's life shows how Jung as a psychiatrist "was interested not only in the specific diseases of the soul, but even more in the mysteries of the human soul itself, for the latter is par excellence behind all the activities of man." Jung remarked to Marie-Louise von Franz that those who suffer and try to implement his thoughts in their own lives would carry on his work, rather than "those who satisfy their ambition by preaching them to others." Shortly before his death, Jung is said to have remarked to Marie-Louise von Franz that the discovery of the unconscious provided humankind with two ways of seeing the world, and this fact, according to Marie-Louise von Franz, would have unforeseeable consequences for all branches of science.

In a modest footnote at the end of her Preface, Marie-Louise von Franz tells us that, throughout her life, she had become convinced by Jung's ideas. She does not, however, consider them to be universally valid, absolute, scientific truth. But it was Jung's view of things that had offered her the most plausible explanations about her own inner experiences. Furthermore, in her therapeutic work, she had seen that many other people felt the same way. In an unpublished manuscript written by Marie-Louise von Franz in 1969, eight years after Jung's death, she tells us what was most valuable to her in her relationship with Jung: "The collective unconscious represents the principle of charity and also of Eros. Its counterpart is the principle of power.... All of us who remember knowing him have learned that he was the most connected person imaginable. Independent and solitary, yet intensely connected at the same time, he not only taught us, but also exemplified, how a person can become individually conscious and, at the same time, be connected to humanity.... Lived consciously, this archetype brings about ... freedom. This freedom, as the highest human emotional value, is, in my opinion, the most precious gift Jung has given us."

With this book, Marie-Louise von Franz demonstrates that certain psychological processes in Jung's life and work are in mysterious correspondence with the inner experience of numerous modern people, which convinced Jung of the existence of a collective human unconscious. For Marie-Louise von Franz, nothing else leads further than Jung's careful and sincere attempt to interpret the manifestations of the collective psyche, common to all human beings. To her mind, Jung's myth also illuminates the meaning behind the new age of Aquarius into which we are now entering.

This revised English edition reflects the revised German edition that was published by the Foundation for Jungian Psychology in 2007. We are greatly indebted to Ms. Alison Kappes-Bates (Hirzel) for her careful work in preparing this new edition.

On behalf of the Foundation for Jungian Psychology, Küsnacht, November 30, 2022.

PD Dr. Hansueli Etter
President

Table of Contents

In patientia vestra possidebitis animas vestras
Luke 21.19

Foreword to the
Second Edition in German

1   Although quite some time has gone by, I believe the content of this book to still be valid. Apart from adding some comments relating to the situation today, no changes have therefore been undertaken.

2   Myths remain vital longer than a human life does, and it is my belief that Jung's myth will come to have more meaning in the future for he has illuminated the meaning of the Age of Aquarius that we are now entering. He does not claim to have found *the* answer to our problems, but I believe he has given us a point of reference we desperately need in the confusing and chaotic time we now live in.

3   I am now left with only the pleasant task of thanking Mrs. Hannelore Isler for her help in revising this text, along with Mrs. Karin Isler for creating the Index. My special thanks go to Dr. René Malamud, who took upon himself the arduous task of bringing the footnotes up to date.*

Küsnacht, May 1995   *Marie-Louise von Franz*

*This revised English edition reflects the revised German edition that was published by our Foundation in 2007. We are greatly indebted to Ms. Alison Kappes for her careful work in preparing this new edition.

◆

Introduction

4 To write about C.G. Jung's effect both in and on the culture of our day is an uncommonly difficult assignment. While outstanding individuals are, as a rule, chiefly or exclusively influential in their own professional fields, in Jung's case, his original, creative discoveries and ideas had to do with the whole human being and have therefore awakened echoes in the most varied areas outside that of psychology: his concept of synchronicity, for example, in atomic physics and Sinology; his psychological interpretation of religious phenomena in the human psyche in theology; his fundamental view of man in anthropology and ethnology; his contributions to the study of occult phenomena in parapsychology – to mention only a few instances. Because Jung's work encompasses so many varied fields of interest, his influence on our cultural life has made itself felt only gradually and, in my opinion, is still only in its beginnings. Today, interest in Jung is growing year by year, especially among the younger generation. Accordingly, the growth of his influence is still in its early stages; 30 years from now we will, in all probability, be able to discuss his work in very different terms than we do today. In other words, Jung was so far ahead of his time that people are only gradually beginning to catch up with his discoveries. There is also the fact that his perceptions and insights are never superficial but are so astonishingly original that many people must overcome a certain fear of innovation before they are able to approach them with an open mind. Furthermore, his published works include an enormous amount of detailed material from many fields, and the reader must work through this wealth of information in order to be able to follow him.

5   Jung once remarked that "anything that is good is expensive. It takes time, it requires your patience and no end of it."[1] Since this was the spirit in which he worked, it is not surprising that Jung's influence has been slow in making itself felt. The reader must pay close attention to his patient reflections, involving the painstaking elucidation of much factual material, in order to understand what Jung is aiming at.

6   In addition to the above considerations, there is a further characteristic which distinguishes both Jung's personality and his work quite fundamentally from all other cultural achievements up to the present time. This lies in the constellation of the "unconscious" whose creative nature Jung was the first to scientifically discover.[2] He allowed this unconscious to have a say directly in what he wrote, especially in his later work ("Everything I have written has a double bottom," he once said.) So that the reader finds, on the one hand, a logically understandable argument, but on the other, he finds himself simultaneously exposed to the impact of this "other voice" of the unconscious that either grips him or frightens him. This "other voice" can be heard, for example, in Jung's special way of reviving the original etymological meaning of words[3] and in how he allows both feeling and imaginative elements to enter into his scientific exposition.

7   These circumstances make it difficult to assess Jung's impact on our world with any accuracy for it was, and is still today, two-fold: the effect of his personality and of his work on the one hand, and the impact of that greater entity, the unconscious, to which he was so committed, on the other hand.

8   Like few other important people, Jung bothered very little about world recognition of his work, and he cared less and less about it as he grew older. Simultaneously, he made every possible effort to formulate his ideas in a generally understandable way, to make them accessible to his fellow men. Evidence of this is the very large

---

[1] E.A. Bennet, *C.G. Jung*, London 1961, p. 152.
[2] Freud, as is well known, regarded the unconscious as an epiphenomenon, or secondary phenomenon, consisting of repressed incestuous desires which could just as well be conscious.
[3] Unfortunately, this double aspect of Jung's writings has not been preserved in the monumental English edition of his *Collected Works*, translated by R.F.C. Hull.

correspondence he left behind him, the innumerable letters in which he made every effort to explain his standpoint to the many people who wrote to him with various questions. He did it partly to avoid being left alone with his ideas, but even more because he was convinced that the fate of the Western world depended to a considerable extent on the realization of those ideas. For as he saw it, it is not only the individual who is prone to psychic illness as a result of a wrong attitude toward the unconscious; the same thing can also happen to a nation as a whole. This touches upon yet another point which adds to the difficulty of giving an adequate description of Jung's impact on our culture: His work reaches beyond the academic sphere into all the other areas of life. Jung was interested not only in the specific illnesses of the soul, but even more in the mystery of the human psyche itself, which is the source of *all* human activities. No house was ever built, no work of art ever created, no scientific discovery ever made, no religious rite ever observed without the participation of the human psyche. Even the atomic bomb, which may one day annihilate all of us, had its origin in the psyche of a few physicists. Anything that can be discovered about the natural laws that hold good in the human psyche will also be valid for all aspects of human existence. It is therefore not putting the case too strongly to say that the humanities, the natural sciences, religions, arts, as well as both the sociological and the individual behaviour of human beings, appear in an entirely new light as a result of the discovery of the unconscious. Because of this, both the value we set upon our culture and even, perhaps, its very survival, depends upon our "right" or "wrong" understanding of the unconscious.

9   Strangely enough, Jung's discoveries were less accepted – or were accepted more slowly – within his own profession of academic psychiatry than in many others. Leaders in other scientific fields were the first to make fruitful use of his discoveries and ideas, and it has always been the individual person who reacted to what he found in Jung's work. Jung has never been fashionable; his work has never been the source of any sort of -ism: he always rejected

movements and slogans. Two celebrations were held in honour of this great man on his 80th birthday. To the first occasion, invitations were sent to a carefully selected list of guests, all of whom were official representatives of his psychology. This was a rather stiff event that tired him. To the evening party, anyone who wanted to see the great man was admitted: students, patients, Jung's gardener, neighbours from Bollingen – a great variety of "important" and "unimportant" people. The atmosphere was warm and animated, and Jung stayed longer than had been anticipated. On the way home, he said, "Yes, *those* are the people who will carry on my work, single individuals who are suffering and seeking, and who try to take my ideas seriously in their own lives, not the ones who satisfy their vanity by preaching them to others."

10   It would be inaccurate, however, to say that Jung did not exert a considerable influence in his chosen profession. It merely took longer for his achievements to be recognized by other psychologists, and his unfortunate association with Sigmund Freud and their later separation quite unnecessarily aroused so much emotion that the objective issues involved have frequently been overlooked. Something quite different from merely personal problems lay behind that conflict: the fundamental question was whether the unconscious is only an epiphenomenon of consciousness, arising from repressions (Freud), or whether, as Jung thought, it is the autonomous creative matrix of normal, psychic life. Here the basic differences emerged, and they remain today.

11   But what, in fact, *is* this unconscious that played such an unforeseeably far-reaching part in Jung's life and work? Actually, it is just a modern technical expression for an inner experience which is as old as mankind, the experience that occurs when something alien and unknown overwhelms us from within, when the working of inner forces suddenly changes our lives, when we have dreams or inspirations or hunches which we know we have not "made up" but which come to us from a psychic "outside" and push their way into consciousness. In earlier times, these effects were ascribed to a divine fluid (mana) or to a god or demon or "spirit." Such names gave

expression to the feeling of an objective, alien and autonomous presence[4], as well as to a sense of something overwhelming to which the conscious ego has to submit. Jung himself had experiences of such dreams, hunches and effects from very early on in his youth, and he writes about them in his autobiography, *Memories, Dreams, Reflections*[5]. Although he may have had more numerous and intense experiences of this sort, and perceived them and taken them more seriously than is the rule, they are by no means rare. In the past, and even today among people who live close to nature, they are a part of the normal occurrences of life. Every primitive medicine man depends on his visions and dreams; every hunter knows about supernatural promptings and hunches; every genuinely religious person has at some time or other during his life had such inner experiences. Even within the context of our Western civilization, far more people than we know of have these kinds of experiences, though they rarely speak openly about them for fear of being met by the rationalistic rejection by the people around them. Jung was even interested in the taboo, so-called parapsychological manifestations of the psyche. Brought up in a rural environment during his early childhood, he found them familiar, as they are to all people who live close to nature, and they awakened his curiosity. His first published work, his dissertation[6], deals with such phenomena. Jung discovered that the most important of the "spirits" who manifested themselves during the sittings described was an as yet unintegrated part of the personality of the young medium, and that this part became, in the course of her later growth, an essential part of herself and thereafter ceased to appear autonomously as a "spook." Thus, an important step in the direction of his later work was taken during this early period: he gained the insight that there are objective psychic phenomena which, though unconscious, nevertheless belong to the personality, and that they are not repressed but are nascent psychic contents. He devoted the entire body of his later

---

[4] Cf. C.G. Jung, *Memories, Dreams, Reflections* (henceforth *Memories*), Ed. A. Jaffé, London 1989, p. 335 f.
[5] 1st Ed., Great Britain 1963.
[6] C.G. Jung, "On the Psychology of So-Called Occult Phenomena," Collected Works (henceforth *CW*) Vol. I, §§ 1 – 150.

work to the further investigation of this mystery of the creative aspect of the unconscious psyche.

12 People who have had their own major or minor experiences of the unconscious generally understand without difficulty what Jung means when he describes it. For intellectuals, however, who seek exact definitions, the concept of the unconscious is a stumbling block. We are not in a position to predicate anything about the ultimate nature of these phenomena, for the simple reason that the psyche that is observing them is the same psyche that produces the experience. We must, therefore, in all honesty resign ourselves to an attempt to order and describe these experiences without concluding anything definite about their ultimate nature. One may say that Jung's understanding of the unconscious marks the end of 19th-century scientific rationalism. This, in my opinion, is the basic cause of all the disputes that have never ceased to flare up concerning his work. On closer consideration, however, this point is in fact not really material. The leading natural scientists of our time have long since discarded the illusion that man can acquire an absolute, permanently valid knowledge of nature – atomic physicists have resigned themselves for a long time now to describing matter, instead of defining it – and the time has come for psychology to make a corresponding advance. Present basic research in all the scientific disciplines inclines more and more to support the reasonable view that even in the so-called exact sciences, like physics or mathematics, there can be no absolute truth and that the researcher's mental and general psychological condition, and along with it the *Zeitgeist* (spirit of the time) and the communicability of what one's investigations have revealed, all play a relativizing part. In psychology there is a further difficulty in that the object of the science, the psyche, is at the same time that which practices the science. In other words, we have no Archimedean point outside the psyche. Jung reached this insight early in his career and was deeply convinced of the relativity of all scientific knowledge. "As I saw it, a scientific truth was a hypothesis which might be adequate for the moment but was not to be preserved as an article of faith for all

time."[7] His own theories were for him never more than "suggestions and attempts at the formulation of a new scientific psychology based in the first place upon immediate experience with human beings."[8] "I have set up neither a system nor a general theory, but have merely formulated auxiliary concepts to serve me as tools. ..."[9] For "I have never been inclined to think that our senses were capable of perceiving all forms of being. ... All comprehension and all that is comprehended is in itself psychic, and to that extent we are hopelessly cooped up in an exclusively psychic world."[10] Thus, there can be no generally valid truth, although a *true description* of psychic data can indeed be made, which can also be communicated to others, provided the data are relevant to general, human experience. If this were not the case, we would all be isolated in hopeless subjectivity and would only be able to talk past one another. That this is not the rule is in part owing to the fact that when one gives expression to ideas that are "in the air" or which are constellated psychologically within the collective, then they are apt to meet with a certain acceptance.

13   But this acceptance of the unconscious has duplicated our image of the world with unforeseeable consequences for all scientific disciplines. The subjective state of the observer can no longer be dismissed as it was in the past, and even computers are dependent upon the psychology of their programmers. This new awareness brings us back full circle – but on a higher level – to the situation in which *homo religiosus* of earliest times felt himself exposed to certain unknown psychic powers, both good and evil, and with which he had to learn to come to terms.

14   As he had no wish to conceal the subjective element in his work, Jung gave a graphic description, in his *Memories, Dreams, Reflections*, of the gradual emergence of his conscious ego (which he called "No. 1") out of the objective-psychic background ("No. 2"). During this process, it gradually became painfully clear to him that

---

[7] *Memories*, p. 174.
[8] Foreword to Jolande Jacobi, *The Psychology of C.G. Jung*, New Haven and London 1973.
[9] C.G. Jung, "Religion and Psychology: A reply to Martin Buber," CW 18, §§ 1499 – 1513.
[10] *Memories*, p. 385.

the majority of people around him tried as hard as possible to forget their "No. 2," that is, the unconscious, and were offended when he wanted to talk about it. Moreover, his loyalty to the relation to the inner "genius" or "daimon," as one might also call it, provoked mistrust and aversion in many people, almost as if he himself appeared to them as that daimon of the unconscious of which they were so afraid. This still seems to me to be the case, more or less, even today: the name of Jung seldom leaves people cold; one almost always comes up against emotionally charged rejection or enthusiasm whenever one mentions him. Only rarely does one meet with detached appraisal.[11] On closer examination, however, these reactions are generally directed at that god or demon, the unconscious, whose existence many modern people do not wish to recognize, for which reason they frequently make all sorts of quibbling objections to depth psychology, without noticing that they are motivated by fear. Jung's work is therefore conspicuous as a stumbling block in the contemporary intellectual scene. It is too fundamental, in a sense, to be modern.

15   What Jung said in praise of Freud, that he was inspired, is also true of Jung himself. He was an inspired person, in the sense that he was gripped by his numinous inner experiences. As he writes, "… at the source of the great confessional religions as well as of many smaller mystical movements we find individual historical personalities whose lives were distinguished by numinous experiences." Such people are not pathological, however, for the "significant difference … between merely pathological cases and 'inspired' personalities is that sooner or later the latter find an extensive following and can therefore transmit their effect down the centuries … they are talking of something that is 'in the air' and is 'spoken from the heart.'"[12] "The wise man who is not heeded is counted a fool,

---

[11] As L.L. Whyte writes, in *The Unconscious before Freud*, the concept of the unconscious has many antecedents in Western philosophy and is conceived in many different ways. Jung is scarcely mentioned in this volume, unfortunately, and then incorrectly interpreted, but the reader can at least obtain a picture of the pre-Freudian conceptions of the unconscious in philosophy. Friedrich Seifert, in *Seele und Bewusstsein*, attempts to give Jung his place in the history of philosophy. This work is very much worth reading, especially since the author has had practical psychological experience. His criticism of Heidegger (p. 246) seems to me quite just, and is recommended.
[12] Cf. *Mysterium Coniunctionis*, CW 14, § 782.

and the fool who proclaims the general folly first and loudest passes for a prophet and Führer, and sometimes it is luckily the other way round."[13] Whenever a great many people are persuaded or converted through the effect of a conspicuous personality, it always turns out that he is consciously formulating precisely those ideas and views which will serve to compensate[14] some general psychic distress, and that these images have broken through from the unconscious as part of his personal experience but are also "constellated" in the unconscious of many other people. Throughout the course of history, such inspired personalities have almost always presented their own inner experiences as new *religious* ideals and truths, more often than not with the "metaphysical" claim of being the one ultimate revealed truth. Even philosophies and scientific theories are not always without such claims to general validity. But we ought to realize how pitiably relative are all our convictions, even the deepest ones, in face of the historical and international multiplicity of religious images and "ultimate" truths. For this reason, Jung, though he was an inspired personality, consciously and expressly rejected any such "religious" or other "absolute" claim to validity for his ideas and truths. "In view of this extremely uncertain situation," he writes,[15] "it seems to me very much more cautious and reasonable to take cognizance of the fact that there is not only a psychic but also a psychoid[16] unconscious, before presuming to pronounce meta-physical judgments. ... There is no need to fear that the inner experience will thereby be deprived of its reality and vitality." This places the individual at the centre of the field of attention.[17]

16   In the following pages, I shall not enter into the many superficial, ephemeral personal disputes about Jung's work. Instead, I shall try to place both Jung as a man and the influence of his work in a wider historical perspective, that of the history of our Western culture.[18]

---

[13] Ibid., § 783.
[14] "Compensate": to complete a conscious one-sidedness, or balance it, in the direction of wholeness.
[15] *Mysterium Coniunctionis*, CW 14, § 788.
[16] That is, an unconscious behind which something unknowable and trans-psychic is at work.
[17] *Mysterium Coniunctionis*, CW 14, § 788 – 789.
[18] An excellent account of Jung's theories in relation to immediate philosophical trends can be found in Peter Seidmann, *Der Weg der Tiefenpsychologie in geistesgeschichtlicher Perspektive*.

Whereas, with few exceptions, Jung's own contemporaries were, if anything, alienated by his work, later generations have moved so far, with the changes in our *Zeitgeist*, that it is easier for them to understand it. But the wheel of time will have to revolve still further before the wider public will begin to see what Jung meant. Even before the First World War, Jung, during a lonely crisis, lived through an inner death and spiritual renewal, of the sort which, after two great world catastrophes, has today become more common among cultivated Europeans and Americans. It is increasingly clear that our cultural values have been undermined, so that even among the masses, and especially among today's youth, there are individuals who are seeking, not so much the destruction of the old, as something new on which to build. And because the destruction has been so widespread and has gone so deep, this new foundation must be located in the depths, in the most natural, primordial and most universally human core of existence. When I once remarked to Jung that his psychological insights and his attitude to the unconscious seemed to me to be in many respects the same as those of the most archaic religions – for example, shamanism, or the religion of the Naskapi Indians, who have neither priest nor ritual but who merely follow their dreams which they believe are sent by the "immortal great man in the heart" – Jung answered with a laugh, "Well, that's nothing to be ashamed of. It is an honour!" The pastor's son, for whom the church now meant only death,[19] came early to the painful recognition that ecclesiastical religion could give him no answers. Instead, he found the way to illumination in the depths of his own soul, in the same place where modern youth, for example, are looking for it today, though for the most part through drugs rather than through direct conscious confrontation. The basis and substance of Jung's entire life and work do not lie in the traditions and religions which have become contents of collective consciousness, but rather in that primordial experience which is the final source of these contents: the encounter of the single individual with his own god or daimon, his struggle with the overpowering

---

[19] *Memories*, p. 73. ". . . the church is a place I should not go to. It is not life which is there, but death."

emotions, affects, fantasies and creative inspirations, and obstacles which come to light from within. It is only natural, therefore, that the majority of those who understand it are people for whom the life of all those doctrines that are preached, taught, and believed in has lost its meaning and who are therefore forced, as Jung himself was, to bend down without prejudice and look into the despised corner of their own unconscious psyche for signs that might point the way.

17   Whoever has observed, over the last decade or so, the development of unconscious influences on the *Zeitgeist* and on the present crisis in our culture, can see that those same archetypal images that live behind Jung's work and that gripped him are having an ever greater impact on the masses these days, that Jung's "myth" is becoming manifest all over the world in a virulent and to some extent negative form, and that Jung's conscious attitude towards and confrontation with the contents of this myth are by no means everywhere known or popular. The reasons for this will be discussed later, but here it is necessary at least to glance at the effects of Jung's "myth" as he lived it, partly parallel and partly in opposition to the spiritual currents of our time. This is also why I have not taken the dates of Jung's external biography or a chronological or systematic presentation of the development of his ideas as the leitmotif or theme of this book[20], but have instead tried to follow the basic melody of his inner myth.[21]

---

[20] It is not the intention of this volume to spare the reader a study of Jung's work. A short survey can be found in Gerhard Wehr, *Portrait of Jung*, or E.A. Bennet, *What Jung Really Said*.

[21] As he reads the following pages the reader will notice that Jung's ideas carry conviction for me. This should not be understood as meaning that I regard them as universally valid, 'absolute' scientific truths. However, since my youth, I have myself had inner experiences for which Jung's discoveries have offered me the most illuminating explanation to date, and I have seen that it is the same with many people. Thus, I am convinced on the one hand that certain background processes in Jung's life and work parallel those of numerous modern men and women, and on the other hand that Jung's careful and honest attempt to interpret them leads farther than any other explanation known to me.

Chapter 1

The Underground God

Nietzsche's cry, "God is dead!" – which was much discussed in the press not long ago[1] – gives succinct expression to an experience that troubled Jung when he was still a boy. Born on July 26, 1875, in Kesswil (Thurgau), he lived his early years in the parsonage at Laufen, and at a very early age felt oppressed by the sombre atmosphere around him. Unavoidably, he witnessed burials in the nearby churchyard and was told that "Lord Jesus had taken them to Himself", and through a misunderstanding of a child's prayer that he was taught, he even came to the conviction that Jesus was a "man-eater."[2] However, this darkening of the Christ-image cannot be accounted for merely by such outer events, but was also the result of the general atmosphere prevailing in a Christian household at that time, a psychic atmosphere in which religious faith had lost its original vitality and had, to a large extent, rigidified into a collective-conscious way of living. Jung's father, Pastor Johannes Paul Achilles Jung, had, in the depths of his being, gradually lost his faith; he tried desperately and with great suffering to replace it with a consciously assumed point of view. Jung's mother, on the other hand, assumed a dual attitude, as is often the case with people in whom feeling comes first. On the surface, she took part in the collective Christian way of life, but, at bottom, her own personal *religio*[3] was that of nature, animals, the waters, the forest. From time to time, her son had

---

[1] Especially *Time* Magazine, 8th April 1966. In this connection cf. William Braden, *The Age of Aquarius*, pp. 263 ff. (I am indebted to Fowler McCormick for calling this book to my attention.) Instead of the "God is dead" motif, certain theologians (Ernst Bloch; Jürgen Moltmann, *Theologie der Hoffnung*) have recently proclaimed a "God of hope." The "God is dead" movement originated with T.J. Altizer (*The Gospel of Christian Atheism*). Altizer used the writings of Mircea Eliade as support, ignoring the work of Jung, though he must have known of it.

[2] *Memories*, p. 25.

[3] In the sense of careful attention to and respect for a dominant or "supreme" value.

surprising, shocking, and helpful glimpses into these depths, although she never discussed such matters with him.

19   But what does it really mean when people say that "God is dead"? If there is a God independent of human experience, one may suppose that such a fashionable catchword would not bother him much! The point at issue is rather the fact that our image of God, or our definition of him, is dead for us although for past generations the word was a name for something that was alive in the highest degree and represented for them the supreme value. The "something" that was so alive in their image of God – the psychologically effective power that evoked in them an impressive reverence for their "God" – is, however, not dead (as Jung learned later and sought to verify). God was never really "captured" in that man-made image, still less in the definitions, so that he is free to leave them behind and "reveal" himself anew. Instead of saying with Nietzsche, "God is dead," it would have been closer to the truth, in Jung's opinion, to say,[4] "…the highest value, which gives life and meaning, has got lost. God has put off our image and where shall we find him again?"

20   It is by no means rare for a cultural community to lose its "god" and to fall thereby into a severe social and psychological crisis; it is a typical occurrence and has often repeated itself throughout the course of history. Hence, the gods of many religions "die": this motif even has a central place in the Christian mystery itself, in the image of the crucifixion, the entombment of Christ and his resurrection. "I only know," Jung says therefore[5], "…and here I am expressing what countless other people know – that the present is a time of God's death and disappearance. The myth says he was not to be found where his body was laid. 'Body' means the outward, visible form, the erstwhile but ephemeral setting for the highest value."

21   The Christian myth says further that the value rose again in a miraculous manner, *but transformed.*[6] This insight, which Jung expresses in a work published in 1938, harks back in some ways to a profound experience of his own, namely to his earliest

---

[4] Cf. "Psychology and Religion" (The Terry Lectures of 1937), CW 11, §§ 142 ff.
[5] Ibid., § 149.
[6] Italics by the author.

remembered dream, that he had during his third or fourth year. As Jung later remarked[7], the first dream that one can recall from childhood often sets forth in symbolic form, the essence of an entire life, or of the first part of life. It reflects, so to speak, a piece of the "inner fate" into which the individual is born. At the centre of Jung's own childhood dream was a mysterious content that was destined to form the fateful background of his life and work. He writes:[8]

22   The vicarage stood quite alone near Laufen castle, and there was a big meadow stretching back from the sexton's farm. In the dream I was in this meadow. Suddenly I discovered a dark, rectangular, stone-lined hole in the ground. I had never seen it before. I ran forward curiously and peered down into it. Then I saw a stone stairway leading down. Hesitantly and fearfully, I descended. At the bottom was a doorway with a round arch, closed off by a green curtain. It was a big, heavy curtain of worked stuff like brocade, and it looked very sumptuous. Curious to see what might be hidden behind, I pushed it aside. I saw before me in the dim light a rectangular chamber about thirty feet long. The ceiling was arched and of hewn stone. The floor was laid with flagstones, and in the center a red carpet ran from the entrance to a low platform. On this platform stood a wonderfully rich golden throne... Something was standing on it which I thought at first was a tree trunk twelve to fifteen feet high and about one and a half to two feet thick. It was a huge thing, reaching almost to the ceiling. But it was of a curious composition: it was made of skin and naked flesh and no hair. On the very top of the head was a single eye, gazing motionlessly upward.

23   It was fairly light in the room, although there were no windows and no apparent source of light. Above the head, however, was an aura of brightness. The thing did not move,

---

[7] Cf. his seminars on children's dreams, given at the Federal Institute of Technology (ETH) in Zurich, 1936/37, 1938/39 and 1939/40.
[8] *Memories*, p. 26 ff.

yet I had the feeling that it might at any moment crawl off the throne like a worm and creep toward me. I was paralyzed with terror. At that moment I heard from outside and above me my mother's voice. She called out, 'Yes, just look at him. That is the man-eater!' That intensified my terror still more, and I awoke sweating and scared to death.

24 Before this dream, the small boy, as mentioned above, had already associated images full of anxiety with the figure of Jesus and, through misunderstanding a children's prayer, had even picked up the notion that Jesus was a "man-eater."

25 I could never make out [Jung continues, in his account of the dream] whether my mother meant, 'That is the man-eater', or 'That is the man-eater!' In the first case she would have meant that not Lord Jesus . . . was the devourer of little children, but the phallus; in the second case that the 'man-eater' in general was symbolized by the phallus, so that the dark Lord Jesus . . . and the phallus were identical.

26 As Jung himself realized, the hole in the meadow represented a grave, whose green curtain symbolizes the mystery of earth with her covering of green vegetation.

27 The abstract significance of the phallus is shown by the fact that it was enthroned by itself, "ithyphallically." . . . the phallus of this dream seems to be a subterranean God "not to be named." . . . Lord Jesus never became quite real for me, never quite acceptable . . . for again and again I would think of his underground counterpart . . . something nonhuman and underworldly, which gazed fixedly upward and fed on human flesh. This dream "was an initiation into the realm of darkness. My intellectual life had its unconscious beginnings at that time."

28 A volume could be written about this mysterious dream symbol, so laden with meanings. In the first place, Jung himself saw in it a birth, the birth of his intellectual life. According to the ancient Roman view, the phallus symbolizes a man's secret "genius," the source of his physical and mental creative power, the dispenser of all his inspired or brilliant ideas and of his buoyant joy in life and, as such, every Roman offered sacrifices to his "genius" on his birthday. Later on, this "genius" often radiated from Jung's personality, in the jovial, "festive" atmosphere he created around him, in his cheerfulness and openness to any and every kind of joke, in his enormous vitality, and above all in his life-long commitment to the inner creative spirit, which drove him relentlessly to ever more research and creativity. This spirit was also the source of an unusually large capacity for love, which both enlivened and burdened his existence. Jung had to an extraordinary degree the gift of empathy, almost to the point of being mediumistic[9]; and of participation, of sympathy, and of human warmth for his family, his friends, his patients, and, in the end, for all mankind. He was always open to any person, as a matter of course, with a wordless acceptance and without reference to race or social standing. But his capacity for love was also a source of many disappointments and of much suffering and was one of the reasons he suffered to the very brink of despair during the two world wars through which he lived, even though, being Swiss, they did not touch him personally. Jung shared this quality of intensive Eros with other Swiss, like Nicholas von Flüe, Henri Dunant, and Pestalozzi[10], all of them men who turned toward their suffering fellow men in an attitude of love and who found their vocation through this attitude rather than in political or academic power struggles.

---

[9] At the moment the wife of one of his colleagues committed suicide – a woman whom he had seen only a few times – he fainted, while the husband, who happened to be talking to Jung at the time, noticed nothing. Cf. for example, an experience noted in *Memories*, 159.
[10] For the relation between Jung's ideas and those of Pestalozzi, cf. P. Seidmann, *Der Weg der Tiefenpsychologie in geistesgeschichtlicher Perspektive*, pp. 119ff, and Jung, *The Practice of Psychotherapy*, CW 16, §539.

29   "Jung was direct and primitively vital to a rare degree," testifies Otto Händler[11], for example. "He met men, things and ideas with his whole being, in a genuine confrontation. This quality of greeting openly whatever came his way was bound up with an immediate impressionability and a deep capacity for suffering." One of his pupils[12] writes, "This is the first characteristic one encountered in Jung: his respect for the other person . . . he always gave the same lively attention to whatever I had come to consult him about. . . .The small as well as the larger issues seemed to assume in his mind . . . the quality of glowing but transparent colours, reflecting alight not their own, on a broad canvas." He was a passionate man with a clear mind which could draw on the centuries of human thought, and he possessed that capacity for "wonder" and for never taking anything for granted, which makes everything seem new and fresh. His unusually clear consciousness made it possible for him to bear the loneliness which unavoidably surrounds such greatness; at the same time, it enabled him to give himself unreservedly to his work, his patients, his family, and his friends. What distinguished Jung's personality more than anything else, and which was especially conspicuous when face to face with him, was, in my opinion, his unqualified integrity and outspokenness – an honesty that stood firm even in those areas of conversation in which most people evade the issue in embarrassment and pseudo-tactful politeness. It is true that he also learned, through many disappointments, to shrug diplomatically and keep silent. But whenever he gave his respect or friendship to another person, he related to the other with such utter simplicity and truthfulness that the other was almost forced into awareness of the background darkness in himself. Many of Jung's closest friends were themselves creative[13] and were able to understand something about a fate ruled by the "genius," because they too had been gripped by a "daimon." To other people he remained all his life a sympathetic, natural man, but a man whose "secret" seemed

---

[11] *Wege zum Menschen*, Göttingen 1962. Cf. also G. Wehr, p. 144.
[12] A.I. Allenby, *Contact with Jung*, Ed. By M. Fordham, Tavistock Publications, London 1963, p. 67 ff. Cf. also J.-L. Brunneton, "Jung, l'homme, sa vie, son caractère," *Revue d'Allemagne 7*, No. 70, Paris 1933.
[13] On Richard Wilhelm cf. *Memories*, p. 405 f.

incomprehensible or even, at times, uncanny. Women, who are by nature closer to the principle of Eros than to that of Logos, understood him better as a rule than men did. For this reason, there were many women among the first generation of his pupils who helped to make his ideas known. In the first instance, his own wife encouraged and enriched his work.[14] Among others, special mention is due to Toni Wolff[15], Jung's friend and colleague, who was for many years the President and the animating spirit of the Psychological Club of Zurich, and to M. Esther Harding[16] and Eleanor Bertine[17], founders of the Analytical Psychology Club of New York and later founding members of the C.G. Jung Foundation for Analytical Psychology. Also widely known are Barbara Hannah[18], Rivkah Kluger (Schärf)[19], Frances Wickes[20], Linda Fierz-David[21], Cornelia Brunner,[22] and many others. Aniela Jaffé[23] and Jolande Jacobi[24] share the special merit of having made Jung's work more understandable to the general public.

30   Jung married Emma Jung (Rauschenbach) of Schaffhausen (in 1903). They had five children, four daughters and one son. He loved his family deeply and spent much time with them, and in *Memories, Dreams, Reflections*[25] he reveals how much they meant to him and how they helped him to avoid being completely swallowed up by the demands of the creative demon.

---

[14] See Emma Jung and Marie-Louise von Franz, *The Grail Legend*, Princeton University Press, New Jersey 1998; and Emma Jung, *Animus and Anima*, Spring Publications, Washington 2008.

[15] Cf. *Studies in Jungian Psychology*, Translated by Eugene M.E. Rolfe, New York, in press.

[16] See *The Way of All Women*, Colorado 2001; *Woman's Mysteries*, Colorado 2001; *Psychic Energy*, New Jersey 1973; *Journey into Self*, Sigo Press 1991; *The "I" and the "Not-I"*, New Jersey 1974; and *The Parental Image*, Toronto 2003.

[17] Cf. *Human Relationships*, London 1958; and *Jung's Contribution to Our Time*, New York 1968.

[18] *Striving Towards Wholeness*, C.G. Jung Foundation, New York 1971; "The Beyond," *Quadrant*, Connecticut 1969; *C.G. Jung: His Life and Work*, New York 1976; *Active Imagination: Encounters with the Soul*, Sigo Press 1981.

[19] Cf. *Satan in the Old Testament (Studies in Jungian thought)*, Illinois 1967; *The Archetypal Significance of Gilgamesh*, Einsiedeln 1991.

[20] Cf. *The Inner World of Childhood*, New York 1927; *The Inner World of Man*, New York 1938; and *The Inner World of Choice*, New York 1963.

[21] *The Dream of Poliphilo: The Soul in Love*, New York 1950; *Dreaming in Red: The Women's Dionysian Initiation Chamber in Pompeii*, New York 2005.

[22] *Anima as Fate*, Connecticut 1986.

[23] *The Myth of Meaning in the Work of C.G. Jung*, Einsiedeln 1984; *From the Life and Work of C. G. Jung*, Einsiedeln 1989.

[24] *The Psychology of C.G. Jung*, New Haven 1973; *The Way of Individuation*, New York 1973.

[25] *Memories*, p. 189.

31   In Jung's life, the god of creative Eros turned out to be a demanding spirit that allowed him no peace and drove him relentlessly into deeper and deeper inquiry. At the end of his life, Jung himself confessed, "I have had much trouble getting along with my ideas. There was a daimon in me. . . . It overpowered me, and if I was at times ruthless it was because I was in the grip of the daimon. I could never stop at anything once attained. I had to hasten on, to catch up with my vision. Since my contemporaries, understandably, could not perceive my vision, they saw only a fool rushing ahead.

32   . . . I had no patience with people – aside from my patients. I
           had to obey an inner law. . . .
               . . . In this way I made many enemies. A creative person has
           little power over his own life. He is not free. He is captive and
           driven by his daimon.
           Shamefully
           A power wrests away the heart from us,
           For the Heavenly Ones each demand sacrifice;
           But if it should be withheld
           Never has that led to good.'
           says Hölderlin.
           The daimon of creativity has ruthlessly had its way with me."

33   In his garden in Küsnacht, Jung erected a statue to the phallic god of his first dream, a statue in the form of a *Kabir*, which, in accordance with a later dream, he named *Atma victu* (Breath of Life), and in his country place in Bollingen, he chiselled an ivy-wreath around a phallic cornerstone, which stands on the edge of the lake, with the inscription *Attei tö kallistö* (To the most beautiful Attis). The stone stands among wild anemones, the flower of Attis, a god who symbolized the eternal spring-like glory of life.

34   However, the ancient phallic god of Jung's dream embodied not only the principle of Eros and of the creative. In antiquity he was also known as Telesphoros, a guide of Asclepius, the god of medical

healing.[26] Over the entrance to the sanctuary of Asclepius in Epidaurus, there are images of Eros and Methe: love and ecstasy as healing psychic powers, and Asclepius himself has Telesphoros as a phallic *Kabir* near him or round about him as a youthful double of himself. The name Telesphoros means "he who brings completeness"; he is a god of inner transformation.

35 Jung's intense love of human beings disposed him, as it has many another doctor, to sympathize with patients who did not always deserve it. His grey schnauzer, Joggi, once caught his paw in a door, and as Jung was trying to free it, the dog bit him, simply out of pain. Jung liked to tell this story and then add with a laugh, "Patients do that, too, sometimes." A disturbed and troublesome strange woman once broke in upon the quiet of his country place in Bollingen and exhausted him with her problems. When he was reproached for not having protected himself, he replied gravely, "Life has been so cruel to some people that one cannot pass judgment on them for being warped." All his life, Jung showed the generosity and the magnanimity which are typical of the strong, and it was no accident that African natives named him "the bear" when they saw him climbing down a ladder backwards.[27] (The bear in general is especially associated with Northern medicine men, as a god of the forest from whom they draw their strength.)

36 The principle of Eros, the *compassio* of the medical healer and the creative "genius" must be seen as *the* decisive components of Jung's fate, a powerful impulse that was already revealed in his first dream. But there is something even greater, something of a transpersonal nature, behind the surface, for that first dream also contains an answer to the problem of the death of God, the problem of the age into which Jung was born, the sadness of which cast a shadow over the atmosphere of his earliest childhood. For it is the image of a *grave*-phallus. The ancient Etruscans, Romans, and Greeks used to erect these on a man's grave; it was a symbol of the *after-life of the spirit* and a guarantor of the dead man's *resurrection*.

---

[26] Cf. C.A. Meier, *Ancient Incubation and Modern Psychotherapy*, passim.
[27] They also knew him as "the man of the book" because he knew the Koran. Cf. Charles Baudouin, *Jung, Homme concrêt*, p. 347.

In Jung's dream, the dead man had obviously been a king who now, as a grave-phallus, awaited resurrection. In ancient Egypt, for example, the dead sun-god and king was honoured in this way, as Osiris, and was represented by the phallic *djed* pillar. The erection of this pillar in the grave-chamber signified the resurrection of the dead man, who had become identical with the god Osiris. He was the green or black god of the underworld and also embodied the spirit of vegetation.

37   In ancient Greece, Hermes, the messenger of the gods, was represented as a phallus and, like Osiris, was both conductor and king of the dead. As Kyllenius, he was the god of love and fertility. Hermes is the god of peacemakers, of scholars, of interpreters, of cooks, and of alchemists – all aspects that Jung realized in his own life.[28]

38   In late antiquity, the image of the phallic god Hermes gradually broadened into a cosmic image of a god-man who animates all of nature, a figure of the Anthropos as he was known to the Gnostics, and as he was described in the following words of an Ophite text:[29]

39   'They say, now, that the Egyptians, who of all men except the Phrygians are the oldest, first proclaimed to all other men ... the consecration and the worship of all the gods, as well as the powers of all the gods and their ways of manifesting themselves, and that they possess the holy and sublime mysteries of Isis, which cannot be communicated to the uninitiated. These mysteries, however, have as their object nothing other than the phallus of Osiris. . . . By Osiris they understand the water. . . . They say of the substance of the seed which is the source of all becoming that it is nothing in itself but produces and creates all becoming, since they say, "I become what I will, and I am what I am." Therefore, is it

---

[28] On Jung's attempts at peacemaking, see below. The other activities are well known. One thing, though, should be added: that Jung was an absolutely first-rate cook, who cooked for hours at a time with real devotion. Part of being a good cook, of course, is being a gourmet. He loved to let his guests guess what ingredients had gone into a soup or a sauce; I remember a *boeuf braise à la marseillaise* with a sauce of 16 ingredients!

[29] Cf. Hans Leisegang, *Die Gnosis*. p. 122 ff.

that he is unmoved, yet moves everything. For he remains what he is, even though he creates all things and becomes no created thing. This alone is good, and there is no temple where the hidden (that is, the phallus) does not stand naked before the entrance, erected from below upwards and wreathed with the fruits of all becoming. . . . And the Greeks have taken over this mystical symbol from the Egyptians and kept it until today. We see, therefore, that the Herms were worshipped by them in this form. The Kyllenians, however, paid homage to him especially as the Logos. They say, namely, "Hermes is the Logos". He is looked upon as Hermeneut[30] and creator of that which was, is and will be, and is held by them in honor, made known by means of a statue representing the male sexual member which strives from the lower to the upper things. . . . In the sanctuary at Samothrace, however, there are the statues of two naked men who are stretching both hands heavenwards and their sexual members point upwards, like the image of Hermes in Kyllene. These statues, though, are images of the original man and of the reborn pneumatic man, who is identical with the former. The Phrygians also call him a corpse because he is buried in the body as in a tomb in a grave. The same Phrygians also, in the opposite sense, call him by the name of God. . . . That is the man-named, thousand-named, unknowable, toward whom every creature is always and ever striving, each in his way."

40 This gnostic Anthropos-figure was a divine spirit *permeating all of nature*, a symbol of the "union of spiritually alive and physically dead matter,"[31] and he personified that secret which the alchemists and the Hermetic philosophes were always seeking in nature. This "subterranean" or "underground" – that is, hidden in the depths of the psyche – god-image which appeared to him in his first dream marked Jung's religious outlook for the rest of his life. In *Memories*,

---

[30] That is, translator, interpreter.
[31] Cf. *Memories*, p. 237.

he tells us how he was more and more disillusioned by and alienated from the collective Christian religious views that his father, the Church and his fellow men preached and seemed to believe. They often spoke, with an undertone of disbelief and doubt, of a "metaphysical" God as though this were a concept or something which should be believed, whereas he himself was utterly convinced that there really is an overwhelming, mysterious, unknowable hidden God, who speaks to the single individual from the depths of his soul and who reveals himself in forms which he himself chooses. This God in the dream is not merely hidden, he is alive in the depths of the grass-covered earth, in nature. Rather like Goethe's "God-nature," Jung referred to nature as "God's world" – an overwhelming mystery all around us, full of the most wonderful and awesome events and forms.

41   Jung loved animals and plants, not only when he was a child but all his life, and he could never see enough of the beauty of lakes, forests, and mountains. Nature was for him of prime importance, and striking descriptions of nature are scattered through all of his works. As quite an old man speaking of the limitations of age, he confesses,[32] "Yet there is so much that fills me: plants, animals, clouds, day and night, and the eternal in man. The more uncertain I have felt about myself, the more there has grown up in me a feeling of kinship with all things." It is as if he had finally been allowed, toward the very end of his life, to give himself in peace to "God's world." Nature was Jung's greatest love, and like his mother, he felt from early youth partially "rooted in deep, invisible ground . . . somehow connected with animals, trees, mountains, meadows and running water."[33] This love stood opposed to the Christian tradition of his father's world, which it compensated.[34]

42   Jung writes, "To 'God's world' belonged everything superhuman – dazzling light, the darkness of the abyss, the cold impassivity of infinite space and time, and the uncanny grotesqueness of the

---

[32] Ibid., p. 392.
[33] Ibid., p. 110.
[34] By compensation Jung understands the function of completing and balancing consciousness by the unconscious. The goal of the balancing process is psychic wholeness. For Jung it is an expression of the psyche's capacity for self-regulation.

irrational world of chance."[35] As a boy, Jung lost himself so deeply in "God's world" that a neurotic crisis occurred, during his school days in Basel, when he was close to being swallowed up by his beloved nature, in an attempt to escape from school problems and the problems of the world of people in general. This crisis revealed, too, how clearly introverted he was, by nature.[36]

43   The phallus in Jung's first dream represents the hidden spirit in "God's world." But who is the *king* who lies buried there? Another youthful experience of Jung's sheds some light on this question. During his school years he noticed more and more – much as he enjoyed the comradeship of his fellow pupils – that contact with the collective estranged him from himself. He felt divided and uncertain in the "big world" and these feelings led him to a step he did not understand at the time:[37]

44   I had in those days a yellow, varnished pencil case . . .with a little lock and the customary ruler. At the end of this ruler I now carved a little manikin, about two inches long, with 'frock coat, top hat and shiny black boots!' I coloured him black with ink, sawed him off the ruler, and put him in the pencil case, where I made him a little bed. I even made a coat for him out of a bit of wool. In the case I also placed a smooth, oblong blackish stone from the Rhine, which I had painted with water colours to look as though it were divided into an upper and lower half. . . . This was *his* stone. All this was a great secret. Secretly I took the case to the forbidden attic at the top of the house. . . and hid it with great satisfaction on one of the beams under the roof. . . . No one could discover my secret and destroy it. I felt safe, and the tormenting sense of being at odds with myself was gone. In all difficult situations, whenever I had done something wrong or my feelings had been hurt . . . I thought of my carefully

---

[35] *Memories.*, p. 91.
[36] By introverted Jung understands the type of person who habitually and by temperament gives more weight to the inner object than to the outer.
[37] *Memories.*, p. 36 f.

bedded-down and wrapped-up manikin and his smooth, prettily coloured stone.

45 "This manikin," explains Jung,[38] "was a little cloaked god of the ancient world, a Telesphoros such as stands on the monument of Asklepios and reads to him from a scroll." It is identical with the phallus of the childhood dream and forms "a first attempt, still unconscious and childish, to give shape to the secret"[39] of the dream. But why does Jung place quotation marks around the words frock coat, top hat, and shiny black books? These words point back to those darker experiences of his earliest years, for it was *this* kind of dress that was worn by the people he saw at burials and which also clothed the corpse of a man who had been washed down the Rhine and which he had seen as he was coming from a *church service*. Finally, they refer to the sight of a Catholic priest, dressed in solemn black, which had given the boy Jung a hellishly traumatic fright, as he tells in *Memories*. For he took the black-clad man for one of those "Jesuits" of whom his father spoke with alarm and with whom he associated the word "Jesus."[40] This terrifying apparition was now united, through self-amplification, with the phallic king, into the carved black figure, above ground a nightmare for the small boy, underground as a buried royal being, transformed into a hidden nature-god of creativity.[41] Thus, the dark, uncanny "Jesus," associated with man-eaters and death, is secretly the same as the buried king of the first dream, though in death he has been transformed into a healing, positive power and is even the guardian of the life-force and of Jung's personal secret. In connection with the first dream, Jung said, as mentioned previously, that he could never determine whether his mother's statement, "That is the man-eater" meant "That is the *man-eater*", meaning Jesus, or "*That* (unlike Jesus) is the man-

---

[38] Ibid., p. 38.
[39] Ibid., p. 37.
[40] Ibid., p. 25 f.
[41] In *Memories*, p. 39, Jung writes, "Ultimately, the manikin was a *Kabir*, wrapped in his little cloak, hidden in the *kista*, and provided with a supply of life-force. . . . But these are connections which became clear to me only much later in life. When I was a child, I performed the ritual just as I have seen it done by the natives of Africa; they act first and do not know what they are doing."

eater." In fact, the reason for this is clear. It is a paradox; he both is and is not Jesus. For when the "god" dies (and as a dying god he turns dark and negative in the upper world) he goes down to the secret depths of the underworld, there to be *transformed*. His first resurrected appearance is in the form of a phallus. The strange connection of the Christ-image with the figure of this subterranean nature-spirit, which on the one hand seems to be identical with Christ but on the other appears as a hidden adversary of Christ, engaged Jung's attention all his life.[42] In a work to be discussed later,[43] he calls Christ the archetype of (collective) consciousness, the hidden adversary as a personification of the unconscious, or of "God's reflection in physical nature."[44] The latter appears when the former has darkened and "dies," not as an adversary but as a transformation-image of exactly the same psychic content during its period of latency in the unconscious. The carved black manikin which was such a consolation to the boy is reminiscent of the black Osiris of the ancient Egyptians, "he with the strong phallus," the buried sun-god as he would appear in his coming resurrection, when he would eat all the other gods and, in this fashion, become *one* universal god.[45] This dream and the carved manikin are thus answers from the depths of the psyche to the deadly paralyzing Christian atmosphere in which Jung grew up, answers not only to his personal situation but also to a problem which today – nearly a hundred years later – is shaking our culture more and more deeply.

46   The "pagan" depths of nature and of "God's world," where the buried king of Jung's first dream lives in a hidden form, later sent Jung another dream that resolved his doubts concerning the choice of his future profession. Jung was drawn in equal measure both to the humanities, especially to archaeology, and to the natural sciences, and he long postponed the decision about which course he should follow. Then he had a dream in which he dug the bones of

[42] Cf. *Psychology and Alchemy*, Ch. III, 5: "The Lapis-Christ Parallel," CW 12. §§ 447 – 515.
[43] "The Spirit Mercurius," *CW* 13, §§ 129 – 303. Here § 299.
[44] Ibid., § 283.
[45] For more detail, cf. Helmuth Jacobsohn, *Das Gegensatzproblem im altägyptischen Mythos* (1955), pp. 171 f..

prehistoric animals out of an old grave mound, and shortly thereafter a second one, of the greatest significance:[46]

47 "Again, I was in a wood; it was threaded with water-courses, and in the darkest place, I saw a circular pool, surrounded by dense undergrowth. Half immersed in the water lay the strangest and most wonderful creature: a round animal, shimmering in opalescent hues, and consisting of innumerable little cells, or of organs shaped like tentacles. It was a giant radiolarian, measuring about three feet across. It seemed to me indescribably wonderful that this magnificent creature should be lying there undisturbed, in the hidden place, in the clear, deep water. It aroused in me an intense desire for knowledge."

48 These two dreams decided Jung in favour of natural science. What Jung did not know then, and only discovered later through his work on alchemy, was that the image of the radiolarian represented in another form that same psychic power which had appeared to him as the grave-phallus and as the little black man in the coffin – a power which Paracelsus aptly named "the light of nature."[47] The round, radial shape indicates not only a light, but also an orderedness which, so to speak, lies hidden in the darkness of nature. It is once again that *God-image*, as it appears in mother nature, which has now come up out of the earth but still remains hidden within the forest.

49 The "light of nature" was taken, from the Middle Ages on, as a second source of knowledge, along with the Christian revelation. Starting from the conception of a world-soul which permeates the universe, William of Conches (1080 – 1154), a Platonic Scholastic, developed a theory of the *sensus naturae*, which could be described as an unconscious, instinctive supernatural knowledge possessed by animals as well as by human beings. The Scholastics took over this idea, mostly from the *Liber sextus de Anima* of Avicenna (Ibn Sina), who found in this instinctive – we would say "unconscious" – knowledge an explanation of the natural gift of prophecy and

---

[46] *Memories*, p. 104 f.
[47] C.G. Jung, "Paracelsus as a Spiritual Phenomenon," CW 13, §§ 148 ff.

telepathic capacities in human beings. William of Conches then associated this kind of knowledge with the Holy Ghost, somewhat as Abelard did, and this conception was shared by Guillaume de Paris, Wilhelm d'Auvergne, Albertus Magnus, and most Western alchemists. This *lumen naturae* or *sensus naturae* was regarded by them chiefly as the *source of all knowledge of nature*[48]. According to Agrippa von Nettesheim, from the light of nature "gleams the light of prophecy came down to the four-footed beasts, the birds, and other living creatures" and enabled them to foretell future things.[49] Paracelsus entertained the same conception as Agrippa; in contrast to most of his predecessors and successors, however, he held that this light was not buried in the human body but in one's "inward body" which, he says, "is always truthful" or real. He continues[50], "Moreover, the light of nature is a light that is lit from the Holy Ghost and goeth not out." It is invisible. Man, however, is "a prophet of natural light and *he learns* the lumen naturae *through dreams:* as the light of nature cannot speak, it buildeth shapes in sleep from the power of the word' (of God)."[51]

50   Jung could not have known of this traditional idea of a light of nature at the time, but the conclusion to which his feeling inclined him, that the dream pointed to the study of nature, was obviously correct. From then on, he felt himself committed to the "light of nature" and rightly considered himself an empirical natural scientist. All his life he remained faithful to the conviction that the facts of nature are the basis of all knowledge. What many extraverted investigators failed to understand about him was that for him nature is not only outside but also within: the human psyche, too, is a piece of nature, like the "inward being" of Paracelsus, an objective Something that is not "made" by our subjective ego but which it confronts as an objective other.

---

[48] Cf. C.G. Jung, "On the Nature of the Psyche," CW 8, § 393.
[49] *De occulta philosohia*, Coloniae 1533, p. LXVIII, quoted in CW 8, §393. Descartes, too, believed in such a natural light. Cf. Marie-Louise von Franz, "The Dream of Descartes," *Timeless Documents of the Soul*, pp. 55 ff.
[50] Cf. C.G. Jung, "On the Nature of the Psyche," CW 8, § 391.
[51] Ibid. For more detail, see C.G. Jung, "Paracelsus as a Spiritual Phenomenon," CW 13, §§ 145-168.

51   In the symbolism of alchemy, which will be discussed later, the adept must firstly find the initial substance and in it the "spirit of nature." When he submits this to the alchemical transformation process, it first disintegrates into the *nigredo*, the blackness of death. The next stage, that is often called the *cauda pavonis* (peacock's tail), is marked by a play of iridescent colours. Jung's little black man in the pencil case represents, so to speak, the *nigredo* condition of that inner "god" who was to govern his life, and this *nigredo* was reflected in the boy's consciousness as doubt, depressions, and uncertainty. The luminous giant radiolarian shining in the forest is, as it were, the *cauda pavonis* – this interplay of colours – and, according to the alchemists, represents the first sign of the "resurrection" of the *prima materia – an activation of feeling*. This development had its parallel in Jung's student years, which came after this dream and which were far happier than his school years. His spirits revived, he made friends, especially with Albert Oeri (later a *Nationalrat* – a National Councilman), whom he had known since his boyhood, and began to develop that exuberant love of life and that liveliness of spirit which were later so characteristic of him. Oeri has left a witty and warm-hearted picture of Jung as a student, which shows how intensely he lived at that time and how he gradually found himself.

52   The three symbols which governed Jung's early life – the dream-image of the underground phallus, the fantasy of the little black man, and the dream-image of the luminous radiolarian in the darkness of the forest – were psychic powers which left their stamp on Jung's youth. What Jung did not know at the time, however, was that these symbols also alluded to that Western cultural tradition which he was to discover consciously only much later, namely alchemistic and Hermetic philosophy, and in which he later found his spiritual ancestors. He did encounter this tradition, however, in *one* form at this time: in Goethe's *Faust*, which his mother brought to his attention when he was in the Gymnasium.[52] "It poured into my soul like a miraculous balm." He was deeply impressed by Mephistopheles, in whom he saw not just a "devil," but a figure who, he

---

[52] *Memories*, p. 78.

"vaguely sensed, had a relationship to the mystery of the Mothers," that is, to the world of nature. "At any rate Mephistopheles and the great initiation at the end remained for me a wonderful and mysterious experience on the fringes of my conscious world." Jung became aware only much later that Mephistopheles does not personify the devil of the Christian imagination but is rather a parallel to the alchemical Mercurius, that "godlike companion" of the lonely adept, who reveals to him the mysteries of nature. Mephistopheles also initiates the intellectual, weary scholar Faust into the world of Eros and leads him beyond the life he has lived into the depths and down to the Mothers and mysteries of the "god in nature."

53   Although it has been known for a long time that the young Goethe, under the influence of Fräulein von Klettenberg, took an active interest in alchemy and in Hermetic philosophy[53], it is especially to Rolf Chr. Zimmermann's recent work that we owe more exact knowledge concerning this interest, as well as the specific books on the theme which were read by Goethe.[54] Of special interest here are the work of an anonymous Austrian catholic, the *Aurea Catena Homeri*, and Welling's *Opus mago-cabalisticum et theosophicum*, but also his doctor, Johann Freidrich Metz, who cured him with his own "elixir" and who was deeply immersed in alchemistic ideas and views[55]; and his participation in Freemasonry cannot be overlooked. Fräulein von Klettenberg introduced the young Goethe into the circles of certain southern German pietists, and, curiously enough, they, too, received inspiration from alchemistic and Rosicrucian ideas by way of Jakob Böhme and Franz Baader; thus, Goethe read the works of Samuel Richter, known as "Sincerus Renatus," who, in 1709, published a *Wahrhafte und vollkommene Bereitung des philosophischen Steins*[56], as well as, somewhat later, a *Theo-Philosophia Theoretico-Practica*, which took up ideas of Weigel, Paracelsus and Jakob Böhme. He also knew Friedrich Christoph

---

[53] Cf. R.D. Gray, *Goethe, the Alchemist: A Study of Alchemical Symbolism in Goethe's Literary and Scientific Works*. (A superficial study.)

[54] R. Chr. Zimmermann, *Das Weltbild des jungen Goethe*.

[55] Ibid., p. 172 ff.

[56] Ibid., p. 105.

Ötinger, who was interested in chemistry (which means alchemy) and the natural sciences.[57] The latter was also devoted to the ideas of Jakob Böhme, and in his Hermetic *Philosophia perennis*, he attempted to combine alchemical symbolism and Hermetic philosophy with the Christian *Weltanschauung*. Thus, "Chymie" was young Goethe's "secret love" and so remained even throughout his Strasbourg period, as a letter dated August 26, 1770, testifies[58]. These Hermetic ideas formed Goethe's "private religion," which he took care to conceal but from which he received his deepest and greatest inspiration.[59]

54   For the rest of his life, and despite certain moral criticisms of the character of Faust, Jung kept his great admiration for Goethe and, indeed, loved him as one loves a kindred spirit.[60] He often quoted Napoleon's remark about Goethe: "C'est un homme qui a beaucoup souffert." Like Goethe, he was alone and ruled by the genius of creativity, and just as Goethe, isolated, far removed from the everyday life around him, suffered from the basic problems of our cultural tradition, and expressed them in his work, so Jung, too, drew on the same mainstream of psychic images on which Goethe had based his "private religion."[61] It was only much later in his life than was the case with Goethe, however, that he also discovered the historic tradition that helped him to understand these images, that is, alchemy and Hermetic philosophy. For a long time, those symbols that he had seen remained the isolating secret of the growing youth, a secret he dared not share with anyone. As an artist, Goethe was never obliged to admit the jeering mob into the realm of his alchemistic private religion; it infiltrated his work in symbolic disguise. For Jung, who as a thinking type felt himself both drawn to and responsible to the scientific world, it was more difficult to find

[57] Ibid., p. 144 ff.
[58] Ibid., p. 195.
[59] Cf. especially the chapter, "Christliche Hermetik und die Nicht-christilichkeit von Goethe's 'Privatreligion'" in Zimmermann, pp. 210 ff.
[60] On Jung's alleged descent from Goethe, cf. *Erinnerungen*, p. 400. (German edition only.)
[61] R. Chr. Zimmermann deserves credit for also having shown the general continuing life of alchemistic ideas in the 18th century, both alongside and together with the contemporaneous beginnings of scientific rationalism. That was the century to which Jung felt so closely related in his youth that he frequently almost fancied he was living in it.

a form in which to communicate his innermost convictions. He once attempted to give them expression in the style of a poetic "proclamation" or "announcement," in the *Septem Sermones ad Mortuos*, but later regretted its publication as being too personal. Next, he tried to assume the scientific style of the contemporary psychological world, but he was never able entirely to give up poetic language. Too much that seemed unsayable was in this way merely hinted at. It was only after he had discovered the old alchemists that he finally found a *form* into which he was able to mould even his most personal experiences and convictions in accordance with the Western historical tradition and a form in which he could communicate them.

55   From the late Middle Ages onwards, little by little in the alchemical tradition there was being prepared a fundamental transformation of outlook which is, in fact, nothing more nor less than a new image of God and man, an image that brings the official Christian image of God and man into a new fullness and greater completeness. This transformation is a process in the collective psyche which is a preparation for the new aeon, the *Age of Aquarius*. This new image of God appears in Jung's first dream of the underground phallic god-king, awaiting in this hidden form its eventual resurrection. This secret stamped Jung's whole life, and it became his fate.

Chapter 2
The Storm-Lantern

56   It was not until he was in his middle years, when "Zarathustra passed him by," that Nietzsche learned that "One becomes two." Jung, on the other hand, had this experience very early in life: *he became aware of a second living psychic presence*, that presence which today we call the unconscious, and which appeared to him as a second personality within himself. In his *Memories*, as already noted, he describes the two poles of his existence as "No. 1" and "No. 2." The former was his own human ego, but the latter was the activated, and therefore perceptible, unconscious. Jung writes[1]:

57   Somewhere deep in the background I always knew that I was two persons. One was the son of my parents, who went to school and was less intelligent, attentive, hard-working, decent, and clean than many other boys. The other was grown up – old, in fact – sceptical, mistrustful, remote from the world of men, but close to nature, the earth, the sun, the moon, the weather, all living creatures, and above all close to the night, to dreams, and to whatever 'God' worked directly in him. I put 'God' in quotation marks here. For nature seemed, like myself, to have been set aside by God as non-divine, although created by Him as an expression of Himself. Nothing could persuade me that 'in the image of God' applied only to man. In fact it seemed to me that the high mountains, the rivers, lakes, trees, flowers, and animals far better exemplified the essence of God than men. ...

---

[1] *Memories*, p. 61 f.

58   The world of No. 2 was "another realm . . . in which anyone who entered was transformed and suddenly overpowered by a vision of the whole cosmos, so that he could only marvel and admire, forgetful of himself. Here lived the 'Other', who knew God as a hidden, personal, and at the same time supra-personal secret. Here nothing separated man from God; indeed, it was as though the human mind looked down upon Creation simultaneously with God."[2] In his school years Jung was not yet able to make a clear distinction between the two personalities[3] and sometimes claimed the world of No. 2 as his own. But "there was always, deep in the background, the feeling that something other than myself was involved. It was as though a breath of the great world of stars and endless space had touched me, or as if a spirit had invisibly entered the room – the spirit of one who had long been dead and yet was perpetually present in timelessness until far into the future."

59   As No. 1, Jung[4] saw himself as "a rather disagreeable and moderately gifted young man with vaulting ambitions . . ." No. 2, on the other hand, "had no definable character at all; he was a *vita peracta*, born, living, dead, everything in one; a total vision of life. Though pitilessly clear about himself, he was unable to express himself through the dense, dark medium of No. 1, though he longed to do so. . . ." No. 1 regarded him as a "region of inner darkness," whereas in No. 2 "light reigned, as in the spacious halls of a royal palace." No. 2 "felt himself in secret accord with the Middle Ages, as personified by *Faust*, with the legacy of a past which had obviously stirred Goethe to the depths. For Goethe too, therefore – and this was my great consolation – No. 2 was a reality . . . . *Faust*[5] . . . was the living equivalent of No. 2, and I was convinced that *he* was the answer which Goethe had given to his times."[6]

---

[2] Ibid., p. 62. Jung continues: "The play and counterplay between personalities No. 1 and NO. 2, which has run through my whole life, has nothing to do with a 'split' or dissociation in the ordinary medical sense. On the contrary, it is played out in every individual. Since time immemorial, it has always been religions that speak to man's No. 2 personality – to the 'inner man.'" (Note by editor: This latter sentence does not exist in the English translation of *Memories*. It has therefore been translated and added by said editor.)

[3] Ibid., p. 85.

[4] Ibid., p. 106 f.

[5] The play, not the character, is being referred to here.

[6] *Memories*, p. 107.

60   We know from the lives of many creative people that, through-out their youth, they lingered for a while in a second "other world," or that they secretly felt themselves to be identical with a per-sonification of this other world.[7] This kind of close contact with the collective unconscious constitutes, so to speak, both the wisdom and the folly of a young person. However, if one remains caught in this situation (past about the 25th year), it leads to a neurosis which might be called the *puer aeternus* neurosis[8], a sort of unadaptedness, possibly with a touch of genius, which frequently results in the early death of these people.

61   At the beginning of Jung's university career, he came to a *turning-point* which foreshadowed the end of this vacillation between the two worlds. It was precipitated by a fateful dream[9]:

62   It was night in some unknown place, and I was making slow and painful headway against a mighty wind. Dense fog was flying along everywhere. I had my hands cupped around a tiny light which threatened to go out at any moment. Everything depended upon my keeping this little light alive. Suddenly I had the feeling that something was coming up behind me. I looked back and saw a gigantic black figure following me. But at the same moment I was conscious, in spite of my terror, that I must keep my little light going through night and wind, regardless of all dangers.

63   "When I awoke," Jung continues, "I realized at once that the figure was a 'spectre of the Brocken,' my own shadow on the swirling mists, brought into being by the little light I was carrying. I knew, too, that this little light was my consciousness, the only light I have. My own understanding is the sole treasure I possess, and the greatest. . . .This dream was a great illumination for me. Now I knew that No. 1 was

---

[7] The Brontë children, for example, or Robert Louis Stevenson. Cf. in this connection Barbara Hannah, *Striving towards Wholeness*.

[8] Cf. Marie-Louise von Franz, *Puer Aeternus*. There is also a good depiction of the problem in Bruno Goetz's novel *Das Reich ohne Raum*. Cf. further James Hillman, "Senex and Puer," *Eranos-Jahrbuch* 36, 1968.

[9] Quoted in *Memories*, p. 107 – 110.

the bearer of the light, and that No. 2 followed him like a shadow. My task was to shield the light and not look back at the *vita peracta*; this was evidently a forbidden realm of light of a different sort. . . .

64   I recognized clearly that my path led irrevocably outward, into the limitations and darkness of three-dimensionality." This dream revealed to Jung that "in the light of consciousness the inner realm of light appears as a gigantic shadow. . . . Now all at once I understood . . . that cold shadow of embarrassment which passed over people's faces whenever I alluded to anything reminiscent of the inner realm."

65   *This recognition and turning-point remained decisive for Jung's entire life* and it protected him during his student years from a crisis that today menaces the greater part of the youth of an entire continent. Well acquainted with the "inner light" and the darkness of their No. 2 through the use of hallucinogenic drugs, many lose their foothold in No. 1 and so are destroyed. To the extent that they turn their backs on the darkness of three-dimensionality, they also lose the "little light" of ego-consciousness, the only thing they have that can guide them forward into the future.

66   The shadow of estrangement mentioned by Jung, that passed over people's faces when he spoke of the reality of the unconscious, was also reflected on him for his school friends nicknamed him "Father Abraham." This is not uninteresting, since later in life he was so often referred to as a mystic or a prophet or the bringer of an *ersatz* religion, a fact which annoyed him intensely. People who saw him in this light knew nothing about the turning-point in his life, that crisis when he once and for all renounced any kind of identification with No. 2 and thus definitively renounced the role of one who preaches or proclaims the realm of "inner light." On the contrary, he endeavoured to describe that inner world objectively with detachment as an autonomous phenomenon *sui generis*.[10] Thus, for instance, in the introduction to his *Answer to Job*, which is personal and full of emotion, he emphasized that he was describing

---

[10] Cf. in this connection G. Wehr, *C.G. Jung*, p. 122, and especially p.84. Willem A. Visser 't Hooft, for example, accuses Jung of this sort of thing in *Kein anderer Name*, pp. 34f.

a purely subjective experience. "I deliberately chose this form because I wanted to avoid the impression that I had any idea of announcing an 'eternal truth'. The book does not pretend to be anything but the voice or question of a single individual who hopes or expects to meet with thoughtfulness in the public."[11]

That Nietzsche did *not* make a decision when he reached this crucial turning-point exasperated Jung. "Just as *Faust* had opened a door for me, *Zarathustra* slammed one shut, and it remained shut for a long time to come."[12] Jung recognized of course that Zarathustra was Nietzsche's No. 2, just as Faust was Goethe's. In Jung's eyes Nietzsche's error lay in the fact "that he fearlessly and unsuspectingly let his No. 2 loose upon a world that knew and understood nothing about such things,"[13] and the more he felt the estrangement between himself and his contemporaries, the more he fell back upon an inflated style, full of heaped-up metaphors and rhapsodic enthusiasm, in an effort still to convince the others. When the ego, however, identifies to that degree with the greater inner presence, No. 2, the result is a "puffed-up ego and a deflated self[14]." History is full of examples of such figures: Sabbatai Zevi, Hitler, Manson, Leary, and all the other pathological demagogues and religious pseudo-prophets. They have inflicted infinite damage on the world because they have transformed normal inner experiences into morbid poison through inflated identification with them. Because of this the world is inclined to reject *all* the possibilities of inner experience, not understanding that whether the inner phenomena function destructively or not depends on having the right attitude towards it. This is where it becomes so eminently important to protect the integrity of that little light of individual consciousness. In a long series of seminars, Jung later elucidated Nietzsche's *Thus Spake Zarathustra*, sentence by sentence, and

---

[11] C.G. Jung, *Answer to Job*, CW 11, p. 358.
[12] *Memories*, p. 124.
[13] Ibid., p. 123.
[14] C.G. Jung, *On the Nature of the Psyche*, CW 8, §430. "Self" is the word Jung later used for the centre of No. 2.

interpreted its images.[15] In the "rope-dancer" he saw a symbol of Nietzsche himself daring too much by wishing to actualize the "Superman," with the consequence that he lost touch with the ground under his feet, with normal everyday life. The rope-dancer's fall is like a premonition of Nietzsche's later psychic illness. The "buffoon" causes him to fall: "You are blocking the way of a better man than you!" This buffoon is Nietzsche's No. 2 turned negative, so to say, and therefore destructive, because Nietzsche did not stand firm in his ordinary human ego but lost his way on the dizzy heights of wild speculation.[16]

68   The result of such defective discrimination between consciousness and the unconscious is that if the ego chooses to parade as the "announcer" of unconscious inspiration, then the unconscious becomes contaminated with human inadequacies and prejudices, because these had not previously been integrated into the conscious personality. The water of the unconscious spirit is muddied, so to speak, by personal and all-too-human contents and then overflows into consciousness. Jung analyzed *Thus Spake Zarathustra* in order to arrive at a clear distinction between what is genuine inspiration in the work and what appears to be distorted as a result of Nietzsche's unresolved personal problems, chiefly those due to his inflation.[17] Since Nietzsche identified with the Superman, the "higher" men want to drag him down to the collective sphere of average humanity and finally the "ugliest" man emerges as an expression of the regulating influence of the unconscious. But the "roaring lion" of Zarathustra's moral conviction forces all these influences back into the cave of the unconscious. Thus, the regulating influence of the unconscious is suppressed, but not its secret counteraction that Nietzsche projected onto one or another adversary from then on. He found his first opponent in Wagner, but he soon concentrated all his wrath against Christianity, and in particular against St. Paul, who in some ways suffered a fate similar to Nietzsche's. As is well known,

---

[15] Cf. C.G. Jung, *Nietzsche's Zarathustra*. Notes of the Seminar Given in 1934-1939.
[16] Cf. C.G. Jung, "*Picasso*," CW 15, § 214.
[17] Cf. C.G. Jung, "On the Psychology of the Unconscious," CW 7, §§ 36 – 41.

Nietzsche's psychosis first produced an identification with the "Crucified Christ" and then with the dismembered Zagreus. With this catastrophe, the counteraction at last broke through to the surface. In reality, Nietzsche identified with the adversary of the official Christ-figure which explains his "pagan" and anti-Christian leanings. He was overwhelmed by the unconscious which, in his day, was surging up with great power.

69 Another personality who is again being quoted frequently these days is G.W.F. Hegel, in whom the same problem of not differentiating between one's ego and the unconscious led to the production of an equally unhealthy ideology. Although Hegel did not fall into a psychosis, his work also suffers from a lack of differentiation between conscious and unconscious. The self-revelation of the unconscious is set forth in Hegel's writings as if the ego were doing the thinking[18], even proposing that the state, with its power apparatus, should promulgate these truths. In other words, he fell victim to a spiritual power claim, which is why, not surprisingly, he felt a special admiration for Napoleon. What happened to him is what Jung calls 'the attempt to dominate everything by the intellect'[19] – including the unconscious. In order to avoid the necessity of admitting that one is exposed to uncanny autonomous psychic influences from the unconscious, and thereby to circumvent the *experience* of these influences, one interprets them in an "artificial . . . two-dimensional conceptual world in which the reality of life is well covered up by so-called clear concepts."[20] The inner experience of the spirit is thus poisoned by the power drive. A further danger, implicit in this attitude towards the unconscious and evident in many Marxist thinkers deriving from Hegel, is that if the autonomy of the unconscious is not recognized then it insinuates itself into conscious thought processes in the

---

[18] Cf. C.G. Jung, "On the Nature of the Psyche," CW 8, § 358. "A philosophy like Hegel's is a self-revelation of the psychic background and, philosophically, a presumption."
[19] *Memories*, p. 167.
[20] Ibid. In the case of Hegel: the idea that the actual self can be grasped by abstract thinking. Cf. F. Ueberweg, *Grundriss der Geschichte der Philosophie* IV, pp. 73ff. Philosophy expresses the absolute spirit (that is, the divine creative first cause of the world) in subjective-objective form. – Ueberweg, p. 85.

form of projections, contaminating the underlying unconscious inspiration.[21] On the one hand this lends to the ideology in question a stirring pseudo-religious effect, but on the other it distorts it with unrealized personal resentments, misjudgements, and limitations.[22]

70   Such contamination of unconscious inspiration can only be avoided through critical discrimination and the renunciation of any sort of claim to spiritual power, that is, by carefully preserving the integrity of the "little light" of ego-consciousness. Jung never tired of stressing the importance of understanding and realizing the significance of this little light, indeed he even found in it the ultimate meaning of our existence.[23]

71   At all events, the conscious ego in the human being is an unfathomable mystery, no matter how familiar and subjective it may seem to us. It appears to be a complex – that is, a psychic nucleus of feeling-toned ideas – with which our feeling of identity becomes bound up in early youth, but which near the end of our life, in old age, becomes increasingly detached. We can never see our own ego objectively or, if at all, then only in its reflection via the unconscious. It comes awake every morning from unknown depths and mirrors the outer world for us in inner images.[24] It is the centre and subject of all personal conscious acts and all willed efforts and achievements in adaptation. It appears to possess a quaternary structure.[25] When

---

[21] I have tried to demonstrate this in my essay "The Cosmic Man as Image of the Goal of the Individuation Process and Human Development," in: Marie-Louise von Franz, *Archetypal Dimensions of the Psyche*.

[22] With Hegel, the unrecognized autonomous unconscious appears in projection as the course of history. Cf. L.L. Whyte, *The Unconscious before Freud*.

[23] Cf. *Memories*, p. 371.

[24] Cf. C.G. Jung, "The Psychology of Eastern Meditation," CW 11, § 935, and *Memories*, p. 413. Composed by A. Jaffé from the so-called Basler Seminar 1934 (unpublished).

[25] Cf. C.G. Jung, *Aion*, CW 9/II, §§ 1 – 12. The ego, according to Jung, rests on a somatic and a psychic base. The former becomes manifest in the form of endosomatic stimuli, some of which cross the threshold of consciousness and become perceptions, that is, psychic, and are associated with the ego, while others remain below the threshold. The psychic base consists in the total field of consciousness on the one hand and the sum total of unconscious contents or inner processes on the other. "It seems to arise in the first place from the collision between the somatic factor and the environment, and, once established, as a subject, it goes on developing from further collisions with the outer world and the inner" – § 6. Thus, the differentiation between subject and object, between inner and outer, gradually takes place. This contribution of Jung's to the psychology of consciousness, here very briefly summarized, received almost no recognition in the wider field of philosophic-academic psychology, because it is concerned with a description of ego-consciousness which *cannot be understood without experience of its mirror-world, the unconscious*. Academic psychology usually tries to describe consciousness from the standpoint of the conscious subject, although it is unable to refer to an Archimedean point outside the thinking ego. Cf. for example, Detlev von Uslar, *Der Traum als Welt*,

Jung later studied the way in which individuals adapt to their environment with their "little light," their ego, he discovered that one could divide these attempts at adaptation into four basic forms of psychic activity or psychological function[26]:

72

1) the sensation function, which consciously registers inner and outer facts, irrationally;

2) the thinking function, by means of which our conscious ego establishes a rational – that is, in accord with reason in general – logical order among objects;

3) the feeling function, which rationally establishes or, alternatively, "selects" hierarchies of value (this is more pleasant, more important, etc., than that); and

4) the intuitive function, which is irrational. It appears to be a kind of perception via the unconscious and seems to be mainly concerned with the future possibilities of what is at hand. (Intuition is not identical with fantasy[27] which Jung regards as a human capacity independent of the functions, just as the will[28] is.)

73 The four functions provide a sort of basic orientation for the ego in the chaos of appearances.[29] "*Sensation* (i.e., sense perception) tells you that something exists; *thinking* tells you what it is; *feeling* tells you whether it is agreeable or not; and *intuition* tells you whence it comes and where it is going."[30]

---

concerning the difficulties of understanding consciousness without empirical knowledge of the dream.

[26] C.G. Jung, *Psychological Types*, CW 6, § 727.

[27] Fantasy can find expression via thinking, feeling, intuition, and perceptions and is therefore probably an ability *sui generis*, with deep roots in the unconscious.

[28] By will, Jung understands that amount or quantum of psychic energy which is disposable by ego-consciousness.

[29] Cf. C.G. Jung, *Psychological Types*, CW 6, § 933, where he writes, "From earliest times attempts have been made to classify individuals according to types, and so to bring order into the chaos. The oldest attempts known to us were made by oriental astrologers. . . ." (Similarly, the physiological typology of antiquity, namely the division into the four temperaments by humors, is closely connected with the still more ancient cosmological ideas.)

[30] Cf. C.G. Jung, "Symbols and the Interpretation of Dreams," CW 18, §§ 416 – 607, here § 503. Cf. also Jolande Jacobi, *The Psychology of C.G. Jung.*

	Thinking		Sensation	
Sensation	Intuition	Feeling		Thinking
	Feeling		Intuition	

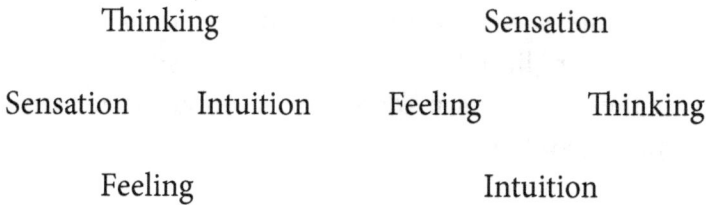

74   In the course of his development, every human being cultivates and differentiates one function more than the others and tends to rely to a large extent on this function for his adaptation. In most cases a second or even a third function will also be developed (in the diagram above, the two functions to the right and left of the principal function), but the fourth (the one which stands opposite the main function in the diagram) nearly always remains largely unconscious, for which reason Jung calls it the "inferior function."[31] Here the light of ego-consciousness turns into twilight. Our attempts to adapt with the fourth function are to a large extent uncontrolled and often fall under the influence of No. 2, the unconscious personality. If, therefore, our highest values and central religious ideas disappear from consciousness, they drop down, so to speak, into the despised and neglected corner of the inferior function, and that is where they have to be rediscovered. The first time Jung consciously tackled the problem of the "death of God" in his work was in his description of the psychological function types, specifically in his interpretation of Carl Spitteler's *Prometheus*. *Prometheus* is concerned with the rediscovery of the lost "treasure"

---

[31] C.G. Jung, *Psychological Types*, CW 6, § 776 f. This does not mean that a normal thinking type, for example, has no feeling, or that a feeling type is stupid, but rather that the fourth function in each case will be primitive, spontaneously arbitrary, intense, undisciplined, and archaic. Moreover, it behaves somewhat in the fashion of the opposite attitude type, which means that, for example, the feeling of an introverted thinking type is extraverted, bound to the object, and the sensation of an extraverted intuitive will be introverted, etc. What lends the matter a kind of fatefulness is the fact that opposite types attract each other in the form of admiring fascination (they often marry) or, more often, they cannot endure each other. The introvert finds the extravert "superficial," and the latter sees the introvert as an unworldly dreamer. The thinking type finds the feeling type stupid and sentimental, the latter takes the thinking type to be a "cold intellectual." To the sensation type, the intuitive is "unreal," whereas the latter finds the sensation type a "flat, spiritless pedestrian creature," etc. Food for one is poison for the other. Judging from my practical experiences, the merit of Jungian typology, even today, lies in the use for which Jung originally developed it, namely that it assists reciprocal *understanding* between individuals and among whole schools and movements. In *Psychological Types* Jung therefore adduces many examples from the history of culture (the struggle over the Last Supper during the Middle Ages, Schiller versus Goethe, etc.) in his effort to illustrate the way in which type differences interact in general.

or "jewel," the "new god" who had dropped down into the realm of the unconscious. This treasure is in the possession of the despised realm of the soul, of the "ugliest man" in Nietzsche's language. The lost value always reappears in the most unexpected place, as the birth of Christ in a neglected stable symbolically affirms.

75   Because its psychological meaning was not understood, this aspect of the myth that gripped Jung and which he lived has, curiously enough, materialized in our culture in the form of *outer* projections. Thus Karl Marx, for instance, sought the lost Self, or the restoration of the "real man" in the "despised" element of society, the working class.[32] Others seek salvation through efforts on behalf of the "underdeveloped" countries; only a few seem to understand that it is just as important to care for the underdeveloped areas of one's own soul, lest unforeseen evils gather there and emerge to destroy our best-intentioned idealistic outer efforts.

76   In his description of the four functions of consciousness Jung came upon a "quaternary" pattern that is of special significance, since he later discovered that the nuclear core of the No. 2 – the unconscious – also generally manifests itself as a quaternary structure. The two parts of the personality – the light of the ego's storm-lantern and the centre of the unconscious – appear, accordingly, to possess a mirror-image-like structure. Both contain light and dark because, even though our ego seems lucid and familiar to us, it nevertheless contains the most mysterious darkness, and although the unconscious appears as a great shadow, it nevertheless contains unexpected light, for it produces, among other things, "illuminating" inspirations. Therefore, Jung says in his later work[33], one could even define the ego as a *"relatively constant personification of the unconscious itself,* or as the Schopenhauerian mirror in which the unconscious becomes aware of its own face. All the worlds that have ever existed before man were physically there. They were a nameless happening, but not a definite actuality, for there did not yet exist that minimal concentration of the psychic

---

[32] Cf. Robert Tucker, *Philosophy and Myth in Karl Marx*, pp. 151 ff.
[33] C.G. Jung, *Mysterium Coniunctionis*, CW 14, § 125.

factor to speak the word that outweighed the whole of Creation: 'that is the world, and this is I!' That was the first morning of the world . . . when that inchoately conscious complex, the ego, the son of the darkness, knowingly sundered subject and object, and thus precipitated the world and itself into definite existence. . . ."

77   Toward the end of his life, Jung had a dream in which the conscious ego appeared as a reflection or projection of the larger inner centre, exactly as if No. 2, the unconscious personality, were dreaming or imagining the conscious life of No. 1. It seems, therefore, as if the light of No. 1, which is dark within, and the light of the unconscious, No.2, which is dark in the outer world, together ultimately form a strange two-fold unity, in which the one cannot exist without the other[34], and ego-consciousness appears to be such an essential part of this totality that in many myths and religions it even stands as *pars pro toto* for the God-image itself. In Indian philosophy, for example, the identity of God and ego "was taken as self-evident. It was the nature of the Indian mind to become aware of the world-creating significance of the consciousness manifested in man."[35]

78   When in his youth Jung decided to direct all his efforts towards keeping alive the "little light" that he carried with him in his dream, he made another decision that set him apart from the average young man. Most people, when they decide – because of pressure from within or from the environment – to grow up and leave behind the romantic dreams of their youth and enter the battle of life with the light of the ego, forget and repress the existence of No. 2 – of the unconscious.[36] Jung, however, took a conscious decision not to deny No. 2[37] or to "declare him invalid. That would have been a self-mutilation and would moreover have deprived me of any possibility of explaining the origin of the dream. For there was no doubt in my

---

[34] This is most clearly seen in cases of severe mental illness, where the little storm-lantern of the ego is obscured or extinguished. The manifestations of the unconscious in the dreams of the patient then deteriorate into a meaningless up-and-down and back-and-forth, without direction or goal.
[35] C.G. Jung, *Mysterium Coniunctionis*, § 131.
[36] In my work, I have called this the "Icarus crash" of the *puer aeternus*, where the romantic youth suddenly becomes a cynical, reality-bound power-driven man; after the hippies, the skinheads! Cf. Marie-Louise von Franz, *Puer Aeternus*.
[37] *Memories*, p. 109 f.

mind that No. 2 had something to do with the creation of dreams, and I could easily credit him with the necessary superior intelligence. . . . He was indeed a spectre, a spirit who could hold his own against the world of darkness.' 'I did not connect this with the idea of any definite individuality. . . . The only distinct feature about this spirit was his historical character, his extension in time, or rather, his timelessness." No. 2 also personifies, in a way, a collective *Zeitgeist* at work in the human unconscious, a spirit which is transformed and revealed throughout the centuries of the history of the human mind.

79   The now-contrasting, now-concordant harmonizing of ego consciousness and the unconscious, the two mirror-worlds between which he tried to steer a middle course, could also be felt in personal meetings with him. His lively, dark eyes would linger kindly and with interest on the visitor, then wander away, as if he were gazing into a darker background and looking for an answer there. In spite of his natural modest manner, one felt as though transported into prescient, magical surroundings and suddenly began to feel that mysterious power in whose hands human fortune rests and from whence come the meaning and the meaninglessness of one's own life. Few people left his consulting room without having been touched by the power of the unconscious and thereby made responsive to the challenge to *also* give attention in all seriousness to their own No. 2, which carries our ephemeral ego-consciousness, changes it, and lends a deeper meaning to it.

◆

Chapter 3
The Physician

Asclepius, the god of physicians, is often accompanied in antique sculpture by the phallic Kabir Telesphoros, "he who brings completeness as a goal," for it is a fact that there is no psychic or even psychosomatic healing without a profound change of attitude. Although Jung's first dream was, so to speak, a call to be a healer of souls, it was only after much hesitation that he found his vocation. He matriculated first in the Faculty of Natural Science at the University of Basel.[1] When, towards the end of his student years (around 1900), it was time for him to specialize, he thought of surgery or internal medicine.[2] But while he was preparing for his final examinations, he read Krafft-Ebing's textbook on psychiatry[3] and there he came upon two observations which provoked "tremendous emotion" in him. One was a reference to the relative subjectivity of psychiatric insights; the other was the assertion that psychoses are "diseases of the personality." That decided him. "My excitement was intense, for it had become clear to me, in a flash of illumination, that for me the only possible goal was psychiatry. Here alone the two currents of my interest could flow together. . . . Here was the empirical field common to biological and spiritual fact. . . . It was as though two rivers had united and in one grand torrent were bearing me inexorably toward distant goals."[4] The radical opposition between the humanities and the sciences which is so characteristic of our culture seemed to him to be at last resolved in a third, in the

---

[1] In this connection, see Franz N. Riklin, "C.G. Jung – ein Porträt," in: *Was weiss man von der Seele?*, pp. 32ff, and Wehr, *C.G. Jung*, p. 19.
[2] For this period of his life, see *Memories*, pp 125 ff.
[3] R.F. von Krafft-Ebing, *Lehrbuch der Psychiatrie*, 4th ed., 1890.
[4] *Memories*, p. 129 f. Cf. also the BBC interview with Stephen Black reprinted in Bennet, *C.G. Jung*, pp. 146 ff.

realm of the science of the human psyche, since it is in the psyche, as we will see later, that matter and spirit merge into one.

81   After finishing his final examinations, Jung joined the staff of the Burghölzli Mental Hospital in Zurich (December 10, 1900) as an assistant. It was, as he says, "a submission to the vow to believe only in what was probable, average, commonplace, barren of meaning."[5] His temperament being what it was, he almost immediately started asking questions which hitherto had received but little attention, in particular the burning question of what actually takes place inside the mentally ill beyond the labelling of diseases by cataloguing their symptoms and diagnoses.[6] This attitude stayed with Jung all his life because for him, psychic illness was always the personal drama of a particular individual, in spite of all the categories of disease. The personal history "is the patient's secret, the rock against which he is shattered. If I know his secret story, I have a key to the treatment."[7] To find this key requires, first of all, "long and patient human contact with the individual."

82   "It cannot be assumed," Jung acknowledges in the last paper he wrote[8], "that the analyst is a superman who is above such differences, just because he is a doctor who has acquired a psychological theory and a corresponding technique. . . . There is no therapeutic technique or doctrine that is of general application, since every case that one receives for treatment is an individual in a specific condition." It is much more important to establish a relationship of trust than it is to demonstrate a clinical theory. "The doctor has something to say, but so has the patient."[9] Every treatment, for Jung, was *dialogue* and *encounter*. The treatment is also never merely logotherapy (Victor Frankl) because to therapeutic encounter, as understood by Jung, belong all those irrational imponderabilia, such as tone of voice, facial expression, gestures, and – by no means least

---

[5] *Ibid.,* p. 133.
[6] Ibid., p. 135.
[7] Ibid., p. 138.
[8] C.G. Jung, "Symbols and the Interpretation of Dreams," CW 18, § 497.
[9] *Memories*, p. 153. See in this connection Wehr, p. 129. Wehr correctly stresses the fact that it is wrong to attribute to Jung an I-It experience, in contrast to Buber's I-Thou experience: Jung always (not just to a greater extent in his later years, as Wehr thinks) gave the I-Thou relation a central importance.

– the unconscious itself "which *really is unconscious*." The sayings of Paracelsus which Jung quotes in his paper "Paracelsus the Physician" to describe the art of therapy might also justly be applied to him:[10] "Where there is no love, there is no art." "Thus the physician must be endowed with no less compassion and love than God intends towards man." The physician is "the means by which nature is put to work." What the physician does is not his work. "The practice of this art lies in the heart; if your heart is false, the physician within you will be false."[11]

83   I know of a woman patient of Jung's who stipulated as a condition of beginning treatment with him that he never talk to her about his theories or ideas or interpretations; she wished only to talk to him about his everyday life, for example, what he did during his holidays, etc. Although it was a difficult condition for him, he agreed – and the treatment was a great success. This is simply an example of the extent to which he always adapted to his analysands – even when it went against his own nature and temperament.[12] Eros was the principle which guided him in his medical work. On one occasion, after a young woman patient had confessed with great embarrassment that she had a "transference" to him, he remained gravely silent for a while, then, as it was a fine day, suggested they go for a walk in his garden. As if by accident, he paused when they came to a patch in which the most varied and rare wildflowers were growing together. He pointed to the flowers and said, "You see, I have some rare and beautiful plants. I offer them the soil. If they like it, they can stay here and bloom and grow. If they don't, well then, nothing can be done." This was his answer to her. He did things of this kind almost without conscious intention; he simply followed a spontaneous prompting from the unconscious and did or said whatever came to him from nature. In fine weather he liked to work in his open summer-house, where his eyes and ears were always

---

[10] C.G. Jung, "Paracelsus the Physician," CW 15, § 42.
[11] Ibid., § 42.
[12] In the face of such evidence, as noted above, the curious charge made by Hans Trüb in *Heilung aus der Begegnung* that Jung showed his patients too little feeling needs no answer. Trüb was a feeling type; to this type the thinking type often mistakenly appears to be, as noted above, a "cold intellectual" which is, however, a projection of the feeling type's own inferior thinking function.

open to the sights and sounds of nature. He noticed at what point in the conversation his dog sighed or a wasp flew into the room or a high wave pounded against the wall. When, as often happened, these small events harmonized with what was being discussed at the moment, he would call attention to it with an amused wink. Indeed, the physician is "the means by which nature is put to work."

84   From the beginning of his practice, Jung treated his patients with this total relatedness. At the same time, however, he carried on his research and experimental work. He set up a kind of laboratory for parapsychology in the Psychiatric Clinic at Burghölzli in 1904/5 and his boss, Eugen Bleuler (senior), supported him in this whole-heartedly and generously. Around this time, he finished his dissertation, *On the Psychology and Pathology of So-called Occult Phenomena*, Leipzig 1902, and somewhat later his *Studies in Word Association*. Though very different in subject matter and treatment, these two early works are nevertheless closely related on a deeper level. During his student years, Jung had read a great number of the books then available on spiritualism[13], "for I could not help seeing that the phenomena described . . . were in principle much the same as the stories I had heard again and again in the country since my earliest childhood. The material, without a doubt, was authentic. But the great question of whether these stories were physically true was not answered to my satisfaction. Nevertheless, it could be established that at all times and all over the world the same stories had been reported again and again." Such things "must be connected with the objective behaviour of the human psyche. . . . The observations of the spiritualists, weird and questionable as they seemed to me, were the first accounts I had seen of objective psychic phenomena."[14] It was in these studies that the ego, or Jung's No. 1, tried for the first time to approach the utterances of No. 2 as objective statements.

85   Two poltergeist phenomena (the sudden, causeless splitting of a table and the breaking of a knife) awakened Jung's interest and

---

[13] He names, among others, Zoellner, Crookes, Swedenborg, Duprel, Eschenmayer, Passavant, Justinus Kerner and Görres – *Memories*, pp. 120 ff.

[14] *Memories*, 119 f.

curiosity[15] and he decided, while still a student, to attend some séances centring around a 15-year-old girl who was subject to somnambulistic and spiritualistic manifestations. (During his Burghölzli period, Jung and Eugen Bleuler often attended séances with a male medium.) He carefully recorded everything said by the medium and came to the conclusion that a second, wiser, and more mature part of the medium's own personality was speaking, a part of her which as time went on "grew into" the medium, so to speak, because the girl herself began to exhibit increasingly the qualities of the spirit presence which in the beginning had behaved autonomously.[16] As a result of this experience he was disposed for a long time to regard all spiritualistic phenomena in general as autonomous "partial souls" which in principle belong to the conscious personality.[17]

86   The investigations which Jung then took up at Bürgholzli, his studies in word association, belong in this context. Franz Riklin, Sr., who had been working with Gustav Aschaffenburg in Germany, brought news of Wilhelm Wundt's association experiment to the doctors at Burghölzli; he himself hoped to be able to discover possible brain lesions through its use[18]. Jung took up this experiment with enthusiasm, but he changed it radically: for him, it presented the possibility of demonstrating the presence, the influence, and the structure of those "partial souls" that he now called "feeling-toned complexes." Together with Franz Riklin, Sr., Carl Peterson, Charles Ricksher, A. Lang, Ludwig Binswanger, and others, he started wider experimental work which would make it possible to identify different reaction types, reaction similarities, and types of diseases, and to develop a juristic evaluation of this experiment for use in the diagnosis of facts.[19] In this work Jung finally found a solid scientific

[15] For details, see *Memories*, p. 125 ff.
[16] Cf. C.G. Jung, "On the Psychology and Pathology of So-called Occult Phenomena," CW 1, §§ 1 – 150.
[17] Cf. C.G. Jung, "The Psychological Foundation of Belief in Spirits," CW 8, §§ 570 – 600.
[18] The experiment consists in principle in giving the test person a hundred stimulus words and asking for the quickest possible word association. Delay in answering, as well as the so-called psychogalvanic effect, etc., show where there are "holes" in the field of conscious associations, behind which the unconscious complexes are to be located.
[19] Cf. C.G. Jung, "The Psychological Diagnosis of Facts," CW 1, §§ 478 ff. As a result of this work, originally published in 1905, he was invited, with Freud, to lecture at Clark University in Worcester,

experimental basis for his intuitive insights into a person's No. 2, that is, into the autonomous activity of the unconscious. Although he extended his research during this period into the psychosomatic field, he decided never to regard the bodily concomitant phenomena as *cause* of the complex-indicators, which would have been tantamount to a materialistic interpretation of the complexes; he considered the physical reactions as *concomitant* phenomena, and he never had reason to change this view. In contrast to his father who, in a crisis of doubt concerning his faith, began to accept a materialistic interpretation of psychic contents[20], Jung rejected a materialistic derivation of psychic phenomena, for the fundamental reason that we do not know what "matter" is, just as we also do not know what "objective psychic" is, nor what "spirit" is. These can be described only indirectly, by means of the traces they leave in our conscious minds, but they cannot be defined in themselves. "Matter and spirit both appear in the psychic realm," he writes in a later paper[21], "as distinctive qualities of conscious contents. The ultimate nature of both is transcendental, that is, irrepresentable, since the psyche and its contents are the only reality which is given to us *without a medium.*" Thus, one could even define the psyche as a quality of matter, or matter as the concrete aspect of the psyche. "In consequence of the inevitability of psychic phenomena, a *single* approach to the mystery of existence is impossible, there have to be at least two: namely, the material or physical event on the one hand and its psychic reflection on the other,"[22] so that one is hard put to it to decide what is reflecting what. In this way, Jung rejected every attempt to interpret existence materialistically or spiritually.[23] For

---

Massachusetts, in 1909. Cf. also C. A. Meier, *Die Empirie des Unbewussten*, and the literature there cited. This work was later continued by Franz Riklin, Jr., the late distinguished President of the C. G. Jung Institute in Zurich, who died in 1969.

[20] *Memories*, p. 115 f.

[21] C.G. Jung, "On the Nature of the Psyche," CW 8, § 420. Cf also "Symbols and the Interpretation of Dreams," CW 18, § 583 f.

[22] C.G. Jung, "Ein Brief zur Frage der Synchronizität," *Zeitschrift für Parapsychologie und Grenzgebiete der Psychologie,* V:I (1961). For trans., see letter to A.D. Cornell, 9 Feb. 1960, in *Jung: Letters,* ed. Adler, vol. 2. Cf. also in connection with the concepts of spirit and matter, Jung in *Man and His Symbols,* pp. 94 f.

[23] In the sense that everything is "spirit" and that matter is ".only concretized 'spirit.'"

psychology "is not concerned with things as they are 'in themselves,' but only with what people think about them."[24]

87   Although in this early period Jung regarded "spirits" as being "only" psychic complexes, he changed his position in his later work. It is difficult to see how a "place-bound" spook, for example, could have been evoked "only" through a person's complexes. Jung finally expressed a certain doubt, therefore, as to whether an exclusively psychological method could explain such phenomena.[25] Somewhere deep in the ground of being, the psyche and the microphysical conceptions of the space-time continuum meet. "This opens up the whole question of the trans-psychic reality immediately underlying the psyche." This problem, however, will be discussed below. In that early period, Jung dedicated himself to the empirical study of purely psychic reality and put aside the possible "material" or "spiritual" substrate of both as for the time being unknowable. In this way he protected his psychological position from being influenced by the ephemeral ideological assumptions of the prevailing *Weltanschauung*.

88   Through his studies in word association at Burghölzli in Zurich, Jung discovered the psychic complex, as he called it – that is, he was able to demonstrate that there are emotionally charged nuclei in the psyche that can be entirely unconscious, partly unconscious, or conscious. They consist of a "core" that tends to autonomously amplify itself by attracting more and more related feeling-toned representations or ideas. Complexes can be inferiorities (father complex, mother complex, inferiority complex, money complex, etc.) and these are the kind generally referred to in today's popular parlance, but they are also the focal or nodal points of psychic life in the positive sense of the word.[26] It is probable that our whole personality was originally built up little by little out of such complexes. "Since the human body is built up by heredity out of a

---

[24] C.G. Jung, "The Psychological Foundations of Belief in Spirits," CW 8, § 585, n. 5.
[25] Ibid., § 600, footnote.
[26] C.G. Jung, *Psychological Types*, CW 6, § 925.

multitude of Mendelian units, it does not seem altogether out of the question that the human psyche is similarly put together."[27]

89   These were, very briefly, Jung's professional interests and accomplishments up to the time he met Sigmund Freud whose published works he had been reading since 1900.[28] In spite of the unpopularity of Freud's discoveries at the time, Jung nevertheless made up his mind to champion them[29], although he did not share all of his views himself.[30] Near the end of his life he wrote about him:[31]

90   Freud's greatest achievement probably consisted in taking neurotic patients seriously and entering into their peculiar individual psychology. . . . He saw with the patient's eyes, so to speak, and so reached a deeper understanding of mental illness than had hitherto been possible. In this respect he was free of bias, courageous, and succeeded in overcoming a host of prejudices. Like an Old Testament prophet, he undertook to overthrow false gods, to rip the veils away from a mass of dishonesties and hypocrisies, mercilessly exposing the rottenness of the contemporary psyche. . . . The impetus which he gave to our civilization sprang from his discovery of an avenue to the unconscious. By evaluating dreams as the most important source of information concerning the unconscious processes, he gave back to mankind a tool that had seemed irretrievably lost.

---

[27] C.G. Jung, "Archaic Man," CW 10, § 141.

[28] He writes (*Memories*, pp. 269-270): "From the start of my psychiatric career the studies of Breuer and Freud, along with the work of Pierre Janet, provided me with a wealth of suggestions and stimuli. Above all, I found that Freud's technique of dream analysis and dream interpretation cast a valuable light upon schizophrenic forms of expression. As early as 1900 I had read Freud's *The Interpretation of Dreams*. . . . In 1903 I once more took up *The Interpretation of Dreams* and discovered how it all linked up with my own ideas."

[29] Cf. C.G. Jung, "Freud's Theory of Hysteria: A Reply to Aschaffenburg," CW 4, §§ 1 – 26. In 1906 Jung started a correspondence with Freud which lasted until 1913. Cf. *The Freud/Jung Letters*. In 1906 Jung sent Freud his *Diagnostische Assoziationsstudien I* (including papers 1 -3 and 5 in *Experimental Researches*, CW 2) and in 1907 his *Über die Psychologie der Dementia praecox* ("The Psychology of Dementia Praecox"), CW 3, §§ 1 ff. Cf. *Memories*, pp. 165 ff; and Wehr, pp. 23 ff.

[30] Cf. Wehr, p. 23 f.

[31] C.G. Jung, *Memories*, p. 192 f.

91   Oddly enough, it was the same basic mythical theme, the phallic god, that had gripped both researchers, and both men were motivated to their very depths by a great love for humanity, by their *compassion medici*. Nevertheless, when it came to the question of that unconscious power, they had to take different paths.

92   I do not wish to bring up once again all the personal details of Jung's break with Freud here.[32] It should be clear enough from the facts presented above, however, that Jung was not a pupil of Freud's who defected, as has often been erroneously reported, but that he had already developed the basic features of his own life-work before his meeting with Freud. What brought these two great pioneers together was their common recognition of the unconscious as a fundamental, now empirically demonstrable, psychic reality. The separation was necessary, broadly speaking, because Freud concentrated on the physical and biological background of the unconscious and on a causal explanation of its manifestations, while Jung conceived the psyche in terms of polarity, in the sense that both the drive (the biological aspect) and its restraints (the so-called spiritual or cultural aspect) belong to the very nature of the unconscious, and that the causal explanation of its manifestations must be complemented and completed, so to speak, by the final or teleological explanation.[33] For Freud, sexuality in the last analysis is rooted in a biological drive; for Jung, sexuality, although indeed a biological occurrence, is also the expression of a "chthonic spirit," which is "God's other face," the dark side of the God-image (phallus dream). In view of Freud's emotion when he discussed sexuality, Jung suspected that for Freud, too, sexuality was really a "god," but one which he was unable consciously to accept.

93   Later, Jung also tried to explain the opposition between Freud and himself as a typological difference in temperament. Freud's thinking corresponded to an extraverted approach to scientific research, whereas Jung's approach was that of an introvert.[34] In the

---

[32] The reader can find an orientation concerning Jung's standpoint in *Memories, Dreams, Reflections,* pp. 169 – 193 and in *Man and His Symbols,* part I; and on Freud's standpoint in Ernest Jones' *Life and Work of Sigmund Freud.* Cf. also *The Freud/Jung Letters.*

[33] Cf. Liliane Frey-Rohn, *From Freud to Jung,* and the further literature cited there.

[34] For the first time in a lecture on the question of psychological types, at the 1913 Psychoanalytic

case of an extravert, it is the outer object which most interests the subject, while with the introvert, attention will flow from the object back to the subject. Jung compared this movement and counter-movement of psychic energy with Goethe's concepts of *systole* and *diastole*. Both attitudes are present in everyone; the type is determined merely by the fact that the one or the other attitude customarily predominates. The attitude can change with the passage of time. The introvert, generally speaking, is characterized by a "hesitant, reflective, retiring nature that keeps itself to itself, shrinks from objects (and) is always slightly on the defensive."[35] The extravert, on the other hand, has an open, forthcoming disposition that "adapts easily to a given situation, (one that) will often venture forth with careless confidence into unknown situations." Jung himself was unmistakably an introvert. As such, he helped to gain a great appreciation of the introverted undercurrent in our culture, which often undervalues the introverted attitude to life. At the same time, he also helped us to understand better the more introverted outlook of most Eastern cultures. Jung's differentiation of types has been so widely recognized that the two concepts have entered the vocabulary of ordinary speech. Yet the Jungian and Freudian schools are still opposed to one another at this time, probably by reason of the typological difference. The Freudian outlook has to date gained almost exclusive prevalence because it is closer to the predominantly extraverted orientation of our sciences. It is only in recent years that a tendency has arisen to give more serious consideration to the subjective factor, but this has happened not so much in psychiatry as in atomic physics, while among academic psychologists, Jung is still referred to as a "muddled" mystic.

Congress in Munich. Developed in *Psychological Types* (1921), which appeared at almost the same time as E. Kretschmer's *Körperbau und Charakter*. Cf. Wehr, pp. 49 f. The evaluation of Freud's thinking as extraverted does not mean that Freud, as a man, was himself extraverted. In my opinion he was an introverted feeling type and his thinking was accordingly extraverted.

[35] C.G. Jung, "The Psychology of the Unconscious," *Two Essays on Analytical Psychology*, CW 7, §§ 62 and 79 ff. Cf. also Wehr, p. 71. The further typological differentiations developed by Jung are less well known and until now have remained more in the context of therapy and diagnosis of the Jungian school, primarily because a certain degree of differentiation in the observer is required in order to recognize them. Cf. in this connection Heinz Remplein, *Psychologie der Persönlichkeit*, cited by Wehr, p. 56.

94   Unfortunately, many malicious rumours have been spread abroad concerning the relations between Freud and Jung, and one of these is the oft repeated slander that Jung was a National Socialist and/or anti-Semitic. I knew Jung personally from 1933 until his death and I never perceived the slightest conscious or unconscious trace of any such attitude. On the contrary, he frequently inveighed against Hitler and Nazism in quite unambiguous terms. He had numerous Jewish refugees among his analysands (some of whom he treated gratis). A repetition of the facts here seems to me superfluous.[36] A word or two concerning Aniela Jaffé's treatment of the theme, however, does seem necessary.[37] The author gives a true and faithful account of all the facts, as well as of all the actions which could be chalked up as Jung's mistakes and which he later looked upon as such. His great mistake, according to Jaffé (and, later, in his own opinion), lay in talking too much. She correctly emphasizes the fact that Jung was too optimistic, "which proves once again the truism that a great scientist is not necessarily a good politician." Jung once confessed to Leo Baeck himself, "I slipped up" (on the slippery ground of politics). Jaffé uses this occasion to speak of a "shadow" of Jung's which, in her account, was mixed up in the matter.[38] To me, this seems to be an opinion taken from thin air for, quite obviously, as she herself says elsewhere, the mistake was because of Jung's "therapeutic" optimism, or in other words, to the passion with which he gave himself to his medical work. Wherever what was dark and destructive broke through, whether in the individual or in the collective, he always tried, with the passionate intensity of the born physician, to save whatever there was to save. When a friend once remarked to him that he was much too optimistic with regard to a certain ill-tempered and malicious patient and always thought, *now* she is going to improve, he answered, "I know. I know. You are right. But how could I treat people if I do not go on hoping?" And he

---

[36] The reader will find the best account of the facts in E.A. Bennet, *C G. Jung*, pp. 56 ff; and in Barbara Hannah, *C.G. Jung*. Cf. also Ernest Harms, "Carl Gustav Jung, Defender of Freud and the Jews," *Psychiatric Quarterly*, 20 (1946), pp. 199 ff; and Wehr, pp. 114 – 16.
[37] A. Jaffé, *From the Life and Work of C.G. Jung*, pp. 78 ff.
[38] Ibid., p. 90.

confesses in a letter[39] (dated April 1946) that he had had illusions about people. He could never have imagined that such abysmal evil could come to the surface and break out. It was not a hidden shadow element but rather the "therapeutic" optimism of his temperament which misled Jung into his "mistake."

95   The phallic god of Jung's childhood dream is also, as Hermes, the divinity of heralds and peacemakers, and because Jung hoped to save the situation in Germany, which was heading into a mass psychosis, he did not remain silent, which would have perhaps been wiser. On one other occasion his hopes were dashed. A year or two before the end of the war, a German doctor who was in no way sympathetic to National Socialism but whose professional work gave him access to an important personage in the Führer's headquarters, approached Albert Oeri, Carl J. Burckhardt, and Jung with the plea that they help him convey to England an offer of capitulation that he had been able to persuade Hitler to make. Jung went to work at once, in the hope of saving both sides much suffering. But Hitler suddenly changed his mind and the German doctor had to take hasty refuge in Switzerland to avoid being executed as a defeatist. Jung said sadly to the English pupil whom he had expected to send to England on this mission, "This evil is so abysmal that it can only end in total destruction. Even the innocent people who are left can no longer be spared the suffering that is coming now." It was not some unconscious shadow element but a deep and intense *compassion medici* which disposed Jung to this "mistake." His natural optimism often brought him disappointments, in important and unimportant matters, but it also enabled him to achieve transformations in therapy which a more sceptically disposed physician could not have brought about. In the mythologem of the physician, interestingly enough, Asclepius is led by his passion for healing to rebel against the god's decree and for this offense he has to pay dearly.

96   War was abhorrent to Jung and towards the end of his life, he often said that he would not be able to survive the outbreak of a third world conflagration. However, since he knew that the Swiss military

---

[39] Ibid., p. 95 ff.

would never be used in an offensive action, he had a most positive attitude towards the Army. He was proud of his rank as Captain in the Medical Service, and whenever there were military parades in the neighbourhood, whether large or small, he often went to watch them.

97   Hermes, the god of peacemakers, dominated not only Jung's adaptation to the world around him, but first and foremost his way of dealing with his patients. He had no interest in "training" or "educating" a patient according to any kind of method. Instead he always tried to help him find peace with himself by mediating the messages sent by the patient's own unconscious. He felt that his was the role of obstetrician, so to speak, or midwife, assisting in bringing into the light of day a natural inner process of coming into one's self. This process follows a different path with each individual since individual human beings and individual fates are so infinitely varied. The physician is thus truly a *hermeneut*, an interpreter who translates the symbolic dream-letters the patient receives out of his own psychic depths during the night. In this respect Jung's work resembled that of the old shamans and medicine men among primitive peoples. The shaman or medicine man also seeks with his own means (trance, oracles, etc.) to learn what the "spirits," that is, the activated unconscious or certain complexes, want from the person who is suffering, so that they can be propitiated through appropriate rituals, expiatory rites, sacrifices, etc., or driven away if these "spirits" are alien to the personality. The shaman is able to do this because, during his initiation ordeal, he himself has struggled with the spirit-world, the unconscious, and has come to terms with it, so that he has learned to understand the language of spirits and of animals. The shaman himself does not heal; he mediates the healing confrontation of the patient with the divine powers.

98   Although he expressly never employed a schematic therapeutic method or technique[40], Jung did describe certain typical phases of

---

[40] The reader who is interested in the details of this non-technical approach in Jungian psychology will find them in Wolfgang Hochheimer's excellent book, *The Psychology of C.G. Jung*. Hochheimer correctly points out that this approach has some things in common with Rogers' "non-directive" method.

the analytic process. He distinguished *four* characteristic stages[41]: confession, elucidation, education, and transformation.

99   This first step or stage, *confession,* has its prototype in the confessional practices of almost all the mystery religions of antiquity and the historical continuation of these practices in the Catholic Church. This means that the patient becomes conscious of and confesses to the doctor everything concealed, repressed, and guilt-laden, which isolates him from the society of his fellow men. Repressed contents can be thoughts, wishes, or also emotions and affects. "It is as if man had an inalienable right to behold all that is dark, imperfect, stupid and guilty in his fellow men – for such, of course, are the things we keep secret in order to protect ourselves .... There is a saying from the Greek mysteries: 'Give up what thou hast, and then thou wilt receive.'"[42] This first stage of catharsis (purification) serves to bring into consciousness the shadow, that is, the dark inferior aspects of our personality. Healing, however, does not always set in at this stage; in many cases the patient regresses after confession to a childish dependence either on the doctor or on his own unconscious.[43] This dependence (transference) has its source for the most part in unconscious fantasies. In contrast to the repressed material, these fantasies are contents which have never become conscious; in fact some of them have never been capable of coming into consciousness. In order to make these contents conscious, Freud, like Jung, used the dream interpretation method, but Freud employed a more reductive method: he traced the dream contents causally back to early childhood impulses and impressions.[44] This is the stage of *elucidation.* Once these contents are assimilated into consciousness, the next task is that of *education,* or self-education *as a social being.*[45] With this education it might appear that everything necessary in the way of psychotherapy had been accomplished, were it not for the fact that "normality," though

[41] C.G. Jung, 'The Problems of Psychotherapy', CW 16, §§ 114 – 174, here § 122.
[42] Ibid., § 133.
[43] A condition that Freud calls fixation.
[44] Whereas Jung employs the so-called synthetic method as well; cf. below.
[45] C.G. Jung, "The Problems of Psychotherapy," CW 16, § 150. Here the standpoint of Alfred Adler comes into play.

it is indeed a solution for some people, is nevertheless a prison for others. "To be 'normal' is the ideal aim for the unsuccessful," writes Jung[46], "for all those who are still below the general level of adaptation. But for people of more than average ability ... the moral compulsion to be nothing but normal signifies the bed of Procrustes – deadly and insupportable boredom, a hell of sterility and hopelessness." It seems to me that there are more and more people today who are suffering, as Jung realized[47], from what he called a facultative or optional neurosis – that is, they are normally adapted socially, or could be, but they find it impossible to go along with the neurotic misorientations of precisely this assumedly "normal" collective. Jung writes[48], "Among the so-called neurotics of our day there are a good many who in other ages would not have been neurotic – that is, divided against themselves. If they had lived in a period and in a milieu in which man was *still linked by myth with the world of the ancestors, and thus with nature truly experienced and not merely seen from outside*, they would have been spared this division with themselves." The picture of the world described from the outside, as provided by the natural sciences, and by mere intellectual speculation, is no substitute. In my opinion, this problem is becoming more acute with each passing year and a revolt particularly by the younger generation against the pseudo-normality of our banal and shallow academic rationalism is gathering force. In their quest for the lost myth many are turning to the teachings of the East[49], others want to go back to nature, while still others are trying to find a breakthrough to immediate experience and the unconscious via drugs. Thus, the present neurotic split is constantly drifting into greater crises. One scarcely knows any longer if the more normal people are not those who refuse to adapt to a time which is out of joint, but of course there are a great many genuinely neurotic and lazy individuals who make use of this argument to cloak their actual social inferiority.

---

[46] Ibid., § 161.
[47] C.G. Jung, *Memories*, p. 166.
[48] Ibid. Italics added.
[49] One thinks, for example, of the Beatles' guru or of the spread of Zen Buddhism in America, as well as of the many different kinds of yoga practiced in both Europe and America.

100   If, however, the case is not one of such a maladapted individual but of a normal person who is suffering from the neurotic deformations of our time, the physician cannot come to his aid with treatment aimed at achieving normality. Instead he must "meet" the patient with his whole personality and lay himself open to the irrational forces from both the patient's and his own unconscious. But most important of all he must himself "be the man through whom [one wishes] to influence others." In the fourth stage, therefore, the physician must first of all apply to himself whatever system he believes in. The analysand can be transformed only to the extent that the doctor has been himself transformed. The doctor's own ethics and his own attitude towards life become therefore the central point of his endeavour. The self-education and self-development undertaken by the therapist, however, go far beyond the scope of the consulting room. The physician must also treat the healthy, as the guru or the teacher usually does in Eastern cultures.[50] From then on, compulsion must be replaced by development, by growth into maturity. Jung later called this maturation process individuation. Individuation is difficult to describe scientifically because it includes so many individual variations, as the name itself implies. Nevertheless, if a sufficient number of cases are observed, it is possible to discern certain general features.[51]

101   On his first encounter with his own unconscious, the European or American who has been brought up in a Christian atmosphere usually discovers those inferior and "dark" qualities that have been repressed, or that he has tried consciously to suppress. The unconscious first appears, so to speak, as the "shadow" of that personality that the ego believes itself to be. Both Sigmund Freud and Alfred Adler were chiefly concerned with this aspect of therapy. The shadow, however, does not always consist of inferior aspects of the personality. Hedwig Boye[52], for example, observed a number of criminals who had lived out their darker side uninhibitedly and

---

[50] Cf. C.G. Jung, "The Problems of Psychotherapy," CW 16, § 167 f.
[51] Cf. in particular C.G. Jung, "The Relations between the Ego and the Unconscious," CW 7, §§ 266 – 406, and Marie-Louise von Franz, "The Individuation Process" in: *Archetypal Dimensions of the Psyche*, p. 202 – 359.
[52] Hedwig Boye, *Menschen mit grossem Schatten*.

discovered that the shadow figure in the unconscious exhibited moral and noble traits. In the analysis of an East Indian, I, too, had an opportunity to observe that the unconscious tended to separate the light from the dark parts of the personality, rather than to unite them, as it does with us, because, as a result of the general attitude of the conscious mind of the Indian, they were too much mixed up with each other, which, of course, is just as much a form of unconsciousness as is the repression of one side or the other.

102   Once the "inferior" aspects of the ego-personality have become conscious and have been integrated[53], a contra-sexual aspect of the unconscious generally then comes to light.[54] If the conscious personality has been more committed to the Logos aspect of life, as is usually the case with men, then the Eros aspect appears personified in feminine figures in dreams. Conversely, if the Eros aspect of life has received more attention from the ego, as is generally the case with women, then there will be masculine personifications of the Logos aspect. Jung called these contra-sexual personifications of the unconscious personality the *anima* (in men) and the *animus* (in women).[55] In a man, the anima finds expression principally in the form of specific positive or negative moods or feeling tones, of erotic fantasies, of life impulses and inclinations; the animus of a woman will appear rather in the form of unconscious impulses to action, sudden initiative, autonomous babbling, opinions, reasons, or convictions. On the one hand, these contra-sexual personality components form a bridge in relations with the opposite sex (mostly by way of projections), but they are also a special obstacle in trying to understand one's partner, since the man's anima tends to irritate women and woman's animus tends to irritate men which engenders the so-called "war of the sexes." Most marital difficulties can be traced back to the influence of these unconscious forces.

---

[53] By "integration" Jung understands the conscious and morally responsible incorporation of the unconscious complexes into the total personality.

[54] And with it, the problem of the transference, which will be taken up below.

[55] Cf. in this connection C.G. Jung, *Aion*, CW 9ii; and Emma Jung, *Animus and Anima*. Cf. also Cornelia Brunner, *Die Anima als Schicksalsproblem des Mannes*. Cf. particularly Barbara Hannah, "The Problem of Contact with the Animus," in: *Jungiana*, Beiträge zur Psychologie von C. G. Jung, Series A, Vol. 3, and *Striving towards Wholeness*, passim.

103   If these aspects of the unconscious are withdrawn from the objects onto which they are projected and integrated into consciousness, the unconscious will then reveal a superior personality which, in men, often has the traits of the "master," of the wise old magician, and demi-god, and in women those of the mistress, the great mother, the old wise woman, or of a goddess who is both Kore and Demeter at once. Jung called this aspect of the unconscious *the Self*, borrowing the term from Indian philosophy. The Self appears to encompass all the aspects of the psyche mentioned above, including the ego. Jung's description of his own No. 2, which he discovered in early youth, corresponds to the Self – it is, so to speak, the greater, eternal human being in us. But this figure does not always appear in personified form. It may just as often be symbolized by a mathematical figure, a circular or square image, in which case it is not so much the personal aspects, but rather the aspect of this centre of the personality that creates order or gives meaning that is being emphasized. This symbol of the unconscious – of psychic wholeness – will be discussed at greater length below.

104   Jung suggested that the sequence of transformations described above does not end with the Self. There are probably further powers behind the personification of the Self, but he decided not to attempt further description of them for he thought such a description would not be understood. He was convinced, however, that more and more distant horizons of existence could be opened up to our growing consciousness.

105   It has often been said in Jungian circles that the above sequence can also take place in quite a different order, so that the above schema may by no means be taken as the only possible pattern. Especially in the case of young people, in whom the ego is just being constellated, one sometimes meets with an exact reversal. Jung's description presents, as it were, a gradation of the degrees of difficulty in the process of integration. Becoming conscious of the shadow could be described as work for a beginner, while integration of the animus and anima is a much more advanced endeavour, and few people today succeed in getting beyond that point. The

components described are *present* in every man and woman, but people find them for the most part in projection, or else they identify with them *unconsciously*. If, for example, one knows nothing about one's shadow, one can simply stop and ask oneself what those qualities are in other people that get on one's nerves a bit more than is really called for. That is where the devil is hiding! Animus and anima for the most part pull the strings from behind in love relationships, but they can also be spotted in the effeminacy of a man or in the masculinity of a woman. Throughout the present century, various political "leaders" have offered conspicuous examples of identification with the Self, whereas in earlier times, these "leaders" were more apt to be religious figures with claims to speak for Christ or Satan or God or the Holy Spirit. In a less conspicuous way, however, any overly-authoritative behaviour betokens an identification with the Self, whether it be in science, politics or religion. Identification with the aspects of the unconscious just described is, according to Jung, the reverse of making them conscious.

106   Finally, there is a further kind of identification with unconscious contents that one meets often enough that must be mentioned. There are certain people who suffer from the illusion that they are identical with the social role they enact (that Jung calls the *persona*): the wise "all-knowing" scholar or doctor, the "energetic" officer, the "kind-hearted" nurse, the "fatherly and benevolent" clergyman, etc. A familiar folklore motif has materialized in these individuals, the motif in which the mask (persona) suddenly grows onto the person wearing it and can no longer be detached. Many people, however, have enough insight and sense of humour to avoid this trap and are able quite readily to discriminate between their public role and their personal ego.

107   These differentiating terms of Jung's (persona, shadow, animus and anima, Self) are under no circumstances to be understood as mere intellectual concepts.[56] They are designations for the purpose

---

[56] In *Memories*, (p. 167), Where "the reality of life is well covered up by so-called clear concepts," then experience "is stripped of its substance, and instead mere names are substituted, which are henceforth put in the place of reality. No one has any obligations to a concept; that is what is so agreeable about

of establishing a certain order in the chaos of the most widely varied inner experiences of many men and women, much as one also classifies plants and animals. The term "the cloven hoof," for example, is not a philosophical term, but a descriptive name for a relatively similar group of real, observable creatures. In the same way, what Jung has called the individuation process is an *experience* that is by no means restricted to the context of Jungian therapy. This path to maturity is followed naturally by many people, either alone or supported within the framework of traditional spiritual values. When he treats this kind of patient, the therapist is but a midwife at the birth of a process of growing and becoming conscious, toward which nature herself seems to be striving.

108   "In reality . . . individuation is an expression of that biological process – simple or complicated as the case may be – by which every living thing becomes what it was destined to become from the beginning."[57] The goal of individuation, as pictured in unconscious images, represents a kind of mid-point or centre in which the supreme value and the greatest life-intensity are concentrated. It cannot be distinguished from the images of the supreme value of the various religions; rather, it appears as naturally in the individuation process as it does in the religions, in the Christian world, for example, as an "inner castle" (Teresa of Avila), a four-square city or garden, as the *scintilla animae*[58], as the *imago Dei* in the soul, as the "circle whose periphery is nowhere and whose centre is everywhere[59]," as a crystal, a stone, a tree, a vessel or a cosmic order; or, again, as in Eastern religions, as a golden four-petalled flower, as light, as a "void" filled with meaning. The experience of this highest end, or centre, brings the individual an inner certainty, peace, and sense of meaning and fulfilment, in the presence of which he can accept himself and find a middle way between the opposites in his inner nature. Instead of being a fragmented person who has to cling to collective supports, he now becomes a self-reliant whole human

conceptuality. . . . The spirit does not dwell in concepts, but in deeds and in facts. Words butter no parsnips; nevertheless, this futile procedure is repeated *ad infinitum*."
[57] C.G. Jung, *Psychology and Religion: West and East*, CW 11, § 460.
[58] Cf. Hans Hof, *Scintillae animae*, especially, pp. 185 ff.
[59] On this symbol, see Dietrich Mahnke, *Unendliche Sphäre und Allmittelpunkt*.

being who no longer needs to live like a parasite off his collective environment in an infantile manner, but who enriches it and strengthens it by his presence.[60] The experience of the Self brings a feeling of standing on solid ground inside oneself, on a patch of inner eternity which even physical death cannot touch.

109   In professional psychotherapeutic circles, these discoveries and interpretations of Jung's have found less favour than those of Freud's. Nevertheless, they are spreading, although for the most part in the form of privately operated institutions and societies.[61] In almost all of the larger cities of Europe (for example London, Paris, Bremen, Berlin, Stuttgart, Munich, Zurich, Basel, Copenhagen, Rome, Milan) there are associations of therapists and others interested in the Jungian orientation, and in some of these cities there are also training centres. The same is true in Israel and America. In the United States, there are professional associations and large groups in New York, Chicago, Houston (Texas), San Francisco and Los Angeles, as well as in Brazil (Rio de Janeiro). There are a great many eminent writers who have been pupils of Jung's: Erich Neumann established a wide reputation especially with his *Origins and History of Consciousness*[62], along with Joseph Henderson[63], John Perry[64], Gerhard Adler[65], Michael Fordham[66], E.A. Bennet[67], Bruno Klopfer[68], Wilhelm Bitter, C.A. Meier, Gustav Schmalz[69], and many others[70]. But it is not only those who write books who are to be honoured for their contributions to Jungian psychology: everywhere

---

[60] Cf. in this connection C.G. Jung, "The Development of Personality," CW 17, § 286 and particularly, § 295 ff.

[61] Cf. Esther Harding, "Jung's Influence on Contemporary Thought," *Religion and Health*.

[62] See also Erich Neumann, *The Great Mother; Depth Psychology and a New Ethic; The Child; Amor and Psyche; Art and the Collective Unconscious;* and other works.

[63] Joseph Henderson, *Thresholds of Initiation;* and other works.

[64] John Perry, *The Self in the Psychotic Process*.

[65] Cf. Gerhard Adler, "C.G. Jung," in: *Middlesex Hosp. Journal 63*, No. 4; *Studies in Analytical Psychology; The Living Symbol*.

[66] Michael Fordham, *The Life of Childhood* (later edition *Children as Individuals*); and other works.

[67] E.A. Bennett, *What Jung Really Said*.

[68] B. Klopfer et al., *Developments in the Rorschach Technique;* "Some Dimensions of Psychotherapy," *Spectrum Psychologiae;* and other works.

[69] *Östliche Weisheit und westliche Psychotherapie*, W. Bitter, Ed.; *Komplexe Psychologie und körperliches Symptom*.

[70] My colleagues around the world will perhaps forgive me if I cite only a small random selection. A complete and fairer listing would exceed the scope of this book.

there are the quiet voices who live with Jung's conceptions and communicate them to those around them.

110   Jung's description of the individuation process has not met with much understanding outside of the Jungian school.[71] Hence one sees more and more each year how those "powers," whose coming to consciousness is part of the individuation process, capture an ever greater number of people from behind, leading to the phenomena of primitive possession: the upsurge of the shadow in the increase in criminality and "riots"; the activation of the animus and anima in the comparative effeminacy of many young men and the masculinity of many girls. The unconscious always seems to come through the door with its left foot first – it may be, therefore, that these phenomena are the first hopeful signs heralding a future increase in consciousness. In any case I have found not a few of today's young people seem to have less difficulty in becoming aware of the shadow and of the animus and anima than did the previous generations.

---

[71] The reproach most frequently levelled against Jung is that individuation is an asocial, egocentric exercise. This is by no means the case. The human being, in his instinctual nature, is a social being, and, when this nature is rescued from unconsciousness and related to consciousness, he becomes more socially fit and better related to his fellow men. Individuation, therefore, is by no means the same as individualism. Naturally, it may happen that a person who has sacrificed too much to his social task is forced into a relative withdrawal as a result of becoming conscious of what his unconscious is saying, and people around him may feel that he has become egocentric. Such a withdrawal, however, merely anticipates a much more radical withdrawal, which the unconscious would have precipitated in the form of a heart infarct or of some other kind of 'breakdown'. This problem will be discussed in more detail in Chapter 14.

Chapter 4

Mirror–Symmetry and the Polarity of the Psyche

111   Just as it was suggested in the previous chapter, ego-consciousness – the "little light" – and the realm of the unconscious appear to have a similar basic quaternary structure and to possess a mirror-symmetrical relationship of mutual projection to one another.[1]

112   *Projection* was a concept created by Jung, one that is of great significance. It is not difficult to recognize in everyday life: we repeatedly see in others peculiarities and ways of behaving that we ourselves display without being aware of doing so. Whenever we suffer from an excessive emotional fascination, whether of love or of hate, there is always at bottom a projection. In other words, projection is an involuntary transposition of something unconscious in ourselves into an outer object without our being consciously aware of doing so. The occurrence of projection stems in the last analysis from that universal psychological phenomenon which Jung calls "archaic identity," a state in which primitive man, the child and, to a degree, every adult is not differentiated from his environment; our instinctive empathy with people, with animals, and even with inanimate objects also has its source in archaic identity.[2] In the

---

[1] Cf. C.G. Jung, *Psychological Types*, CW 6, § 783: "Projection means the expulsion of a subjective content into an object; . . . Projection results from archaic *identity* of subject and object, *but is properly so called only when the need to dissolve the identity with the object has already arisen.* This need arises *when the identity becomes a disturbing factor,* i.e., when the absence of the projected content is a hindrance to adaptation and its withdrawal into the subject has become desirable." (Italics added by author.) Jung makes a further distinction between an active and a passive projection, the latter being an act of "feeling-into," the former an act of judgment.

[2] C.G. Jung, "I use the term *identity* to denote a psychological conformity. It is always an unconscious phenomenon . . . a relic of the original non-differentiation of subject and object. . . . It is not an *equation.. . . .* But identity also makes possible a consciously *collective . . . social* attitude." CW 6, §§ 741 – 42. "Lévi-Brühl coined the expression *participation mystique* for these relationships. It seems to me that the word 'mystical' is not happily chosen. Primitive man does not see anything mystical in these matters, but considers them perfectly natural. . . ." C.G. Jung, 'Archaic Man,' CW 10, § 130.

concept of projection, Jung created first and foremost an instrument for use in clearing up many misunderstandings between persons and groups, and in this practical application, the concept is currently in rather wide use. But the withdrawal of a projection, especially when it involves negative contents which are taken as "evil" and which are projected onto other people, is a moral achievement – that is, an achievement in the area of feeling. The need for the withdrawal of a projection is always constellated at that moment when conscious or semi-unconscious doubts about the rightness of one's own way of looking at things arise and when this view is fanatically defended on the conscious level. Doubt and fanaticism are therefore symptoms that indicate that the time is ripe for the withdrawal of some projection.

113   Because the withdrawal of a projection involves considerable moral effort, it is not generally a popular exercise. If a wider acceptance were given to Jung's concept of projection, profound and far-reaching changes would result, for we could no longer, for example, denigrate as "superstitions" the living religion or culture of another people (as so many religious and civilizing missions are still unashamedly doing today). Only that which is outlived and which is being called into question by the people itself may be described as projection and, even then, they cannot simply be dismissed as "error," but rather, people must be helped to see them as *psychic*, rather than as concrete "outer" truths. Many unclarified riddles are still hidden behind the concept of "projection," however, and in my opinion, it is the task of a future psychologist to investigate them.[3] For is not our entire picture of the world a projection (as it is understood by Hinduism or by Leibniz, with his "windowless" monads), and what makes it possible at a particular time for us to withdraw a projection – that is, that act of insight into what was previously projected?

114   The realization of a projection takes place in four stages.[4] On the level of archaic identity, the human being experiences projection

---

[3] M.L. von Franz, *Projection and Re-collection in Jungian Psychology.*
[4] Cf. C.G. Jung, "The Spirit Mercurius," CW 13, § 248, where the process is exemplified in the idea of an "evil" spirit.

simply as if it were the perception of reality. However, if conscious or unconscious doubts should arise from within and if the behaviour of the object conflicts with the individual's ideas about it, then he begins to differentiate between the projected image and the actual object. At the third stage, the individual usually explains the projection as having been an error or an illusion. At the fourth stage, however, he asks himself where that faulty image could have come from and then he has to recognize it as the image of a psychic content which originally belonged to his own personality (unless it was still not in evidence in his own psychology, in which case external factors once again have to be taken into account and the circle begins anew.)

115   The history of chemistry and physics may serve as an example: in antiquity, learned men – alchemists, that is – made many fantastic statements about matter that they took to be "truthful" descriptions of it. Later, it was noticed that quite a number of them were wrong, and new models – modern scientific hypotheses – for the ultimate nature and behaviour of matter were found. Previous statements were dismissed as "superstitious" errors. Jung then discovered that it was precisely in these "errors" that the statements of the alchemists described *psychic* contents, and that although they did not hold true when applied to the behaviour of matter, they did offer an adequate picture of certain psychic contents of the unconscious.[5] Although little notice has been taken of Jung's view so far, contemporary research into the fundamental problems of the sciences has already come very close to them, since today it is generally recognized that scientific knowledge is based on the creation of models in the researcher; but *the preconscious origins of our conceptual models, which are observable in dreams, are not closely examined*, so that the aspect of the projection which is peculiar to each model is still to a large extent ignored. The appearance of a projection is probably connected with the mirror-symmetrical relationship between the ego-complex and the centre of the unconscious personality. Closely

---

[5] More on the subject of alchemy in Chapters 11, 12 and 13.

connected with this is the capacity of consciousness to *reflect* (!), from which all higher consciousness emerges.

116   Today, the concepts of symmetry and polarity dominate to a large extent, if not exclusively, the field of atomic physics and hence broad areas of the natural sciences, especially biology[6], and, from the beginning, Jung experienced the psychic field in this way: on the one hand as a polarity between ego-consciousness (No. 1) and the unconscious (No. 2), and on the other hand as a polarity between matter (biological basis) and spirit (that is, the form-giving, ordering factor).

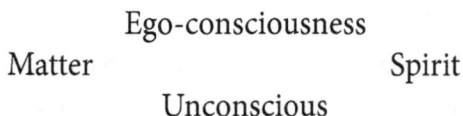

Ego-consciousness

Matter   Spirit

Unconscious

117 Just as in the natural sciences polarities are now generally described as symmetries because the poles are interchangeable, so the idea gradually forced itself on Jung that in the psychic realm as well it was conceivable that the poles might change into each other. On the practical level, however, symmetry is a question of polarity, often of genuine opposites.

118   In his reminiscences, Jung presents a dramatic description of the first type of polarity, of how consciousness and the unconscious polarize each other, and in this respect his convictions coincided with those of Sigmund Freud. They did not coincide, however, in respect to the second kind of psychic polarization, namely, the state of tension between spirit and matter, since ultimately Freud was convinced that psychic processes have their origins in matter. What Jung understood by the word "spirit" should therefore be looked at rather more closely.

119   In the German language, the word "Geist" (here translated as "spirit") has many different applications: it is used, for example, to indicate something that contrasts with matter, something imma-

---

[6] Because of the relativization of the parity principle. Cf. in this connection Karl Lothar Wolf, "Symmetrie und Polarität," *Studium Generale*, pp. 221 ff. Cf. further Vilma Fritsch, *Links und Rechts in Wissenschaft und Leben*, pp. 153 ff.

terial, that some philosophers identify with God or regard as the basic substance in which psychic processes occur. By *Geist*, Wilhelm Wundt understood "inner being, when taken as unconnected with outer being." The word *Geist* is applied by other philosophers to certain psychic capacities, like thinking or reason, the totality of intellect, will, memory, fantasy, and ideal strivings, or to a certain attitude of consciousness. The word *Zeitgeist* (spirit of the time or age) generally points to ideas, judgements, and motivations which are common to a collective. The idea of *Geist* displays a tendency towards personification: one speaks of the spirit of Pestalozzi, of Goethe, etc., almost in the sense of a survival of the soul of someone who has died. This is a relic of the original use of the word *Geist*.[7] The German word *Geist*[8] probably has more to do with something frothing, effervescing, or fermenting. . . ." Jung then sums up[9] the meaning of the word *Geist* (spirit) as being a functional complex which originally, on the primitive level, was felt as an invisible, breath-like "presence." When, therefore, something psychic happens in the individual which he feels as belonging to himself, that something is regarded as his own spirit; but if something psychic happens that seems to him strange, then it is somebody else's spirit, which can also be regarded as a still unintegrated aspect of the unconscious. This spiritual aspect of the unconscious possesses the power of spontaneous motion, and independently of outer sensory stimuli it produces images and sudden thoughts in the inner world of the imagination and even orders them in a meaningful way. One can observe this most clearly if one thinks of that unknown Something that produces dreams. From scraps of the previous day's experiences, from all sorts of memory elements and other unknown sources, there is composed in a dream a series of images and scenes which usually strikes the conscious mind at first as so alien that one is inclined to dismiss the dream as nonsense. On closer examination, however, this composition turns out to be a highly intelligent, meaningful statement about inner processes, often superior to those

---

[7] Cf. C.G. Jung, "The Phenomenology of the Spirit in Fairytales," CW 9/I, § 385.
[8] In English and in this context *Geist* means "spirit."
[9] Ibid.

made by consciousness. "Spirit," therefore, according to Jung, is in the first instance the composer of dreams: a principle of spontaneous psychic motion that produces and orders symbolic images freely and in accordance with its own laws.

120   The phenomenon of "spirit" can now also be elucidated by research into behavioural psychology. Zoologists, as is well known, refer to "elementary behaviour patterns"[10] by which is understood specific instinctive motor "patterns," common to both animals and human beings, such as hate, love, parental care in breeding time, aggression, and the like. Irenäus Eibl-Eibesfeldt, for example, takes a cross-section of various forms of greeting and kissing among human beings, in an attempt to reconstruct a generally human "elementary behaviour" form, in order to compare it with those observed in animals, and which could in his opinion be traced back to a few basic elementary primordial drives or urges, to the drive to care for the young at breeding season, for example, which latter drive, when used for greeting, would then acquire a transposed significance.

121   The "urge" to the realization of such instinctive patterns of behaviour is to be observed in human beings not only from outside, through comparison with their usual behaviour, but also *from within*: almost simultaneously with people's elementary behaviour patterns but in the inner field of vision, there appear fantasy images, sudden thoughts or notions that are heavily charged with emotion, "inspired" ideas and feelings (that is, value reactions) which are, like physical impulses to action, also similar or even the same in all human beings. One need only compare love poems or battle songs from all over the world, or myths and fairytales of the most diverse peoples, to discover that they all follow some basically identical pattern. *The dynamic that produces such inner symbolic patterns in the psyche is what Jung understands by the word "spirit."*

122   These inner processes give drives their specific *form*[11]. Among primitive peoples, we can observe that the factors that inhibit

---

[10] Cf. Konrad Lorenz, *On Aggression*, and Irenäus Eibl-Eibesfeldt, *Liebe und Hass*.
[11] It is by no means true that in the animal kingdom drives like aggression, sexuality, etc., are boundless: they are held down to certain limits by counterimpulses, for example by inhibition of the impulse to attack in the presence of an enemy's submissive attitude, by sexual periodicity, etc.

instinctual drives generally consist of traditional usages and in religious rituals and customs. The latter are, so to speak, "magic" customs or beliefs that not only express the form of the drive but also trigger it.[12] They constitute the basic elements of all religions, and out of this primordial association of drive with symbolic image, the close association between instinct and religion in the broadest sense can be explained. Thus, Jung says[13], "Religion on the primitive level means the psychic regulatory system that is coordinated with the dynamism of instinct" – the psychic regulatory system being the form-giving spirit. Primitive man, however, experiences the spirit as an autonomous Other, just as Jung himself in his youth first perceived it as a mysterious "objective psychic" presence. With the growing development of consciousness, certain aspects are then sensed as belonging to the personality[14], as a function of one's own psyche or as one's "own" spirit. The autonomous, still-surviving remnants of this point of view are preserved by the religions in the idea of an "objective spirit," in the idea, for example, of the Holy Ghost or of the "evil spirit" (Satan) in Christianity. In this respect, the religions serve as a reminder of the primordial character of spirit.[15] Between the poles, ego-consciousness/unconscious, and between the poles, matter/spirit, there exists an energy gradient which leads to psychic *flow*.[16] Jung therefore regarded psychic life, exactly as Freud did, as an energic process; in contrast to Freud, however, he did not regard this energy as psychosexual libido but rather as being *in itself entirely indefinite as to content*.[17] Only in the

---

[12] Cf. C.G. Jung, *Mysterium Coniunctionis*, CW 14, § 602.

[13] Ibid., § 603.

[14] In my book, *Number and Time*, I have tried to explain this in the light of the history of mathematics.

[15] Jung constantly warned against the danger of the illusion that one *owns* the spirit. "Spirit threatens the naïve-minded man with inflation, of which our own times have given us the most horribly instructive examples. The danger becomes all the greater the more our interest fastens upon external objects and the more we forget that the differentiation of our relation to nature should go hand in hand with a correspondingly differentiated relation to the spirit, so as to establish the necessary balance. If the outer object is not offset by an inner, unbridled materialism results, coupled with maniacal arrogance or else the extinction of the autonomous personality, which is in any case the ideal of the totalitarian mass state." C.G. Jung, "Phenomenology of the Spirit," CW 9/I, § 393.

[16] Thus, Jung sees psychic life as a tension between the two poles of matter and spirit, originally seen in the primordial images of Mother Earth and Father Spirit. Cf. "Symbols and the Interpretation of Dreams," CW 18, § 583 f.

[17] Cf. C.G. Jung, *Symbols of Transformation*, CW 5, Part 2, Chapter 2; and "On Psychic Energy," CW 8, §§ 54 ff.

field of actual experience does it appear as power, drive, wish, will, affect, work-achievement, etc.[18] At present, psychic energy is not quantitatively measurable. Its psychic intensity can only be estimated by way of the feeling function (for example, the intensity of certain thoughts or emotions).[19] The *quality* of an affect can also be clearly felt. "We can perceive the slightest emotional fluctuations in others and have a very fine feeling for the quality and quantity of affects in our fellow-men."[20] (One might add to this that even animals, dogs for example, have the capacity to assess the intensity of our emotions.)

123   As is well known, physical energy obeys the law of entropy: every expenditure of energy is accompanied by a certain lowering of the gradient, with an irrevocable loss of energy in the form of heat.[21] Psychic energy also seems to obey this law, at least to some extent. It remains to be proven, however, whether the *spiritual* dynamic of psychic energy obeys the law of negentropy, that is, whether it can build up a higher gradient, but it does not appear to be impossible. Without being acquainted with Jung's work, and proceeding from purely cybernetic considerations, the French physicist Olivier Costa de Beauregard recently postulated a cosmic "infra-psychism" that obeys the law of negentropy.[22]

---

[18] Cf. Jung's fundamental exposition, "On Psychic Energy," CW 8, §§ 6 ff. Psychic energy probably is in a relation of reciprocal interaction with physical energy. Thus, psychic energy probably behaves in accordance with the principle of equivalence, which states that "for a given quantity of energy expended or consumed an equal quantity of the same or another form of energy will appear elsewhere." Whether it follows the principle of constancy is uncertain, because we are able to observe only partial systems.

[19] The affect can be better measured indirectly from its physical syndromes, such as the pulse curve, the respiration curve or by the psychogalvanic phenomenon. Cf. C.G. Jung, "Experimental Researches," CW 2, §§ 1015 – 1311.

[20] Cf. C.G. Jung, "On Psychic Energy," CW 8 § 25.

[21] Ibid., § 35.

[22] For more detailed discussion cf. my *Number and Time*, pp. 17, 207 ff. Cf. also Nathan Schwartz, "Entropy, Negentropy and the Psyche." According to Jung, a psychic symbol or a symbolic act is, so to speak, a machine for the transference of energy, perhaps also for its increase. The spring ceremony of the Wachandi of Australia may serve as an example. "They dig a hole in the ground, oval in shape, and set about with bushes so that it looks like a woman's genitals. Then they dance round this hole, holding their spears in front of them in imitation of an erect penis. As they dance round, they thrust their spears into the hole, shouting. 'Pulli nira, pulli nira, wataka!' (not a pit, not a pit, but a c....!). During the ceremony none of the participants is allowed to look at a woman. By means of the hole the Wachandi make an analogue of the female genitals, the object of natural instinct. By the . . . shouting and the ecstasy of the dance they suggest to themselves that the hole is really a vulva.... There can be no doubt that this is a canalization of energy and its transference to an analogue of the original object by means of the dance (which is really a mating-play, as with birds and other animals).... The magic image or the symbol is hence the machine which transforms the psychic energy." C.G. Jung, "On Psychic Energy," CW 8, §§ 83 ff.

124   Psychic energy moves in a polar pattern, on the one hand between extraversion and introversion, on the other in regressive and progressive pulsations. The latter is a movement in time and forward into life (inwards and outwards) in the sense of further development, while the former is a temporary withdrawal to past life-forms in order to bring up values left behind in the past and incorporate them into the present psychic situation, or in order to be able to dispose of their energy for new undertakings ("*reculer pour mieux sauter!*")[23]

125   Yet another pair of polar concepts commended themselves to Jung as useful in the observation of psychic phenomena – those of causality and finality. On the one hand every psychic occurrence may be traced back, causally, to past events (for example, to traumatic childhood experiences, as Freud demonstrated); on the other hand, many can be understood only if we consider them from the view of their purpose or goal.[24] Both these antinomian approaches to understanding are necessary, in Jung's opinion, if one wishes to have a genuine description of psychic events. The two approaches are complementary in the sense expressed by Niels Bohr, who says,[25] "It is a well-known fact that there are biological connections which by their nature are described, not causally, but finalistically, that is, in relation to their goal. One thinks for example of the healing process after an organism has been wounded. The finalistic interpretation stands in a typically complementary relation to a description in accordance with known physico-chemical or atomic-physical laws. . . . The two types of description are mutually exclusive but they are not necessarily contradictory." In exactly the same way Jung thought that psychic processes, and especially dreams, should be described both causally and in respect to their goal or purpose. The psychic healing process can only be understood from the final standpoint, whereas the causal standpoint is more apt to yield a diagnosis.[26]

---

[23] Ibid., § 77 f.

[24] Ibid., § 3 ff. Cf. ibid., § 5, footnote 6.

[25] Speech cited by Werner Heisenberg in *Der Teil und das Ganze*, pp. 129-29.

[26] According to Jung, the latter is, in any case, not as important as it is in physical medicine because diagnosis does not indicate the therapy, as it does in physical medicine; the therapy generally has to be arrived at independently of the diagnosis.

126   Jung's use of the final or energic approach, as well as of the causal, led to very important results in two closely related areas of psychology: dream interpretation and therapy. For Freud, the dream served as a means of *uncovering* repressed, generally infantile unconscious content, and it was hoped that the therapeutic effect would result from this elucidation. For Jung, however, the dream contains much more than that: in symbolic form, it alludes to the goal towards which the psychic energy gradient is striving – that is, the dream contains anticipatory symbolizations of developmental tendencies.[27] That is why the direction in which the therapy is to proceed must be derived from the analysand's own dreams. That is finally the reason why, in Jungian therapy, there *can* be no technique or method and no arbitrary therapeutic goal to which the doctor aspires. Rather, it is a question of seeking to understand the specific energic trends towards healing and growth in each individual patient, in order to strengthen them through the participation of consciousness, and to assist their breakthrough into the conscious life of the patient.

127   The secret poet and director of the dream, however, is, as we have said, the "spirit," the active, dynamic aspect of the psyche. Spirit is the real culture-creating factor in human beings. It is probable that as we ascended from the animal kingdom, it slowly developed and evolved out of an excess of energy that could not find a complete outlet in instinctive behaviour patterns[28] and therefore found no employment in the original unchanged natural environment.[29]

128   This energy began to manifest itself in the creation of symbolic rites and fantasy images. In Jung's opinion, therefore, symbols were not invented or thought up by man, but were produced from the unconscious by way of so-called revelation or intuition.

129   It is probable that a good many historic religious symbols even originated directly in dreams[30] or were inspired by dreams. Ritual,

---

[27] In antiquity, this aspect was at one time considered to be the true meaning of the dream and its interpretation was concerned mainly with the prognosis of future developments.

[28] Cf. C.G. Jung, "On the Nature of Dreams," CW 8, §§ 91-92.

[29] Cf. C.G. Jung, "On Psychic Energy," CW 8, § 91.

[30] Ibid., § 92; and two examples in Marie-Louise von Franz, "The Individuation Process" in: *Archetypal Dimensions of the Soul*, p. 292 – 363.

too, may also have grown from involuntary movements, especially hand movements. We know, for example, that even today among primitive peoples the choice of a personal totem or of a god as a personal guardian or protector is often determined by dreams. In the course of later developments, the tendency to suppress individual symbol formation in the interest of the established collective symbols became more and more noticeable. A first step in this direction is the setting up of a state religion, along with the suppression of polytheistic inclinations and tendencies.[31] But as soon as such official religious forms decay, individual symbol formation begins to be reactivated.

130   It is peculiar to the spirit, or to the symbol-forming function of the psyche, to bring the multiplicity of instinctual drives into a unified structure. Konrad Lorenz, for example, speaks of a "parliament of the instincts"; in man, the symbol-forming function of the unconscious would correspond to the president of such a parliament. This function is the *spiritus rector* of the individuation process described in the previous chapter.

131   Man, in Jung's view, is a natural being, full of, on the one hand, primitive animal instincts and, on the other hand, a spiritual heritage of structural dispositions, created by the symbol-forming function of the psyche, that hold man's instinctive drives in check. "The mind, as the active principle in the inheritance, consists of the sum of the ancestral minds, the 'unseen fathers' whose authority is born anew with the child."[32] While Freud sees the fundamental human conflict as a collision of instinct with collective consciousness, Jung is of the opinion that *both* poles are present in nature, or in the human unconscious, that both of them have always been there and that neither is an epiphenomenon of the other. The recent discovery in the field of behavioural research, that the rudiments of rituals that transform elementary instincts into new forms of application are to be seen even in the animal kingdom, seems to me to lend added

---

[31] Cf. C.G. Jung, "On Psychic Energy," CW 8, p. 92. "The age-old function of the symbol is still present today, despite the fact that for many centuries the trend of mental development has been towards the suppression of individual symbol-formation. One of the first steps in this direction was the setting up of an official state religion, a further step was the extermination of polytheism. . . ."
[32] Ibid., § 101.

weight to Jung's hypothesis. It is still an open question whether animals also perceive inner symbolic mental images; for the time being, we are unavoidably dependent in this respect on the study of human beings since the possibility of verbal communication is not present in animals.[33]

132   According to Jung, the *creative function of the symbol-forming, psychic dynamic – or the spirit – always appears in the single* individual: it is only in the individual that new ideas, artistic inspirations, and constructive hunches and fantasies are created, that are sometimes then taken over and imitated by the group of which the individual is a part. This opinion of Jung's is also supported by behavioural research: it has been observed that only single animals try out new behaviour variations at first (for example, remaining in a particular spot for the sake of the food offered instead of migrating in the traditional way) and, in the event that they seem to be successful, they are then imitated by the group. *The creative spirit thus appears to be unconditionally bound up with the principle of individuation.* The group contribution consists more in the refinement and consolidation of new forms of behaviour.[34]

133   Seen in this context, it is clear why the dream, that most frequent and most important manifestation of the symbol-forming dynamic of the psyche, plays such a central role in Jung's psychology.[35] Along with inspirations and involuntary fantasies, it is the real manifestation of the spirit. Even at the time he entered the university, when he pondered upon the significance of his dream of the storm-lantern, Jung was struck by the superior intelligence of the dream that seemed to suggest a meaningful new attitude towards life. In the course of his later development, he continued to find out more and more about the "light of nature" that revealed itself in dreams.

---

[33] If current American attempts to investigate the "speech" of dolphins and chimpanzees should succeed, they might shed some light on the situation.

[34] It has been asserted that teams or groups can also function creatively, but upon closer observation it turns out that there, too, the single person must "do his own thing," as the hippies say. Small innovations and stimulations sometimes come from a group, but the genuine, important creative action always originates in a single person pursuing his own life-way. Cf. Donald C. Pelz and Frank M. Andrews, "Autonomy, Coordination and Stimulation in Relation to Scientific Achievement," *Behavioral Science.*

[35] And is seen quite differently in the Freudian school and in existentialist theory.

Thus, throughout his life he worked out certain angles of approach for coming closer to this inner source of light.[36]

134   First of all, it is advisable to keep firmly in mind all the personal associations to each individual dream image which come to mind. If this is done, then a wider connection (context) between the single images and scenes becomes apparent. In the event that universal mythological symbols appear – for instance, fire, heaven, stars, tree, etc., – and no special personal associations occur to the dreamer, one can, or must, then frequently bring in mankind's associations, i.e., the widespread collective historical understanding of such symbols. Most dreams also have a dynamic structure that rewards attention: it is similar to that of classic drama, in that the dream begins with an exposition (naming of time and place and principal characters), followed by a plot of complications (beginning of action in time, naming of the "problem"), a *peripeteia* (the back-and-forth and up-and-down of the treatment) and a *lysis* (or catastrophe), that is, a closing note that brings either a solution or a negative shock-effect, at which point the dreamer usually awakens.[37] If all these data are carefully observed, they provide the basis for an interpretation or "meaning" of the dream. This interpretation cannot, however, be a complete or final formulation of the dream's meaning since the meaning of a dream can never be exhaustively formulated. Instead, the interpretation amounts rather to an effort to tune the conscious attitude in such a way that a spark can fly out of the dream and over into consciousness, an "a-ha" reaction is stimulated, with a feeling of shock or illumination. A dream interpretation, therefore, is only correct when it seems "evident" to the dreamer, when it stimulates and also evokes an emotional alteration of the personality. Concentrating on the dream images[38], one talks around them, so to speak, until such a reaction takes place. Although Jung did work out and elaborate certain general scientific principles of his art of interpretation, it follows no single-track "method" but is to some

---

[36] It is with intention that I do not say "methods of interpretation," for it is more a question of an "art" than of a method.

[37] Sometimes the *lysis* is missing, revealing certain conditions which I cannot go into here.

[38] In contrast to Freud's "free association" method, which leads away from the images to the complexes. Cf. C.G. Jung, "Symbols and the Interpretation of Dreams," CW 18, §§ 420 – 426.

extent a practical skill. Even after one has interpreted thousands of dreams, one is always aware of how obscure they often remain and of how much one still has to learn about them. The interpreter's "personal equation" must also be taken into account in the process, since the more developed one is oneself the more meaning one "sees" in other people's dreams.[39]

135   One of Jung's most important contributions is interpretation on the subjective or objective level. Seen on the subjective level, a dream is an inner drama in which we are the spectator and simultaneously every character on the dream stage. All the actors embody projected elements of ourselves, among whom the drama plays itself out. Interpreted on the objective level, the dream gives us, in symbolic form, orientation concerning "objective" people and things that are a part of our waking world (if, for example, we have a warning dream about someone who later proves to be hostile, although we were not aware of that hostility at the time.) Interpretation on the subjective level is nearly always more rewarding, since it is only rarely that one can change the outer world, but with insight, one can bring about changes in oneself. Thus, with dreams of evil figures, for example, it is always more useful to take them as the beam in one's own eye rather than as the mote in the eye of another. Whether a dream should be taken on the objective or the subjective level is seldom unambiguously indicated by the dream itself. The decision is much more *a question of feeling* on the part of the dreamer or of his consultant. Hence, dream interpretation is also an ethical matter, not simply an intellectual procedure. Although a particular interpretation will often bring "illumination" to both dreamer and analyst, this is still no sure proof that it is really right. There is, thank God, another means of control, namely, *the dream series*. If a dream has been "falsely" interpreted, which means in a way that is unhealthy for the dreamer, then a corrective dream will usually appear during one of the following nights and will clear up some of the obscurity of the previous dream. In the end, there is the one

---

[39] I do not want to enter into the philosophical questions here; they are in my opinion prematurely posed. (Cf. Detlev von Uslar, *Der Traum als Welt.*) We have to gain much more experience in this field than we have as yet.

ultimate criterion of success in this art, the question: Does this way of dealing with the dream have a healing effect, or does it not? An objective, generally valid scientific method of interpreting dreams once and for all simply does not exist, in Jung's opinion. The dream remains a mysterious bit of psychic reality[40] which, with understanding, we can only approach but which can never be definitively exhausted by conscious interpretation.

136   Jung's approach to the dream is synthetic and constructive, which means that he attaches more importance to seeking out the purposive healing tendencies in the unconscious than to the causal derivation of the disturbance. Unexpected confirmation of the dream's symbolic representation of such tendencies has come from the purely external dream research being conducted (especially in America) with the aid of the electroencephalogram. If a man is prevented from dreaming, he falls ill. Accordingly, it seems that the dream has a normal, constructive function in the life process, along with the tendency to establish a homeostasis.[41]

137   According to Freud, the dream "disguises" psychic contents, which then need to be uncovered (the dream may say, for example, "walking stick" and mean "penis"). Jung rejected this view. In his opinion, the dream "disguises" nothing but is simply a bit of pure psychic nature; that we cannot necessarily understand it at once is due to the polarity between No. 1 and No. 2 – our ego-consciousness and the unconscious. "We must therefore take it that the dream is just what it pretends to be, neither more nor less."[42] One may – understandably enough – find it vexatious that the dream speaks to us in a relatively incomprehensible language, especially for example in cases where the danger warning is so obscurely put that one understands the warning only after the misfortune has actually

---

[40] Medard Boss gives special emphasis to this, erroneously assuming that it was not Jung's view. Cf. Detlev von Uslar, *passim*.
[41] Cf. W. Dement, "Die Wirkung des Traumentzugs," in: Jutta von Graevenitz, *Bedeutung und Deutung des Traumes in der Psychotherapie*, and the literature there cited, p. 330. Connections between biological research into dreams and the Jungian views are at present being explored by Stefan Vlaikovic, *Biologie des Träumens in teifenpsychologischer Sicht*, an unpublished dissertation. Partial aspects have also been investigated at the C.G. Jung Clinic, Zurich (also unpublished).
[42] C.G. Jung, "On the Psychology of the Unconscious," CW 7, § 162. Cf. also G. Wehr, *C.G. Jung*, p. 108 ff.

occurred. The reason for this is not owing to a "censor" which does not permit the dream to communicate directly, as Freud assumed, but rather, in Jung's view, to the fact that the concentrated brightness of our ego-consciousness has the effect of "dimming" the dream world, just as one scarcely sees candlelight when the electric light is turned on. The condition of unconsciousness keeps ideas and images at a much lower level of tension; they lose clarity and distinctness, their connections with one another seem less consistent, only "vague analogies." They do not seem to fit our logic, nor do they conform to temporal scales. Thus, according to Jung, "a dream *cannot* produce a definite thought. If it begins to do so, it ceases to be a dream because it crosses the threshold of conscious-ness."[43] It symbolizes that bit of spirit which is not yet one's "own" but which is, in its original condition[44], a bit of pure nature, out of which, and away from which, our ego-consciousness, with its concentratedly focussed functions, has grown. The intention behind our effort to understand dreams is to reconnect these more or less differentiated conscious functions with their roots, thereby pre-venting our conscious ego from becoming all too autonomous and concomitantly cut off from the instincts. If this understanding is gained, the dream activity of the unconscious has an animating and creatively inspiring effect on consciousness, and this effect then promotes psychological intelligence and health.

138   Jung's view of dreams is related to a decision he made after his dream of the storm-lantern had brought about a deep inner change: he decided at that time to identify with No. 1, to go on living his life accordingly, but *never to forget No. 2 or turn his back on him*, as so many people do at that time of life. "I have always tried," he writes[45], "to make room for anything that wanted to come to me from within." A denial of No. 2 would have been a self-violation[46] and would have robbed Jung of the possibility of explaining the source of his dreams, in which he sensed a higher intelligence at work. A great many

---

[43] C.G. Jung, "Symbols and the Interpretation of Dreams," CW 18, § 511.
[44] Biological dream research has recently shown that it is very likely that after birth, we gradually emerge from a "permanent" or "eternal" dream.
[45] *Memories*, p. 62.
[46] Ibid., p. 109.

"enlightened" contemporary men and women, however, have allowed themselves to become separated from their No. 2, and, as a result, they have frequently had to find their way back to a new awareness and acknowledgment of the effect of No. 2 in their lives via the suffering of a neurosis, not in order to identify with him or with his wisdom[47], but rather in order to *remain in dialogue with him.*

139   Further observation suggested to Jung that dreams have a certain compensatory relation to consciousness, in other words, they balance the one-sidedness of the conscious orientation[48], more or less as biological processes also do, or they supply what is missing from one's wholeness. In this sense, they are the expression of the *self-regulatory process* in the psychic wholeness of an individual, within which the unconscious appears to have a complementary (as the word is used in physics) relation to consciousness.[49] The stable cooperation of conscious *and* unconscious contents in the life process depends on the transcendent function, which is itself an aspect of the symbol-forming aspect of the unconscious whose purposive tendency is to hold conscious and unconscious together.[50] Our ego-consciousness tends to concentrate exclusively on adaptation to the circumstances of the present. It therefore obscures unconscious material that is not appropriate to adaptation, or else the unconscious contents have too low an energy charge to become conscious or are not yet ready to become conscious. Thus, the ego can easily develop a one-sidedness which does not accord with instinctive totality. It is the transcendent function that makes organically possible the transition from a one-sided attitude to a

---

[47] Ludwig Binswanger and Medard Boss see both the means and the goal of the understanding of dreams (without interpretation) in a total union of the isolated ego with the psychic world common to all mankind. In the Hegelian tradition, they proclaim the *Welt der Dinge* (the world of things). They thereby eliminate precisely that polarity which is so essential to life. Cf. the excellent survey of various views of dreams in Jutta von Graevenitz (Ed.), *Bedeutung und Deutung des Traumes in der Psychotherapie*, pp. 360 ff.

[48] Cf. C.G. Jung, "On the Nature of Dreams," CW 8, §§ 443 – 529; § 483, where examples are given. Earliest mention: "The Psychology of Dementia Praecox," CW 3, §§ 1 – 316.

[49] Cf. C.G. Jung, "The Transcendent Function," CW 8, esp. §§ 137 39.

[50] Cf. ibid., § 132. "This lack of parallelism is not just accidental or purposeless, but is due to the fact that the unconscious behaves in a compensatory or complementary manner towards the conscious." The unconscious contains, furthermore, "all the fantasy combinations which have not yet attained the threshold intensity, but which in the course of time . . . will enter the light of consciousness."

new, more complete one[51], thereby opening up the way for growth by symbolically sketching new possibilities of life. A symbol never points exclusively to something known, but always to complex data *not yet* grasped by our ego-consciousness[52], i.e., it points to a *meaning* we have not yet consciously realized.

140   Intermittent contact with the unconscious is important for the mentally ill because the healing tendencies of the psychic self-regulatory system can come into their consciousness in this way, and in the case of creative talents, a *continual* contact is usually indispensable and also usually present[53], as was the case with Jung himself.

141   The Jungian way of interpreting dream phenomena has been misunderstood in many quarters because of, in my view, the subtle *middle* position it occupies between the poles of the unconscious: spirit and matter, subjective level/objective level, causal-reductive/final-prospective interpretation, etc. Some critics reproach Jung for holding a position which is too remote from the unconscious (Medard Boss, for example), while others reproach him for overvaluing the unconscious.[54] But it is just this subtly balanced, middle position that seems to me to be what is uniquely important about Jung's conception of dreams. It makes it possible to understand the psyche as a living system of complementary opposites, without violating it intellectually with a one-sided approach, so that the door remains open to the adventure of ever-deepening inner experience.

142   What was merely the subject of factional quarrels among the different scientific schools only a short time ago has now become a worldwide problem. The advocates of hallucinogenic drugs are engulfed in a one-sidedly overvalued unconscious, and movements and parties that are politically and rationalistically oriented hope to change the world with only conscious sociological measures. By now, perhaps this split may have deepened to the point where more

---

[51] Ibid., § 145.
[52] Ibid., § 148.
[53] Ibid., § 135.
[54] Mainly exponents of the behaviourist school.

people will listen to Jung as the advocate of a life-giving middle way that must be searched for again and again.

143   Among the advocates of both points of view, one observes how the unconscious is forced into a counter-position by the one-sidedness of the conscious attitude and how destructive this can be. Drug users are often plagued by fearful anxiety dreams and visions which are meant to prevent them from going further into the unconscious (a bad trip!), and the dreams of politically and sociologically oriented world reformers generally criticize their intellectualism, their inflation and their lack of feeling that are concomitant with being too one-sided.

♦

Chapter 5
The Journey to the Beyond

144 The earliest origins of modern psychotherapy known to history lie in the practices of archaic shamanism and in the traditions of the medicine men of primitive peoples. Besides the priest, who is primarily the guardian of existing collective ritual and tradition, there is the figure of the shaman who is characterized by *individual experience of the world of spirits* (which today we call the unconscious) and whose main function is the *healing* of personal illnesses and disturbances in the life of the collective.[1] He is the one who heals the sufferer by means of his own trance, who leads the dead into the "realm of the shadows" and who serves as mediator between them and their gods; in a certain way, he watches over their "souls." "The shaman," writes Mircea Eliade[2], "is the great 'specialist' in the human soul; he alone 'sees' it, for he knows its 'form' and its destiny." His gift of moving freely among the powers of the beyond is sometimes a family inheritance but is more often rooted in an individual experience of vocation. This is generally heralded by a period of psychic disorientation.[3] When called, he sets himself apart, turns contemplative; often he receives his call through a dream experience.[4] Sometimes he falls physically ill and is not restored to health until he begins to shamanize. Psychically, however, the shaman is essentially normal, though usually more sensitive and more excitable than other people. (Even the Romans spoke of *genus irritabile vatum*, the excitable race of seers.)

---

[1] Cf. Mircea Eliade, *Shamanism: Archaic Techniques of Ecstasy*, passim.
[2] Ibid., p. 8.
[3] Such a condition is not to be confused with "possession" or psychic disturbance, as certain historians of religion have mistakenly done. Cf. Eliade, pp. 23 ff.
[4] Ibid., p. 21.

145   The vocational illness is pictured by some peoples as an abduction by a bird that carries the called one off to the underworld where he remains locked up for a time and is often dismembered by the spirits or suffers other tortures. Afterwards the "mother bird" brings him back to the world of human beings, the shaman awakens as from a deep sleep, and from that time on, he possesses the gift of being able to heal other people. This trip to the beyond frequently takes place in a big initiation dream in which the future shaman undertakes long journeys to the gods of the underworld and of heaven.[5] Experiences of dismemberment in the beyond, similar to those of shamans, are also experienced by Australian medicine men, as well as by sorcerers in North and South America, Africa and Indonesia.[6] "Dreams, sickness, or initiation ceremony," says Eliade[7], "the central element is always the same: death and symbolic resurrection of the neophyte." During the journey to the beyond, the initiate receives instruction from the highest divinity of heaven or the underworld, from a dead ancestor or a great shaman of the past, from a female figure with magical powers, or from a magical animal. One initiate, for example, reported that, as he lay suffering, he saw a spirit of a tiny woman who said to him, "I am the 'ayami' (protective spirit) of your ancestors, the shamans. I taught them how to be a shaman. Now I am going to teach you. The old shamans have died off, and there is no one to heal people. You are to become a shaman. . . . I love you; I have no husband now; you will be my husband. . . . I shall give you assistant spirits. You are to heal with their aid, and I shall teach and help you myself. . . . If you will not obey me," she adds, "so much the worse for you. I shall kill you."

146   Thus, many shamans have an invisible heavenly spouse; others have as their most important helper the spirit of one of the great dead shamans, an "Old Wise Man," who guides them[8] and, in the trance-state, often speaks directly through their mouths[9]. To be able

---

[5] Cf. ibid., p. 5. Cf. also A. Friedrich and G. Buddruss, *Schamanengeschichten aus Sibirien*, and Georg Nioradze, *Der Schamanismus bei den sibirischen Völkern*.
[6] Cf. Eliade, pp. 53 ff.
[7] Ibid., p. 56.
[8] Cf. ibid. p. 77, and the parallels there given to the motif of the fairy bride in mythology.
[9] Ibid., p. 83.

to see the spirits, whether awake or in dreams, is the most important sign of the shaman's vocation.[10] It often happens that, after such an experience, he can understand the secret language of spirits or animals, especially of birds.[11] The shaman is frequently both the seer and the poet of his people and in the trance-state he may speak in verse. Among the Altaians, for example, when, after a long and fatiguing trip to heaven, a shaman speaks before Bai Ülgän, the highest god, he puts down his drum and calls out[12]:

147
> Prince, to whom three ladders lead,
> Bai Ülgän with the three flocks,
> Blue slope that has appeared,
> Blue sky that shows itself!

148
> Blue cloud, drifting away,
> Blue sky unattainable,
> White sky unattainable,
> Watering place a year away!

149
> Father Ülgän, thrice exalted,
> Whom the moon's axe-edge spares,
> Who uses the horse's hoof!

150
> Thou didst create all men, Ülgän,
> All that make a noise around us.
> All cattle thou has forsaken, Ülgän!

151
> Deliver us not to misfortune
> Let us withstand the Evil One!
> Show us not Körmös [the evil spirit]
> Give us not into his hand!

---

[10] Ibid., p. 84.
[11] Ibid., pp. 96 f.
[12] Ibid., pp. 196 – 97.

152
>   Thou who the starry heaven
>   Hast turned a thousand, thousand times,
>   Condemn not my sins!

153   A delightful hymn of a Yakut shaman runs[13]:

154
>   The strong bull of the earth, the horse of the steppe,
>   The strong bull has bellowed!
>   The horse of the steppe has trembled!
>   I am above you all, I am a man!
>   I am the man created by the Lord of Infinity!
>   Come, then, O horse of the steppe, and teach!
>   Appear, then, marvellous bull of the Universe, and
>   answer!
>   O Lord of Power, command!
>   O Lady my Mother, show me my faults and the roads
>   That I must follow! Fly before me, following a broad
>   road;
>   Prepare my way for me!

155   Among many peoples, the shaman discovers, over and over again, his own songs and melodies.[14] Along with the ascent to the god of heaven, there is also a descent down seven successive "levels" to the black Erlik Khan, Lord of the Underworld. The shaman brings him sacrifices and wine and puts him in a favourable humour, so that he promises to bestow fertility.[15] Otherwise the main purpose of the shaman's descent is to bring back the soul of a sick person or to escort a dead man to his proper place in the beyond.[16]

156   In shamanism and in the initiation experiences of primitive medicine men, there appears an age-old religious phenomenon, retained in part, at least, in later higher cultures, namely the motif of the "celestial journey of the soul" that is taken by every soul after

---

[13] Ibid., pp. 230 – 31.
[14] Ibid., p. 201.
[15] Ibid., pp. 200 ff.
[16] Ibid., pp. 208 ff.

death but which some elect take even during their lifetime in a state of ecstasy[17]. In Judaism such a journey is described in the first book of Enoch, that relates how Enoch, near the end of his life, is carried off to heaven by the spirit, sees God and receives certain revelations.[18] Similar celestial journeys are also described in the second book of Enoch, in the so-called Apocalypse of Baruch, which in a still older form is mentioned by Origen (*De Principiis* II, 3-6), and in the Apocalypse of Sophonias quoted by Clement of Alexandria. Sophonias is also lifted up to heaven by the spirit (*pneuma*) and sees the majesty of God.[19] Even the Apostle Paul (II Corinthians 12:3,4) is proud of having been "caught up to the third heaven" and "into paradise" – not knowing "whether in the body . . . or whether out of the body" – and to have "heard unspeakable words there."[20] In later rabbinical writings, one reads[21], "Four pressed into paradise, namely Ben Asai, Ben Soma, Acher and Rabbi Akiba. . . . Ben Asai saw and died, Ben Soma saw and was struck (that is, mentally disturbed). Acher cut down the plantations.[22] Rabbi Akiba alone came out again in peace." Aside from references by some early fathers of the Church, reports of this sort of event do not appear very often later on, a fact that can be attributed to the tendency of the Church, referred to in the previous chapter, to repress the formation of individual symbolism.

157   More often than in Judaism, however, one finds in the Gnostics[23] and in Iranian traditions, as late as the time of the Mithraic mysteries, depictions of the journey to heaven where, indeed, a trip to the beyond in a state of ecstasy was part of the initiation into those mysteries: "I shall behold today with immortal eyes, mortally created from mortal mother's womb, immortal Aion and Lord of the Fiery

---

[17] Cf. Wilhelm Bousset, *Die Himmelsreise der Seele*.

[18] Even older, perhaps, is the account of the Prophet Levi's ascension, in the so-called Testament of the Twelve Patriarchs, and the lost original text which tells of the ascent of Isaiah to God. Ibid., pp. 9 – 11.

[19] This idea of the ascension to heaven was also known to the Essenes. Cf. ibid., p. 12.

[20] Cf. ibid., pp. 13 ff.

[21] *Talmud Babylonicus*, Traktat Chagiga, 14b, cited by Bousset, p. 14.

[22] This probably means that he introduced heresies (Bousset, p. 15), because he believed in two, instead of one, divine powers (p. 16). On further Jewish traditions, cf. ibid., pp. 21 f.

[23] Ibid., p. 30.

Crown," begins the instruction given in the so-called Mithraic liturgy.[24]

158   Mircea Eliade points out that the primordial features of the celestial journey of the shamans also existed in ancient Greece. The doctor-priests, Abaris and Aristeas of Proconnesus, healed and prophesied while in an ecstatic trance state. Hermotimos of Clazomenae is supposed to have left his body for four years and travelled afar, after which he was endowed with "much mantic lore and knowledge of the future." Epimenedes of Crete slept in a cave on Mount Ida and learned "enthusiastic wisdom" there. Among the Thracians and Scythians, the smoke of common hemp was used as a means of inducing ecstasy, in order to gain experiences of the beyond. When Plato fell into a cataleptic trance on the battlefield, the "other world" was revealed to him and he learned the secret of fate and of life after death. The legend of Timarchus contains similar material.[25] He descended into the cave of the healer-god Trophonius and experienced there the splitting of the seams of his skull, from which his soul emerged to wander about the beyond. In the Hellenistic period, Hades was oddly blended with the celestial habitations of the blessed spirits and localized in the same spot. [26]

159   From ancient Iran there are accounts of such celestial journeys in which the ecstatic person experiences what, under normal conditions, would be in store for the soul after death. In the *Book of Artay-Viraf* there is a description of the suffering of Artay-Viraf for seven days from tetanus: during this time, his soul wanders through the celestial spaces, crosses the bridge to the beyond and gazes upon the sites of damnation and of blessedness. Ancient Persian images and ideas of this kind lived on in the legend of Mohammed's journey to heaven. In the Roman *Somnium Scipionis*, described by Macrobius, Scipio is instructed in the secrets of the beyond by the spirit of his dead ancestor; and the so-called *Oracula Chaldaica* depict at great length an initiate's visionary journey to the beyond. There the ultimate goal is a "formless fire" whose voice can be heard

[24] The *Pariser papyrus magicus*, published by Albrecht Dieterich, *Eine Mithrasliturgie*, pp. 55 ff.
[25] Plutarch, *De genio Soractis*, 22, 590B.
[26] Cf. Bousset, p. 59.

by the mystic. There are also traces of this tradition in Hermetic literature, in the *Poimander*, for example.[27]

160   This kind of religious experience was retained in the *alchemical* tradition much longer than in the Christian Church. In his quest for the divine secret of the *materia*, the alchemical adept was vouchsafed the truth in visionary dream-initiations (Zosimos) or ecstatic celestial journeys (Krates).[28]

161   Jung's report of his experiences after separating from Freud strikes one as being an astonishing parallel to this form of primeval experience of the spirit-world, that is, of the unconscious. His "journey to the beyond" occurred in his mid-life years (December 1913) when he was 38 years old. "For in the secret hour of life's midday ... death is born. ... Waxing and waning make one curve."[29] While in the first half of life, consciousness grows out of the purely natural basis provided by the instincts[30] and strives primarily for the goal of social adaptation and achievement, a fundamental change takes place in middle life – it is as if the sun, after crossing the meridian, drew in its rays, in order to illumine itself, after having squandered its light on the world. "For a young person it is almost a sin . . . to be too preoccupied with himself; but for the ageing person it is a duty and a necessity to devote serious attention to himself."[31]

162   During this fateful period of his middle life, Jung had dreams with the recurring motif of the dead from the historical past coming to life, or of a dove, transformed into a little girl, coming to him as a messenger from the realm of the dead[32] (like the "tiny woman" of the shaman's trance). The inner pressure continued to increase and out of sheer despair he began to play with stones on the lakeshore, building with them a miniature village with a church, in order to provide some release from the pressure of his fantasies.

---

[27] *De genio Socratis*, 22; cir. Bousset, p. 63, and the additional examples given there.
[28] Cf. C.G. Jung, "The Visions of Zosimos," CW 13, §§ 85 – 144, and "Transformation Symbolism in the Mass," CW 11, §§ 344 – 375.
[29] C.G. Jung, "The Soul and Death," CW 8, § 800.
[30] C.G Jung, "The Stages of Life", CW 8, § 772 f.
[31] Ibid., § 785.
[32] For details, see *Memories*, pp.195.

163   He did this from time to time for the rest of his life. When he
reached an impasse, then he painted a picture or with a chisel struck
out of a stone the image which seemed to him to lie within it.
"Sometimes," he once said, "I know so little about what the
unconscious demands that I simply leave it to my hands, so that
afterwards I can think about what I have shaped." This is a method
also used by certain medicine men, among the Navajo Indians of
North America, for example. The Navajos say that there are three
ways of discovering the invisible in an illness, the will of the spirits,
or the future: watching the stars; listening (inwardly); or "motion-
in-the-hand," that is, a spirit who causes one to make involuntary
movements with the hands.[33] But creative play still did not reduce
the pressure of Jung's inner fantasies. In the outer world, too, an
increasingly ominous psychic situation was developing, for this was
the period just preceding the outbreak of the First World War. As a
shaman often suffers from the plight of his people, so Jung was
afflicted with dreams of blood-baths and catastrophes in Europe –
dreams which he was only able to understand after August 1, 1914.
During the Advent season in 1913, he made up his mind to take the
decisive step of venturing directly into his fantasies and attempting
to write them down. *He decided to take the journey to the beyond.*
"Suddenly it was as though the ground literally gave way beneath
my feet, and I plunged down into dark depths."[34] He found himself
standing on solid ground in utter darkness. Before him was a cave
into which he waded through deep, ice-cold water. Under a red
crystal, he found hidden a still deeper current, flowing with great
force in which was floating the corpse of a blond young man. Behind
the corpse, a giant black scarab, then a streak of blood. Jung
understood that this was an allusion to a hero myth: the murdered
or dismembered sun-hero and the symbol of his resurrection, the
scarab – but why the blood? But it was precisely the vision of blood
which recurred, over and over. Then in the spring of 1914 he
dreamed three times in a row "that in mid-summer an arctic cold

---

[33] Cf. L.C. Wyman, "Origin Legend of Navaho Divinatory Rites," *Journal of American Folk-Lore,* 49,
pp. 134 ff.
[34] *Memories,* p. 202 f.

wave came and the country froze into ice. . . . There were no people anywhere . . . everything green and living froze." In the third dream, however, there was an unexpected ending: "There stood a tree, bearing leaves, but without fruit (my life-tree, I thought), whose leaves had been transformed by the action of the frost into sweet grapes full of healing juice. I plucked the grapes and gave them to a waiting multitude of people."

164   When the First World War broke out, Jung made full use of that time of stress by investigating the unfathomable contents of the unconscious – as he continued his journey into the beyond – so that later he could render them accessible to others in his work and in his books. At the time, however, he did not yet know the degree to which his own experiences reflected the collective situation and he sought in vain for explanations on the personal level. The murdered sun-hero in his vision refers to the fact that our conscious ideals had become invalid and that the naïve enlightened rationalism of the 19th century, its belief in progress and its ambivalent desire for expansion, were at an end. Through the scarab, however, a representation of the power of the unconscious, a transformation of consciousness was being prepared; in the Egyptian motif, the scarab creates, in his egg, the new sun-god, the new dominant of conscious-ness, and pushes him up over the horizon of the eastern sky. But it appears that such deep and far-reaching transformations of the consciousness of a culture are, historically, never possible without monstrous blood sacrifices.

165   During the first half of his life, Jung participated to a certain extent in the optimistic faith in progress which was characteristic of his day and age. When he joined forces with Freud, he believed that together they could develop a new, scientific knowledge of the psyche, an enterprise that would not only benefit many sick people but would also transform the entire consciousness of our culture. Then he had a dream toward the end of December 1913, which showed him that the "sun-god" must be killed, not only in the collective but also in himself. He writes[35]:

---

[35] Ibid., p. 204.

166   I was with an unknown, brown-skinned man, a savage, in a lonely, rocky mountain landscape. It was before dawn; the eastern sky was already bright, and the stars were fading. Then I heard Siegfried's horn sounding over the mountains and I knew that we had to kill him. We were armed with rifles and lay in wait for him on a narrow path over the rocks. Then Siegfried appeared high up on the crest of the mountain, in the first ray of the rising sun. On a chariot made of the bones of the dead he drove at furious speed down the precipitous slope. When he turned a corner, we shot at him, and he plunged down, struck dead. Filled with disgust and remorse for having destroyed something so great and beautiful, I turned to flee, impelled by the fear that the murder might be discovered. But a tremendous downfall of rain began, and I knew that it would wipe out all traces of the dead. I had escaped the danger of discovery; life could go on, but an unbearable feeling of guilt remained.

167   In commenting on this dream, Jung noted that Siegfried embodied both his own attitude and the attitude of the Germans at that time, for both believed in the power of will and in the power of one's ideals. The young savage, on the other hand, represents primitive man who follows his instincts. The rain announces the resolution of the tension between conscious and unconscious.

168   That is a typical dream of middle life: all the goals of social adaptation and achievement have been attained and now the hero, which is the midday sun, must die in order to avoid blocking the way for new life. Siegfried's chariot, made of the bones of the dead, shows us how many other possibilities of life have been sacrificed in the interest of what has so far been achieved by consciousness. At that time, Jung had been *Privatdozent* for psychiatry for eight years at the University of Zurich. But after writing his book *Wandlungen und Symbole der Libido* (1911), he had felt more and more resistance to academic intellectualism, and at the time of his journey to the

beyond and the death of the "hero", he gave up his university career in order to give free rein to new inner possibilities.

169   Only after the dream of the death of Siegfried did the way lay open to Jung for pressing forward more deeply into the beyond. "It was like a voyage to the moon, or a descent into empty space. . . . I had the feeling that I was in the land of the dead."[36] With the passage of time, certain figures coming to him from the unconscious began to crystallize out, so to speak, and in part they were personifications of the unconscious itself. Of special importance to him were the figure of a woman (named Salome, who was blind and who corresponds to the fairy bride of the shaman), and various personifications of the "Old Wise Man," who gave him important advice about the continuation of his inner experiences. The most important of these latter figures was named Elias, who was then superseded by the figure of Philemon, whom Jung later painted on the wall over his bed in Bollingen. Philemon was a man with the horns of a bull (cf. the shaman's song quoted above) and the wings of a kingfisher and he carried four keys. He embodied a "superior insight" coming from the unconscious. "Philemon," says Jung[37], "brought home to me the crucial insight that there are things in the psyche which I do not produce, but which produce themselves and have their own life. . . . In my fantasies I held conversations with him, and he said things which I had not consciously thought. . . . He said I treated thoughts as if I generated them myself, but in his view thoughts were like animals in the forest, people in a room. . . . 'If you should see people in a room, you would not think that you had made those people, or that you were responsible for them.' It was he who taught me psychic objectivity, the reality of the psyche. . . . At times he seemed to me quite real, as if he were a living personality, like an invisible guru or teacher."

170   Laurens van der Post once spoke in a lecture of meeting a Zulu prophet and medicine man who told him the story of his initiation. He had dreamed during this initiation that he should throw his

---

[36] Ibid., p. 205.
[37] Ibid., p. 207 f.

porridge into the river. When he did this a flock of birds flew up and caught every flake before it touched the water. That was the sign of his vocation. Then he told van der Post that the medicine man's task is to maintain a balance between the masculine and the feminine principles in society. He illustrated this with the story of a girl who threw everything of value in her possession into the water and, through this sacrifice received from the "old woman" who lived in the water blessing and fertility for herself and for all her people. Jung, said van der Post, had brought his knowledge of our epoch and of many cultures back to the water of the unconscious, thus fulfilling for our time the role of medicine man. The blind girl he met on *his* journey to the beyond is the feminine principle, which modern man has rejected and which has therefore become blind. Jung's journey to the beyond is an anticipation of a rebirth of our world, just as Dante's journey anticipated the spirit of the Renaissance. Jung's journey, however, led him deeper and farther than Dante's, into a still more profound rebirth of our *Zeitgeist*.[38]

171   The shamans and medicine men of primitive peoples keep their experiences to themselves and hand them on only to younger shamans. Their patients do not participate in the journey to the beyond; instead they abandon themselves passively to the healer. The healer's monopoly, which consists in the fact that only *he* has dreams and travels to the land of the spirits, has been to some extent invaded in the course of cultural development. In the ancient incubation resorts of Asklepios and other gods of healing, the priests observed not only their own dreams but those of their patients as well, and sometimes the patient had to make his own "descent into the underworld" in order to find healing.[39] There was also the institution of the so-called Katoché, where the procedure was similar to that in the Asklepeia: a layman could voluntarily place himself in "confinement" or in the "possession" of a god; while there, he wrote down his dreams, which were then interpreted by the priests. In this

[38] Cf. the abridged version of van der Post's lecture in the *Bulletin of the Analytical Psychology Club of New York*, 33:3 (March 1971).
[39] Cf. C.A. Meier, *Ancient Incubation and Modern Psychotherapy*.

custom lie one of the roots of the later Christian monachism and eremitical life.

172   Jung never thought of keeping his discovery to himself in order to strengthen his prestige. Instead, he taught this way of dealing with the unconscious, which he called "active imagination," to many of his patients.

173   In principle, active imagination consists in suspending the critical faculty and allowing emotions, affects, fantasies, obsessive thoughts, or even waking dream-images to come up from the unconscious, and in confronting them as if they were objectively present.[40] These contents often express themselves in a solemn or pompous way, "a hellish mixture of the sublime and the ridiculous," so that at first consciousness may be shocked and feel inclined to dismiss the whole thing as nonsense. Anxiety may cause a kind of "cramp" of consciousness, or one may fall too far into the unconscious and go to sleep. An alert, wakeful confrontation with the contents of the unconscious is, however, *the* essence of active imagination. This calls for an *ethical commitment* in relation to the manifestations from within[41], otherwise one falls prey to the power principle and the exercise in imagination is destructive both for others and for the one imagining.[42] It becomes a kind of black magic. Fantasies can be objectified by writing them, by drawing, painting, or (rarely) by dancing them. A written dialogue is the most differentiated form and usually leads to the best results.[43]

174   Too one-sided an emphasis on the aesthetic quality of the images obstructs the realization of their *meaning* and should therefore be avoided, according to Jung.[44] On the other hand, impatience to get to the meaning as quickly as possible must be checked by patient

---

[40] Cf. C.G. Jung, "The Transcendent Function," CW 8, §§ 131 ff.

[41] *Memories*, p. 213.

[42] On the primitive level, this happens to the so-called black shamans.

[43] Cf. Marie-Louise von Franz, "Active Imagination in the Psychology of C. G. Jung," in: *Psychotherapy*, pp. 146 – 162; and Barbara Hannah, "The Healing Influence of Active Imagination in a Specific Case of Neurosis." Cf. also Nise da Silveira, "Expérience d'art spontané chez des Schizophrènes dans un Service thérapeutique occupationel."

[44] Cf. C.G. Jung, "The Transcendent Function," CW 8, § 174. One tries to snatch the meaning out of a few hints too quickly and misses those contents that might have come to light in a genuine confrontation. The danger of the aesthetic tendency is an overvaluation of the formal aspect, and the danger of the eagerness to understand is an overvaluation of the content.

attention to the formal aspect. But when the two concerns operate together rhythmically, then the transcendent function, which strives to unite conscious and unconscious, operates with greatest effect.[45] "Active imagination" is the most effective means through which the patient can become independent of the therapist and learn to stand on his own two feet. However, he must then undertake the inner work on his own, for no one else can do it for him.[46] One begins to understand that every fantasy is a genuine psychic process or experience which happens to one, and one thus becomes the active and suffering protagonist in an inner drama. But if one merely looks at the inner images, then nothing happens: one has to enter into the process with one's own personal reactions. There are those who do this in fact but with a fictitious personality, that is, their reactions are not genuine reactions but are "acted," while somewhere in the background there is the thought that this is all "just fantasy"; then, too, nothing happens and inner development comes to a standstill.

175   If one "understands" the images and thinks that this is done with cognition, then one succumbs to a dangerous error. For whoever fails to take his own experience as an ethical commitment falls victim to the power principle.[47] If, on the other hand, one enters genuinely into the inner happenings in a sober spirit of ethical commitment and serious search for greater consciousness, then the flow of inner images commences to contribute to the growth of personal wholeness, that is, to individuation and to the creation of an inner security which is strong enough to withstand the assaults of both outer and inner problems. "He alone has a genuine claim to self-confidence, for he has faced the dark ground of his self and thereby has gained himself."[48]

176   The first detailed description of active imagination which Jung published was in his commentary on *The Secret of the Golden Flower*, translated by Richard Wilhelm into German in 1929.[49] In the reading

---

[45] Cf. ibid., § 179.
[46] Cf. C.G. Jung, *Mysterium Coniunctionis*, CW 14, § 406.
[47] *Memories*, p. 218.
[48] Cf. C.G. Jung, *Mysterium Coniunctionis*, CW 14, § 406.
[49] Cf. C.G. Jung, "Commentary on 'The Secret of the Golden Flower," CW 13, §§ 1 – 84; cf. also "The Relations between the Ego and the Unconscious," CW 7, §§ 202 – 406.

of this Eastern guide to meditation, it became clear to Jung that he had set out quite spontaneously along an inner way that had not only been known in the East for hundreds of years but had over many centuries been developed into a structured inner path. In fact, it is true that the technique of active imagination does have deeply rooted similarities to the most varied forms of Eastern meditation (yoga, etc.), although the differences should by no means be overlooked. The way of active imagination is *not programmed* and is *completely individual*. The guide does not take on the task of guiding the process, as in the case of the Eastern teacher (guru), but only supervises the process at the beginning, in order to be sure that the student, or pupil, does not wander off into one of the two dead ends described above, that of intellectual interpretation or that of aestheticism. In every other respect, the whole thing is a unique inner happening. In respect to this lack of structure, the inner path discovered by Jung comes close to Zen Buddhism, but here, too, there is an important difference. Most Zen masters expressly decline to take serious account of dreams, which they look upon as fragments of illusion which must be overcome. Jung, on the other hand, regards dreams as "messages from the Self" that support the way of meditation.[50] It must be noted, however, that there were a few Chinese Zen masters, for example Han Shan (1546 – 1623), who took their dreams to be beacons along the path of their struggle for enlightenment.[51]

177   Although the wisdom of the East made a profound impression on Jung, nevertheless he constantly warned Westerners against imitating its yoga techniques and other practices.[52] He looked upon such imitation as theft and as a disregard of our own psychic heritage, especially of our shadow. Although we in the West have much to gain from the East, in the way of help in meeting our own spiritual needs, still we cannot shirk the task of working out our own

---

[50] Cf. Marie-Louise von Franz, "Active Imagination in the Psychology of C.G. Jung," in: *Psychotherapy*, p. 156 f.

[51] Cf. "The Story of Ch'an Master Han Shan," in: *World Buddhism* 11:7. I am indebted to Lu K'uan Yü, Hong Kong, for bringing this article to my attention; cf. also Lu K'uan Yü, *Practical Buddhism*, p. 88 ff.

[52] Cf. especially, "Richard Wilhelm: In Memoriam," CW 15, §88 f.

problems.[53] If we approach the unconscious out of our own psychic roots, the first thing we come up against is not the "inner light" but a "layer" of repressed personal contents[54]. Indian (and also Chinese) yoga, however, knows nothing of the moral conflict which the shadow means for us, since the Eastern religions are so much at one with nature that their followers can accept evil without conflict[55]. Only after we have resolved the problem of the shadow can we hope to attain that inner ground that is extolled by Eastern meditation[56], a state of being at one with the divine or universal life-force – from which the Easterner, in contrast to Westerners, has never really been far removed. This warning, however, refers only to the *way* and to the extent that a Westerner may intend to pursue it, not to the *goal*, which is actually *identical* for *both* ways.

178   In his *Memories*, Jung clarifies his personal attitude to the Eastern way.[57] He writes that he does not seek, as the East Indian does, to be freed from nature and the inner opposites. Instead, he seeks that wisdom which comes from the fullness of a life lived with devotion: "Nature, the psyche, and life appear to me like divinity unfolded", and also "the inferno of (the) passions" has to be lived through – in order to be freed of them. Here Jung confesses his Christian spiritual heritage: conflict (represented by the symbol of the cross) may not be circumvented, nor suffering avoided. He liked to quote Thomas à Kempis to the effect that suffering is the horse that carries us fastest to wholeness. Despite this confession, Jung found the Buddha to be a more complete human being than the Christ[58], because the Buddha lived his life and took as his task the realization of the Self through understanding, whereas with the Christ this realization was more like a fate that happened to him.

179   Jung foresaw that the East would exert a growing psychological influence on our culture, while we would intervene drastically in

---

[53] Ibid., § 88.
[54] Cf. C.G. Jung, "The Psychology of Eastern Meditation," CW 11, § 939.
[55] Ibid., § 941.
[56] Ibid.
[57] *Memories*, p. 306.
[58] Ibid., p. 309.

their world with materialism and political destruction.[59] He saw that Buddhism, too, has been weakened by a partial hardening into an outer formula, as Christianity has with the Westerner[60]. This realization (1929) appears to me to be in ever greater measure true today and I have seen for myself that it is sometimes necessary, with the help of Jung's views and ideas, to help Eastern men and women rebuild a bridge to the primordial experience of their own spiritual traditions. "It is clear to me," wrote a Japanese professor, "that Jung can contribute to our spiritual tradition and religion a reality basis that we have partly lost." It appears that in the East, as well as in the West, certain individuals are being called to rediscover the way to the original experience, instead of being satisfied with a mere imitation of the struggle to preserve the tradition, since only that which is genuinely experienced can hold its own against the psychological devastation that we are currently exporting to the East.

180   Interestingly enough there are age-old elements of shamanism in China, too, at the basis of the Taoist-alchemistic forms of meditation.[61] The wise man centres himself, concentrates and thus is able to "rise to higher spheres and descend into the lower, and distinguish there the things which it would be proper to do. . . . Being in this condition, intelligent *shen* descended into them."[62] Seen in this context, Jung's discovery of the technique of active imagination is a return to the oldest known forms of meditation, as they existed *before* the subsequent development into yoga, Buddhistic meditation, and Taoist alchemy. It was as if he had been carried back over the millennia, in one daring leap, to that world in which primordial man, completely naïvely, first began to make contact with the world of the spirit. Still, certain differences are unmistakable: unlike shamans, Jung did not enter this world in a trance-state, but rather in full consciousness and without any diminution of the individual moral responsibility which is one of the attainments of Western culture. This is something new and unique, something that

---

[59] Cf. C.G. Jung, "Richard Wilhelm: In Memoriam," CW 15, § 90.
[60] *Memories*, p. 309 f.
[61] Cf. Mircea Eliade, *Shamanism*, pp. 447 ff.
[62] Ibid.

cannot be compared with the earlier stages of culture that have been described. It makes such heavy demands on the integrity of the meditating individual, however, that it is understandable that not everyone can unhesitatingly follow this path.

181   In spite of his reservations about direct imitation of Eastern methods of meditation, Jung honoured the spirit of the East and valued it highly. His friendship with Richard Wilhelm, moreover, provided him with full access to the spirit which animates the Book of Changes, the *I Ching*, in all its range and depth.[63] For a long time, he used the *I Ching* to obtain responses to questions about doubtful situations, but he gave it up toward the end of his life when he became aware that he always knew in advance, before he threw the yarrow stalks, what the answer would be. In other words, he was so open to the meaning constellated in the unconscious that he was no longer able to use the oracle as a roundabout way via an outer technique. His relationships with the Indologist Heinrich Zimmer and the Sinologist Erwin Rousselle also provided exchanges of highly important insights.[64] His discovery of the principle of synchronicity (to be discussed later), is, in my opinion, a real key to the understanding of Chinese culture. The Zen Upasaka Lu K'uan Yü[65], in Hong Kong, writes appreciatively, "Jung was a great-hearted man, without pride and without prejudice. That is why he made such wonderful discoveries. But such men are very rare today."[66]

182   Aside from the Eastern methods of meditation there is another, somewhat remoter, parallel to Jung's "active imagination", namely, the *Exercitia Spiritualia* of Ignatius Loyola that are practiced in the Roman Catholic Church. These exercises are even more structured than those of the East: each symbol to be contemplated has its

---

[63] For more detail, cf. below. Cf. Jung's foreword to the *I Ching*, included in CW 11, §§ 964 ff.
[64] Cf. The following papers in CW 11: "Psychological Commentary on 'The Tibetan Book of the Great Liberation,'" §§ 759 ff; 'Psychological Commentary on "The Tibetan Book of the Dead,'" §§ 831 ff; "Foreword to Suzuki's 'Introduction to Zen Buddhism,'" §§ 877 ff. Cf. further *Memories*, p. 385 (German edition), and G. Wehr, "Östlicher Geist und westliches Denken bei C. g. Jung und R. Steiner."
[65] Cf. Lu K'uan Yü, *Geheimnisse der chinesischen Meditation*, and "Taoist Yoga," *Alchemy and Immortality*.
[66] Personal communication.

prescribed place in a series, so that the practice of *individual* symbol formation is repressed, instead of being furthered.[67]

183   At the time Jung was experimenting with active imagination, first on himself and later with his analysands, all such inner potentialities for psychotherapy were still virtually unknown. Since that time, however, the situation has changed somewhat. Carl Happich's method, a therapist-directed meditation, is being used, for example, and René Desoille has introduced the technique of the *waking dream*, and most clinics today permit patients to paint, compose or perform musical works, model in clay, and write stories. Contemporary psychotherapy, generally speaking, has found the way to the aesthetic state of creativity[68], but not yet to the next stage of an ethical confrontation with its products, nor to a convinced standpoint or a moral attitude; it appears that this stage is not yet generally understood.[69]

184   The imaginative techniques which have come into such widespread use in psychotherapy in recent years differ from Jung's active imagination in another respect, namely, that of the *directive role* of the therapist, who sometimes prescribes the images to be contemplated (for example, in Happich's method) or who may intervene in some other way to guide the process by means of interruptions or other incidental remarks. Active imagination, on the other hand, is done by the analysand alone. No image, no reaction to the inner images is prescribed for him; it is the lonely way to one's self, unprotected, but also undisturbed by any guiding hand. The role of the guide, which is preferred by some therapists who use other techniques, is dangerous to the therapist himself for it can seduce him into the "pride of the shaman", of which much that

---

[67] Jung comments, point by point, on these exercises in a series of lectures given at the Federal Institute of Technology (ETH) in Zurich (winter 1940/41, privately printed), edited by Barbara Hannah.

[68] Jung's work is, for the most part, studiously ignored. Thus Wolfgang Kretschmer, for example, in his essay, "Die meditativen Verfahren in der Psychotherapie" examines in detail the methods of Schultz-Hencke, Carl Happich, René Desoille, Fr. Manz, etc., without a word about the previous work done by Jung. (*Zeitschrift für Psychotherapie und medizinische Psychologie* 1:3, May 1951). Today there exists a Société Internationale des Techniques d'Imagerie Mentale (SITIM) in Paris, which regularly distributes information and organizes congresses. Here Jung is at least occasionally peripherally mentioned. Cf. further Walter L. Furrer, *Objektivierung des Unbewussten*, and the essay by P. Solié, "Psychologie analytique et Imagerie Mentale," *Action et pensée*, 44, No. 1-2, March-June 1968.

[69] Cf. C.G. Jung, *Mysterium Coniunctionis*, CW 14, § 408.

is evil is reported in primitive myths, and, in addition, it robs the patient of the thing he needs the most which is free inner responsibility. It was in fact a democratic Swiss trait in Jung's character that he so completely renounced any kind of therapeutic power and accorded recognition to the free responsibility of the other person.

185   The medically controlled use of hallucinogenic drugs which has come into practice in recent years is also crippled by the same misuse of power: the power of the unconscious is conjured up through the use of the drug, but it is then the controlling therapist, instead of the experiencing subject, who is responsible for the confrontation.[70] It is true that this experiment can accelerate the resolution of a cramped resistance to the unconscious in a way that dream analysis cannot; but the integration of the contents brought up this way is not often possible. In a letter to a clergyman (April 1954) Jung addressed himself to this question as follows:[71] "I only know there is no point in wishing to know more of the collective unconscious than one gets through dreams and intuition. The more you know of it, *the greater and heavier becomes your moral burden*, because unconscious contents are transformed into your individual tasks and duties as soon as they begin to become conscious. Do you want to increase loneliness and misunderstanding? Do you want to find more and more complications and increasing responsibilities?" The unconscious has its own ways of revealing what is destined in a human life just at that time when it is ready to be integrated. It seemed illegitimate to Jung to seek the holy secret of the inmost light out of simple vain curiosity.[72] In my opinion, however, the current vogue for the use of such drugs might nevertheless constitute a negative preliminary stage, preceding a more enlightened opening-up of the unconscious. At least there are many people today who know what Jung was talking about when he spoke of the unconscious.

---

[70] Cf. in this connection Aniela Jaffé, *The Myth of Meaning in the Work of C. G. Jung*, pp. 68 ff.
[71] Ibid., pp. 72-3.
[72] It can also happen, perhaps, that a spiritually impoverished person may use it as an antidote to his need; but Jung mistrusted this use, too.

186 Shamans and medicine men often set out on the journey to the beyond in order to find a way of alleviating the suffering of their people,[73] and Jung, too, was to some extent forced into this inner way as a result of the dreams of catastrophe, mentioned above, that announced the First World War to him, though he could not have known that that was their meaning at the time.

187 Later he realized that what he had experienced on his inner journey had to do not only with himself but with many other people. "It was then," he writes[74], "that I ceased to belong to myself alone, ceased to have the right to do so. From then on, my life belonged to the generality. The knowledge I was concerned with, or was seeking, still could not be found in the science of those days. I myself had to undergo the original experience, and, moreover, try to plant the results of my experience in the soil of reality. . . . It was then that I dedicated myself to the service of the psyche. I loved it and hated it, but it was my greatest wealth."

188 One great problem which remained for Jung was that of assisting other people to achieve the sort of personal inner experience he had discovered, especially since he had renounced the roles of prophet and preacher, as described above.[75] He had to try, therefore, to capture what he had experienced into the body of his scientific work and at the same time to incorporate it into the contemporary picture of the world.[76] But at first there was no objective form, or objective material, to which he could connect it. He found this when he became familiar with *alchemical symbolism*. Here at last he was able to make a connection with the spiritual tradition of the West; this will be discussed later.

[73] Cf. for example J.G. Neihardt, *Black Elk Speaks*.
[74] *Memories*, p. 217.
[75] The *Seven Sermons to the Dead* might have been an opportunity for assuming such a role, but Jung intentionally renounced this style of writing and referred to the private publication of this paper (not to the conceptions it contains, as Aniela Jaffé appears erroneously to think) as a "youthful folly."
[76] *Memories*, p. 224 f.

◇

Chapter 6
The Anthropos

189   In countless myths of the origin of the world there emerges the figure of a gigantic man pervading the whole cosmos, who represents either the *prima materia* of the world and the basic substance of all later human generations, or what condenses all human souls into a trans-temporal, transpersonal unity. The *Edda*, for example, describes how the gods shape the world from the body of the original giant Ymir.[1] In China, the dwarf-giant P'an Ku was the cosmic original being; when he wept, the rivers were created; when he breathed, the wind; and when he died, the five sacred mountains emerged from his corpse and his eyes became the sun and the moon.[2] The Indian *Rigveda* (X, 19) contains a description of how the whole visible and invisible world came from a primordial being named Purusha (man, person). "Truly he is the inmost self of all things."[3] In ancient Iran, when the corresponding figure of the god-king Gayômart was murdered by the principle of evil in the earliest times, his body disintegrated into the metals of the earth and from his seed there grew a rhubarb bush, from which the first human couple emerged.[4] In Jewish legend Adam was a giant who covered the whole world and "like the wick of a lamp was twisted together from many threads"; thus his soul contains, united within it, the 6,000 souls of all human beings.[5] In similar fashion, Christ, the second Adam, also represents a kind of collective soul, as the one "inner Christ" within the multitude.

---

[1] Arthur Gilchrist Brodeur (Trans.), *The Prose Edda*, pp. 16 f.
[2] Cf. C.G. Jung, *Mysterium Coniunctionis*, CW 14, § 237.
[3] Cf. Marie-Louise von Franz, "The Cosmic Man as Image of the Goal of the Individuation Process and Human Development," in: *Archetypal Dimensions of the Psyche*, p. 133 – 57, here, p. 136.
[4] Sven Hartmann, *Gayomart*.
[5] Cf. August Wünsche, "Schöpfung und Sündenfall des ersten Menschenpaares," pp. 8 – 13.

190   An elaboration of the myth of the original being which is especially important for Western culture is found in the gnostic systems of late antiquity. Highly dramatic accounts are given by various Gnostics of the journey taken by the "Light-Man," the Anthropos, who is identical with the supreme godhead. At first, he travels in a spiritual beyond but then, persuaded by evil star-powers, he falls or flows down into matter and is finally broken up into thousands of sparks of light or is scattered throughout matter as a "crucified world-soul," there to await redemption. His liberation is brought about by the efforts of a Redeemer sent by God, or it may be the task of the single individual to free the pneumatic original being within himself and to return with him to the kingdom of light. This gnostic Anthropos myth lived on, underground, in the alchemical tradition and in Hermetic philosophy, down to the beginning of the contemporary period.[6] Similar elements are also to be found in Jewish images of the Messiah.[7]

191   In the lengthy text of the gnostic sect of Ophites, cited in Chapter 1, the phallus, "which strives from the lower to the upper things," is an image for the Anthropos, sunk in matter and longing to return to the world of light. He is buried like a corpse in matter, awaiting his resurrection, which comes about through the efforts of the single individual in the interest of the development of his "inner man." Thus, he is, on the one hand, the innermost core of the individual psyche, while on the other hand, he is simultaneously a kind of collective soul of all humanity.

192   It is generally agreed today that Jung's greatest discovery was the empirical proof that there is in fact a "collective soul" – the collective unconscious, to use the name he gave it. From early childhood his own dreams had contained the most impressive mythological images which could not possibly have been explained through his own personal memories and for which he found explanatory parallels in religious history only many years later. At the beginning of his

---

[6] Similarly, in the teachings of Adam Kadmon, in the Kabbalah. Cf. Gershom Scholem, *On the Kabbalah and Its Symbolism*, pp. 112 ff. For late Western myths of the original man, cf. Ernst Benz, *Adam: Der Mythus vom Urmenschen*.
[7] Cf. Siegmund Hurwitz, *Der sterbende Messias*.

medical career, he discovered that the same thing was also true of his patients and that even a schizophrenic produced religious images (a tube in the sun through which wind was generated) an exact parallel to one in an ancient text which at the time had not yet been published.[8] Freud, too, had observed similar material; he described such mythological images, coming up from the unconscious, as "archaic residues." For him, they were relics of the past (rather as the appendix is, in the body), while from the first, Jung saw in such images the still vitally important foci of the human psyche. Almost all of the stronger personal complexes have such a collectively human focus as their core. Jung therefore made a clear distinction between two layers in the realm of the unconscious products: one layer of personally experienced, forgotten, or repressed contents; the other consisting of the collective unconscious, which reveals a generally human innate psychic structure.

193   A possible model for a description of the collective unconscious is that of a "field," which, in itself, is invisible, but which can be made visible with the use of suitable means.[9] It would be entirely erroneous, however, to imagine consciousness as a kind of Here and the unconscious as a sort of There because the psyche is, in fact, a conscious-unconscious whole, an "all-embracing One."[10] As mentioned above, conscious and unconscious, as a kind of two-in-one, are the substrate of psychic processes in which now the unconscious predominates, as in dreams, or again the conscious, as in the waking state. The phenomenon of archaic identity, which is *the feeling of being one* with the environment and which is also the basis of all communication between human beings, is ultimately rooted in the existence of the collective unconscious.[11]

---

[8] A. Dietrich (Ed.), *Eine Mithrasliturgie.*

[9] Cf. in this connection Wolfgang Pauli, "Naturwissenschaftliche und erkenntnistheoretische Aspekte der Ideen vom Unbewussten," in: *Aufsätze und Vorträge über Physik und Erkenntnistheorie*, p. 113. The description of the unconscious as a "field" comes originally from William James.

[10] C.G. Jung, "On the Nature of the Psyche," CW 8, § 397.

[11] This has not so far been systematically investigated from the standpoint of information and communication theory. Cf., however, Pascual Jordan, *Verdrängung und Komplementarität*, which assumes, following Jung, that the collective unconscious is the basis of the possibility of human communication.

194   Like "activated points" within an electromagnetic field, centres which can be delimited to a degree (but only to a degree!), and which Jung called *archetypes*, are found in the collective unconscious.

195   A clear distinction must be made here between *archetypes* and *archetypal images*.[12] Archetypes are very probably innate, undemonstrable *predispositions* or structural predispositions in the unconscious that appear in actual experience as the factor that orders or arranges representations into certain "patterns."[13] In his later work, Jung wrote that the archetypes might, in the last analysis, be partly nonpsychic[14], but for the present at least can be described only in terms of their ordering function in the psychic field. In the realm of the conscious-unconscious, the undemonstrable archetypes appear as archetypal representations or ideas, that is, in the form of mythological, symbolic representations which are common to certain collectivities, such as whole peoples or epochs.[15] They are "typical modes of apprehension" which appertain structurally to all human beings[16] and which form at the same time an inner self-image, so to speak, of human instincts or of their structure.[17] Just as the living contents of the psyche appear, at one end of the scale, to "flow over" into physiological processes, so at the other end they "flow" into abstract arrangements or patterns which are not physiological and which belong to the realm of existence described above as "spirit."

196   The archetypes can also be described as "elementary behaviour patterns" of the psyche[18], whose effects are observable only in the subject's field of inner vision but not by comparison with the outer behaviour of many people. In the inner field of vision, the activation of the instincts is accompanied by intense, emotionally laden fantasies or ideas which take possession of the whole personality and motivate it psychologically in a certain direction.

---

[12] At first, Jung did not always distinguish clearly between "archetypes" and "primordial images." This has led to many misunderstandings.

[13] C.G. Jung, "On the Nature of the Psyche," CW 8, § 440.

[14] Ibid., § 418.

[15] Cf. C.G. Jung, *Psychological Types*, § 688-99.

[16] C.G. Jung, "Instinct and the Unconscious," CW 8, § 280.

[17] C.G. Jung, *Aion,* CW 9/II, § 278.

[18] In the sense of I. Eibl-Eibesfeldt, *Liebe und Hass,* passim.

197   At first, Jung regarded the question of the origin of the archetypes as one of heredity, but in his later works, he left the question completely open. In my own opinion, research into heredity and behaviour may soon be able to give us more exact information. In any case, it is only a question of time before behavioural research will be in a position to join hands with Jung's exploration of the archetypes. Up to the present, the principal obstacle in the way of such cooperation has been the fact that researchers in behaviour (Konrad Lorenz, for example) have understood the Jungian archetype as an inherited memory-*image* and have, accordingly, rejected it.[19] The IRMs (innate release mechanisms) in animals are simple, probably almost mathematical basic forms that function as key impulses and are subsumed in the complicated perception of a constant *Gestalt*. Toward the end of his life, Jung saw in natural numbers the most primitive element of the "spirit" and thought that they might be the "key impulse" underlying archetypal images.

198   A second difference, not yet resolved, lies in the fact that even today behavioural research inclines to a materialistic deterministic view of the world, in contrast to Jung's polar conception of reality, but this difficulty does not seem to me to be insoluble any longer. At any rate, Professor Konrad Lorenz assures me that he accepts Jung's theory of archetypes in principle.

199   At the other pole of archetypal research are comparative religion and research in mythology, both of which have inevitably been influenced by Jung's theory of archetypes. The Eranos conferences, initiated by Olga Froebe-Kapteyn at Ascona in 1933, made it possible for Jung to meet with outstanding representatives of other disciplines and to enter into a stimulating give-and-take of ideas. These gatherings were theosophically oriented at first, but they gradually developed into a broad humanistic and scientific discussion centre on a very high level. Jung was invited to the first meeting in 1933 and attended the conferences more or less regularly

---

[19] Cf. Konrad Lorenz, "The Role of Gestalt Perception in Animal and Human Behaviour," in L. L. Whyte, *Aspects of Form*, p. 161; K. Lorenz and P. Leyhausen, *Antriebe tierischen und menschlichen Verhaltens*, pp. 44, 47.

until 1953.[20] There he met with Karl Kerényi, with whom he published several works on mythology; Gilles Quispel, with whom he discussed questions relating to Gnosticism[21]; Henry Corbin, who rediscovered Jung's archetypes in Persian mysticism[22]; Adolf Portmann, who discussed "patterns of behaviour" with him; Hugo Rahner, the specialist in Christian symbolic imagery[23]; Gershom Scholem, the expert in Jewish mysticism; the Egyptologist Helmuth Jacobsohn[24]; Sir Herbert Read[25]; and many other important scholars[26]. Knowledge of Jung's discovery of the collective unconscious and his theory of archetypes, spreading outwards from this circle, was widely disseminated and found wide recognition, but also, as was to be expected, considerable resistance and a good deal of misinterpretation. It was especially unfortunate, for example, that Mircea Eliade uses the same word, "archetype," but in another sense; for him, it is the mythological pattern of the world, projected into a primordial time (*illud tempus*) which, by means of rites, the retelling of myths, and other observances and celebrations, is constantly created afresh in the interest of the enhancement and furtherance of life.[27] In Jung's view, however, these mythological patterns were not archetypes, but rather archetypal representations and rites which form the *contents of the collective consciousness* of a particular people.[28] The archetypes themselves, on the other hand, are the

---

[20] Cf. W.R. Corti, "Vingt ans d'Eranos," *Le Disque vert*, pp. 288 ff.

[21] Together with H.C. Puech and M. Malinine, Quispel published the so-called Jung Codex, *Evangelium Veritatis*, translated as *The Gospel of Truth*; and *De resurrection*. Cf. also G. Quispel, *Die Gnosis als Weltreligion*.

[22] Cf. his beautiful book, *Creative Imagination in the Sufism of Ibn 'Arabi*; see, too, his discussion of "Answer to Job," in: *La Sophia éternelle*.

[23] Cf. Hugo Rahner, *Greek Myths and Their Christian Meaning*.

[24] Cf. Helmut Jacobsohn, "Der Altägyptische, der christliche und der moderne Mythos," *Eranos Jahrbuch*, 37 (1968), pp. 411 ff. and "Das Gegensatzproblem in altägyptischen Mythos," *Studien zur Analytischen Psychologie C.G. Jung*, II, pp. 172 ff.

[25] Cf. his speech, "C.G. Jung, on His 85th Birthday," 26 July 1960; and Nise da Silveira, "Sir Herbert Read, in Memoria," *Quaternio*, and the literature cited there.

[26] Jean Gebser was also much stimulated by Jung at Eranos. Gebser writes (*Abendländische Wandlung*, p. 175): "The future will show whether a psychic process of development will arise from the psychological 'binding-back' (religion), whether the scientific path of subjective knowledge can lead without a break into the heartening universe of objective faith. In the fact . . . that it is no longer exclusively 'psychology' in the scientific sense intended by Freud, but is already in a position to claim to be a theory of the soul – in this fact lies the real meaning of complex psychology."

[27] M. Eliade, *The Myth of the Eternal Return*.

[28] Evan Jan de Vries commits this error in his description of the Jungian point of view. He confuses the collective conscious with the collective unconscious, so that his presentation of Jung's view is completely distorted. *Forschungsgeschichte der Mythologie*, pp. 344 ff.

unconscious dynamisms *behind* such conscious collective representations; they produce them but are not identical with them. Jung emphasizes[29],

200   Another well-known expression of the archetypes is myth and fairy tale. But . . . here we are dealing with forms that have received a specific stamp and have been handed down through long periods of time. The term "archetype" thus applies only indirectly to the "representations collectives," since it designates only those psychic contents which have not yet been submitted to conscious elaboration and are therefore *an immediate datum of psychic experience.* In this sense, there is a considerable difference between the archetype and the historical formula that has evolved. Especially on the higher levels of esoteric teaching the archetypes appear in a form that reveals quite unmistakably the critical and evaluating influence of conscious elaboration. Their immediate manifestation, as we encounter it in dreams and visions, is much more individual, less understandable, and more naïve than in myths, for example. The archetype is essentially an unconscious content that is altered by becoming conscious and by being perceived, and it takes its colour from the individual consciousness in which it happens to appear.

201   Stimulated both by Jung's discoveries and by the views of Karl Kerényi, Raffaele Pettazoni and other investigators, many studies of mythological motifs have appeared recently which demonstrate in a valuable way the living truth and the psychological power of archetypal images and representations. Gilbert Durand's *Les structures anthropologiques de l'imaginaire: Introduction à une archétypologie générale*[30], with the wide range of literature cited, should especially be mentioned in this connection. There is one

---

[29] C.G. Jung, "Archetypes of the Collective Unconscious," CW 9/I, § 6.
[30] Presses Universitaires de France, Grenoble 1960.

danger, however, which it seems to me that none of these works entirely avoids, and that is a certain lack of clarity, owing to the *contamination* of the archetypes. Jung took considerable care to emphasize that the archetypes of the collective unconscious are structures which can be isolated only *relatively*; they overlap to an extraordinary degree, so that in practice it is possible to establish associations of meaning and motif, even of identity, between *every* archetypal symbol and every other one. A rational delimitation of certain cycles of motifs, such as is undertaken by Durand for example, is therefore arbitrary. Archetypal representations, in other words, elude any attempt to grasp them academically, that is, purely intellectually or intuitively. *They are only delimited and genuinely graspable in the actual culture of a people or in the work and experience of an individual.* Without this basis in psychological reality, one can simply describe every archetypal representation as 'everything in everything and in everything else', and go ahead and interpret them at will. Many investigators have drowned in this sea. Because they overlook the feeling-tone that is peculiar to each archetypal manifestation, such a manifestation becomes a mere word or image for them. "Those who do not realize the special feeling tone of the archetype end with nothing more than a jumble of mythological concepts, which can be strung together to show that everything means anything – or nothing at all. All the corpses in the world are chemically identical, but living individuals are not. Archetypes come to life only when one patiently tries to discover why and in what fashion they are meaningful to a living individual."[31] If one attempts to deal with terms like "Great Mother", "Totem Animal", "Tree of Life", etc. in a purely theoretical way, without having experienced their numinosity, then one does not actually know what one is talking about. These terms "gain life and meaning only when you try to take into account their numinosity – i.e. their relationship to the living individual"[32] In my opinion, a good part of current research into mythology suffers from the fact

---

[31] C.G. Jung, *Man and his Symbols*, p. 96.
[32] Ibid., p. 98.

that this relation is missing, even the research that accepts the Jungian idea of the archetypes. In other words, one cannot apply the Jungian theory of archetypes or carry on effective research in this field if it is separated from its basis in practical psychological experience.[33]

202   Although in the last analysis the myth, like the dream, is "its own meaning," one cannot ignore the historical fact that myths do not have the same meaning for people living in the present that they had for past cultures. If they mean anything for us today, then it is their *psychological meaning*. The method which Jung developed for doing this is in principle the same as that used in the interpretation of dreams. It consists chiefly in so-called "amplification," which means that one gathers together motifs as analogous as possible, first from the cultural environment of the mythic symbol, then from other areas, until it becomes apparent that these different motifs are like different facts of the same basic theme. The amplifications are then placed in sequence in the narrative, which itself provides a certain selection of the amplifying images.[34] When the collection of images has thus been enriched, then interpretation follows – that is, the translation into modern psychological language, which means their association to *psychic experience which is liveable in the present*. An interpretation, therefore, is never absolutely "right," but will have, to a greater or lesser degree, a "clarifying" or "illuminating" and enlivening effect. Indeed, the interpretation has no goal beyond that of reconnecting consciousness with the source of energy of the archetype. This source of energy is the original spirit that our consciousness has, so to speak, "differentiated itself away from," losing in the process a part of the primitive energy that is contained in the myth. As with a dream, it appears to be the purpose of the

---

[33] Joseph Campbell, *The Hero with a Thousand Faces*. Even Kerényi follows his teacher, W.F. Otto, inasmuch as he regards the myth or single gods as the ultimate genuine ground of being, which expresses itself in the mythic image. Thus, he demonstrates most valuably the reality of what Jung describes as the collective unconscious (even in its psychoid aspect), but he still misses the relation to the here-and-now of the human being. Much the same thing is true, in my opinion, of the work of Raffaele Pettazoni. Cf. the criticism of Otto in Ulrich Mann, *Theogonische Tage*, pp. 69 f.

[34] If a fox, for example, appears helpful in the context, then the emphasis must fall principally on the positive amplifications, such as cleverness, etc., and less on the equally valid aspect of the "animal sorcerer."

myth to keep alive in our memory our psychological prehistory[35], right down to the most primitive instincts, and the assimilation of the meaning of myths has the effect of broadening and modifying consciousness in such a way as to bring about a heightened aliveness.

203   A merely intellectual interpretation is never satisfactory because the feeling-value of the archetypal content is just as important as its understanding. That is why Jung says[36], "Psychology is the only science that has to take the factor of value (i.e. feeling) into account because it is the link between psychical events and life. Psychology is often accused of not being scientific on this account; but its critics fail to understand the scientific and practical necessity of giving due consideration to feeling."

204   In the Jungian interpretation of a myth, it is, as Jung himself emphasizes, never a question of an "unambiguous" interpretation, but rather one of finding a new expression of the myth in modern language, an expression that can never be quite independent of the nature of the interpreter. It is a question of an "as if" that can never lay claim to absolute validity. This has irritated many scholars and researchers, but nothing can be done about it. It is always a question of whether the interpretation "sheds light" or not. In spite of a good many different reservations, fairytale research has at least partly accepted something of the Jungian hypotheses, especially the idea of the archetypal origin of the fairytale.[37]

205   It is constantly being stressed that the fairytale and the myth, in contrast to the dream, are formations handed down by history, shaped in accordance with aesthetic needs, and of course, the psychologist must agree with this, as did Jung himself.[38] Nevert-

---

[35] Cf. C.G. Jung, "Symbols and the Interpretation of Dreams," CW 18, § 593.
[36] Ibid., § 596.
[37] Cf. the pro and contra in Wilhelm Laiblin, *Märchenforschung und Tiefenpsychologie*, and recently H. E. Giehrl, *Volksmärchen und Tiefenpsychologie*.
[38] Cf. in this connection the solid work of Wolfgang Schmidbauer, *Mythos und Psychologie*, especially pp. 68 ff. In many places, Schmidbauer's criticism of Jung is simply pushing at doors which are already open, and in others, it is based on misunderstanding. Schmidbauer says, for example, that Jung did not describe the spontaneous creative power of the archetype (p. 70)! It produces no representations, which is *not* Jung's view either. Further, he accuses Jung of Lamarcksim and insists that the latter is definitely passé. Whether all teleological ideas are really so completely outdated is still an open question! Further, he accuses Jung of not seeing the sociocultural influences (p. 74), even though he himself has in an immediately preceding passage cited Jung's emphasis on the fact that myths are collectively reworked archetypal representations (p. 68).

heless, criticism of the ambiguity of all interpretations is still unjustified, since this is unavoidable and must even be evaluated positively[39] since the task is simply to find as many ways as possible of reconnecting our consciousness with the latent meaning of these tales. In a hundred years, Jung once remarked, our "modern" interpretations will probably be regarded as amplifying mythologems, and a new interpretation will once again attain validity. This does no damage to the "eternal" myth. We are the ones who suffer when we can no longer connect it to our own psychic life.

206   In any case, it is clear enough that contemporary research into fairytales and folklore takes more and more notice of Jung's hypotheses.[40] But all of this, after all, is only an aid toward a better understanding of certain historical phenomena, through the use of the theory of archetypes. Of much greater importance is the living effect of archetypal powers *today* and their unpredictable influence on the events of our time. For the effect of any single archetype can as well be negative as positive. When they function positively, archetypes are behind every creative human achievement in culture for they are the origin of inspiration in poetry and painting and all the other arts; they are the source of new scientific models and they shape the conceptions and ideas characteristic of a particular day and age.[41] The historian, Arnold Toynbee, understood that the life-cycles of cultures are determined by archetypal forms.[42] Jung attempted to demonstrate in his work *Aion* how, in respect to the last two millennia of our Christian period, the archetypal background processes in the collective unconscious work themselves out in our particular culture. And A. Dupront and R. Alphandéry, taking a shorter period of time, have shown how the archetypal symbol of the "heavenly Jerusalem" and the "grave of Christ," taken as a

---

[39] I am responsible for the Jungian interpretation in Hedwig von Beit's first work, *Symbolik des Märchens*, and in *Gegensatz und Erneuerung im Märchen*. In her second work, *Das Märchen*, she moved away from this interpretation. I stand by my interpretations, which, however, I often expressed somewhat too abstractly, because at that time I had not yet had any psychotherapeutic experience. Cf. Hans Dieckmann, *Märchen und Träume als Helfer des Menschen*.

[40] Cf. for example the studies, written from the standpoint of Jungian psychology, by Gotthilf Isler, *Die Sennenpuppe*, and Adolf Ammann, *Tannhäuser im Venusberg*.

[41] In this sense, J.B. Priestley, for example, was stimulated by Jung. Cf. his *Man and Time*, passim.

[42] Cf. in this connection, Richard I. Evans, *Conversations with Carl Jung*, p. 115. More details below.

mandala[43], exercised a determining influence on the whole period of the Crusades. Even the forms of government developed by particular nations are not uninfluenced by this background and are by no means fully explicable purely by social and economic factors, as is so often asserted. Hans Marti and M. Imboden, for example, have, in my opinion, convincingly shown archetypal representations in the Swiss Constitution and in its idea of the state[44], and Eugen Böhler has shown that even modern economic thinking is strongly influenced by mythological or archetypal representations.[45] Thus, Jung's theory of archetypes is gradually and increasingly becoming the basis of a new general anthropology.[46]

207   The negative influence of an archetype when constellated is manifested in the form of possession, of blind fanaticism, and of ideological rigidity. Jung tried to show that the old archetypal image of Wotan had been reactivated in the National Socialist movement in Germany and had resulted in a warlike state of possession, similar to that of the Turks when they stormed the gates of Vienna with their cry, "No God but Allah."

208   Concealed religio-mythical motivations also lie behind the communist ideology: the idea of a kingdom of peace to be set up on this earth and, even more, the notion of the liberation of the truly or naturally creative human being, represented by the proletariat.[47] Interestingly enough, the archetypal Anthropos-image found in the Gnosis and the Kabbala reappears in Karl Marx, namely the myth of the "light-man," sunk in darkness, who must be freed, but this myth is projected onto society. Capitalists, revisionists, imperialists, and so on are the powers of darkness who oppress the "true human being" who is selfless, farsighted and creative.[48] "The communist

---

[43] *La Chrétienté et l'idée de la Croisade.* Cf. also Helen Adolf, *Visio Pacis, Holy City and Grail*, and A. Dupront's excellent work, "Introduction à l'etude d'un archetype," *La Table Ronde*, December 1957.

[44] Hans Marti, *Urbild und Verfassung*; and M. Imboden, *Die Staatsformen.*

[45] *Der Mythos in Wirtschaft und Wissenschaft; Zukunft als Problem des modernen Menschen;* «Ideologie und Ideal», *Industrielle Organisation*; and other works.

[46] Cf. Erich Neumann, *Ursprungsgeschichte des Bewusstseins*; and Peter Walder, *Mensch und Welt bei C.G. Jung.*

[47] Cf. Robert Tucker, *Karl Marx. Die Entwicklung seines Denkens von der Philosophie zum Mythos*, particularly p. 195 ff; and *Worte des Vorsitzenden Mao Tse-Tung*, p. 48, 140.

[48] Cf. Marie-Louise von Franz, "The Cosmic Man as Image of the Goal of the Individuation Process and Human Development," *Archetypal Dimensions of the Psyche*, p. 133 ff.

world revolution," writes Robert Tucker[49], "is for Marx a revolution of self-change, and act by which man is to end his alienation, restore his lost harmony with himself, and actualize himself as man." The goal is "the complete essential unity of man with nature, the true resurrection of nature, the achieved naturalism of man and the achieved humanism of nature."[50]

209   One wonders why the Christ-image, as an Anthropos figure uniting humanity, was inadequate to the task of liberating "the true man," so that such projections of a differently modified Anthropos-image occurred – and why was the symbolic image of the Buddha unable to protect the East from the invasion of communistic ideology?

210   According to Jung[51], the Christ-image is too one-sidedly spiritual and good to be able to represent man's wholeness adequately. It is lacking in darkness and in bodily and material reality. This was perceived as early as the Middle Ages by the alchemists, the natural scientists of that time, whose attention was directed, not to their own redemption but to the liberation of God from the darkness of matter.[52] The divine Anthropos they sought to free from matter was an image of man in which good and evil, spirit and matter were genuinely united and through which not only man but also all of nature would be made whole. It is this alchemical image of a god-man which is constellated in the collective background of the psyche of contemporary man and which – because it is not recognized – expresses itself in all sorts of singular projections, in Nietzsche's idea of the Superman, in the "true man" of Karl Marx, in Teilhard de Chardin's new Christ-image, to name only a few.[53] At bottom, it is the image of man in the Aquarian Age which is being formed in the collective unconscious. The astrological image of the Aquarian Age is an image of man which, according to Jung, represents the Anthropos as an image of the Self, or of the greater inner personality

---

[49] Ibid.
[50] K. Marx and F. Engels, *Historische-kritische Gesamtausgabe*, Vol. III, p. 116, cited by Tucker, p. 160.
[51] C.G. Jung, *Psychology and Alchemy*, CW 12, § 447 ff.
[52] Ibid., § 420.
[53] Jung said of Teilhard de Chardin's book, *The Phenomenon of Man,* "It is a first-rate book." Cf. also Miguel Serrano, *C.G. Jung and Hermann Hesse.*

which lives in every human being and in the collective psyche. He pours water from a jug into the mouth of a fish, of the constellation of the so-called "Southern Fish," that represents something still unconscious.[54] This could mean that the task of man in the Aquarian Age will be to become conscious of his larger inner presence, the Anthropos, and to give the utmost care to the unconscious and to nature, instead of exploiting it (as is the case today, for the most part).

211   Since the Anthropos also represents the collective psyche of the human race, he is the archetypal source of the feeling of being connected with *all* of mankind.[55] *This connection is of vital importance today* and it is why it is sought by many with fanatical vigour. But when a constellated archetype is not consciously recognized and realized on the inner, personal level, then it seizes upon a person from behind – from the unconscious – and leads to a state of possession. Possession, however, is morbid. Primitive peoples distinguish with great accuracy between a man who is possessed by a "spirit," that is, by an archetypal content, and is therefore sick and in need of treatment, and a shaman or medicine man who knows how to control spirits and can give them free rein to work their powers through him without becoming possessed himself.[56] The effect of archetypal motifs can be blinding or it can be culturally constructive; it can lead to ideologically motivated mass-murder or collective mania, or to the highest spiritual creations. It is a question of the problem discussed in Chapter 2 as to whether or not the individual is able to preserve his ego-consciousness intact, or whether he succumbs to the immense emotional power with which all archetypes are laden, in which case his consciousness disintegrates partially or completely. The many religious wars and ideological battles and persecutions of the past and the present are shattering evidence, today as always, of humanity's openness to possession. In most types of severe illness,

---

[54] *Memories*, p. 371 f.
[55] In the Kabbala, Adam Kadmon consists of the precepts of the Torah, and the Adam-image of the Mandaeans consisted of "the law." Psychologically, this means that at this cultural level, the individual cannot make direct contact with the 'inner man' but must do so through religious precepts.
[56] Cf. M. Eliade, *Shamanism*, p. 5 f.

according to Jung, it is also a question, in the last analysis, of consciousness being overwhelmed by archetypal contents which, because of a particular weakness, it is unable to integrate. The narrower, more rationalistic and rigid the consciousness, the greater this danger. The archetypal content constellated in such individual cases or collective situations is at one and the same time *the* greatest danger *and* the redeeming power, because such a content always comes to life and forces itself upwards from the unconscious when it is needed as a compensation for a one-sidedness of consciousness. However, it can be recognized and integrated only in the individual. If this act of creativity does not occur, then the same content persists, but in the form of a *projection* and the enemy – whatever is blocking this content – is projected onto outer enemies, while the positive content is projected onto a leader or a hero or an elite class. The possibility of it becoming conscious is thereby lost, and a *splintering* of the personality or the society occurs. The myth, described at the beginning of this chapter, of the fall of the Anthropos, the cosmic man, into the multiplicity of the world, mirrors this event, which is why most myths go on to relate that the primordial man who is fragmented in the world must be "gathered together" again and made one. The fact that there are a large number of different archetypes (probably as many as there are instincts) does in fact point to a certain dissociability in the human psyche. This tendency to split up into different archetypal contents is, however, countered in the collective unconscious by an opposite tendency which is revealed by the image of the Anthropos just discussed, and by the mandala symbol, to be taken up in the following chapter. *The Anthropos, seen as mankind's "group-soul," is, namely, an image of the bond uniting all men, or of inter-human Eros,* the preconscious ground of all communication and community among men, as well as being that psychic element which, through its power to compensate and limit, stands opposed to the boundless or one-sided drive to live out any *single* instinct.[57]

---

[57] That is why Jung constantly stressed the fact that we should be less concerned with perfection (in the one-sided Christian sense of the word) than with completeness or *wholeness*, not excluding any essential human disposition, not even the inferior and contra-sexual elements in our psyche.

212   The problem of a collectively human, supranational community forces itself upon us more and more every day as the sole solution to the threatening world-wide splintering into various particular interest-groups. World communism has, indeed, set up such an ideal[58], but with the exclusion of everybody who does not support its ideology and on the basis of identification with the group instead of that of a free and conscious feeling-relation among individuals. As a result – and this is a sign of possession – the exact opposite of the natural goal is achieved, and a *dissolution* of the individual into the mass occurs, instead of a conscious relation to one's fellow men. In other words, the archetype of the Anthropos can operate positively only when it is creatively constellated and conscious in the individual human being. Jung stood alone with this view, against all -isms, fashionable trends, and ideological fanaticism, and was criticized on every side, without ever changing his opinion.

---

[58] Cf. Marie-Louise von Franz, "The Cosmic Man as Image of the Goal of the Individuation Process and Human Development," in: *Archetypal Dimensions of the Psyche.*

Chapter 7
The Mandala

213 When the image of the giant radiolarian, hidden in the centre of the forest, appeared to Jung in his dreams while he was still a student in the Gymnasium, this contributed to his decision to study natural science. Although he could not have known anything about the universal meaning of the dream image at that time, he rightly concluded that it was an indication that he should seek the light of all further knowledge in the secret orderedness of nature. He did not know then that this archetypal image, to which he later applied the Sanskrit word *mandala*, would become one of the central concerns of all his later research.

214 This image-motif made its next appearance with new associations of meaning during the First World War when Jung was Commandant de la région anglaise des internés de guerre (1918/1919). Every morning he devotedly and painstakingly sketched a circular drawing in a notebook, and after a time he noticed that the form of these drawings appeared to mirror his own objective inner condition. If he was "outside of himself" or in a bad mood, then the symmetry of the mandala would be distorted. He writes[1], "Only gradually did I discover what the mandala really is: 'Formation, transformation, Eternal's Mind's eternal recreation.' And that is the self, the wholeness of the personality, which if all goes well is harmonious, but which cannot tolerate self-deceptions. My mandalas were cryptograms concerning the state of the self. . . . I had the distinct feeling that they were something central, and in time I acquired through them a living conception of the self. The self, I thought, was like the monad which I am, and which is my world.

---

[1] *Memories*, p. 220 f.

The mandala represents this monad, and corresponds to the microcosmic nature of the psyche. . . . The mandala is the center. It is the exponent of all paths. It is the path to the center, to individuation." During these years, it became clear to Jung "that the goal of psychic development is the self. There is no linear evolution: there is only a circumambulation of the self."

215   In 1927, Jung dreamed of such a mandala. He painted it and called it a "Window on Eternity."[2] A year later, he painted a similar picture, with a golden castle in the centre.[3] Shortly after that there ensued an extraordinary coincidence: Richard Wilhelm sent him the manuscript of *The Secret of the Golden Flower*, in which Jung enthusiastically recognized a description of the same process at work.[4]

216   Jung's dream about the above-mentioned mandala (1927) went as follows[5]: "I found myself in a dirty, sooty city. It was night, and winter, and dark, and raining. I was in Liverpool.[6] With a number of Swiss – say, half a dozen – I walked through the dark streets. . . . to a plateau above. . . . When we reached the plateau, we found a broad square dimly illuminated by street lights, into which many streets converged. The various quarters of the city were arranged radially around the square.[7] In the center was a round pool, and in the middle of it a small island. While everything round about was obscured by rain, fog, smoke, and dimly lit darkness, the little island blazed with sunlight. On it stood a single tree, a magnolia, in a shower of reddish blossoms. It was as though the tree stood in the sunlight and were at the same time the source of light. My companions . . . obviously did not see the tree. . . . I was carried away by the beauty of the flowering tree and the sunlit island. . . .

217   "This dream brought with it a sense of finality. I saw that here the goal had been revealed. . . . Through this dream I understood

---

[2] See C.G. Jung, "Concerning Mandala Symbolism," CW 9/I, Image 6 and § 654 f.
[3] Ibid., image 36 and § 691. Cf. also *C.G. Jung, Bild und Wort,* A. Jaffé (Ed), p. 91 and 93.
[4] *Memories,* p. 222.
[5] Ibid., 222 f.
[6] Jung commented: "Liverpool is the 'pool of life.' The liver, according to an old view, is the 'seat of life.'" *Memories,* p. 224.
[7] Each quarter of the city was also arranged radially around a central point, a smaller imitation of the greater plan.

that the self is the principle and archetype of orientation and meaning. Therein lies its healing function. . . . *Out of [this insight] emerged a first inkling of my personal myth.*"[8]

218   The symbols of the cosmic Anthropos and the mandala are synonymous; they both point to an ultimate inner unity of the psyche, to the Self. Buddha, the great Eastern symbol of this unity, was always represented in the early days as a 12-spoked wheel; it was only after some contact with Greece that he began to be represented in India as a human figure.[9] In the West, Christ has often been represented in the centre of a mandala, with symbols of the four evangelists. When, in his earlier years, Jung discovered the motif of the mandala-shaped core of the psyche, the Self, he did not know that he had stumbled onto an age-old symbol of the godhead and the cosmos; it was only gradually that he came upon the far-reaching historical parallels to his experience.

219   In our culture, this motif has a long and curious history. It is well known that one of the fateful moments in the evolution of Occidental culture was the genesis of natural scientific thought, which today is invested with such a high, even demonic, priority in world events: the birth of Greek natural philosophy in the seventh and sixth centuries before Christ. During this period a new image of the divine and of the ultimate structure of reality broke through into consciousness and increasingly displaced the personal deities of the Greek pantheon. This image had many and pronounced variations among the different natural philosophers. Nevertheless, given the perspective of time, it is not difficult to discern within it something new, coherent, uniform, namely the idea of an ultimate unitary ground of all being and of its circular or spherical structure, as well as its arrangement in accordance with its own internal laws. While the earliest natural philosophers, like Thales of Miletus, sought chiefly for the basic *substance* of all cosmic being, as early as the school of Parmenides the structural image of a *sphere* (*Sphaera*),

---

[8] Italics added by the author.
[9] The Naskapi Indians, in the Labrador Peninsula, teach that each man carries in his heart Mistap'eo, the "great man," the sender of dreams and the immortal seed, or core, of the individual psyche. But they represented him as a mandala-image rather than as a human figure. Cf. Frank Speck, *Naskapi*.

as the form of the ultimate basic principle of the cosmos, emerged. The natural philosophers probably took this image from the older pantheistic Orphism, in which the godhead was thought of as an all-embracing presence with cyclical or spherical form, encompassing beginning, middle and end.[10] The same image appears again in Empedocles, who believed that when the cosmos is under the dominion of Eros, it is "on all sides like to himself and everywhere without end, Sphaeros, the sphere-shaped, above the loneliness prevailing all around, filled with joyful pride."[11] In Anaximander's case, the world-principle is the *Apeiron* (the limitless), but at the centre of the world there is a "sphere which firmly encircles the cosmos." For Xenophanes, the cosmic god is "limited and spherical," "always and everywhere homogenous," "shaking the universe. . . by the thought-power of his spirit."

220   This primordial image was not clarified, however, until Plato, and later Plotinus[12], when circular motion was characterized as peculiar to the soul and the spirit, and as governing everything, and the cosmos was seen as a perfect sphere, conceived as the likeness of the spherical organism of being, of the world of ideas. It was Plotinus who chiefly mathematically further expanded these representations and handed them on to the Christian era: the centre of all being is the One, the Light which radiates in all directions and into the infinite; this One is surrounded by the spherical covering of the world soul and, further out, by the visible cosmos. But the centre is the "spiritual sphere" (*sphaera noete*) which is unity, wholeness, and the godhead itself.

221   This god is the "all-encompassing," and at the same time lives "inside the depths" at the centre-point.[13] It is to Plotinus's imagery that we owe a famous sentence which constantly appears and reappears everywhere in Hermetic philosophy and in Christian mysticism: "God is a spiritual sphere (or circle), whose centre is

---

[10] Cf. Dietrich Mahnke, *Unendliche Sphäre und Allmittelpunkt*, pp. 243-44.
[11] Ibid., p. 236. Mahnke suggests, instead of "everywhere without end" ("überall endlos"), as W. Kranz translates it, 'völlig unzerstückelt' ('completely undivided'). I find this very illuminating.
[12] Cf. Ibid., p. 227 ff.
[13] Cf. Ibid., p. 220.

everywhere and whose periphery is nowhere."[14] Tradition goes by way of the Neoplatonic *Liber viginti quattuor philosophorum*, via Salomon ben Gebirol to Augustine, John Scotus Eriugena, Alain de Lille and many others, to Meister Eckhart, Tauler, Ruysbroeck, Seuse, Nikolas von Kues, and then to Kepler, Weigel, Reuchlin, Bovillus, Marsilio Ficino, Giordano Bruno, Pascal, Jakob Boehme and Leibniz, to Schelling, Oken, Fichte, Franz Baader and others, a tradition which was unbroken, and which Dietrich Mahnke has set forth brilliantly; his book can therefore be recommended here.

222   Although in earliest times the image of the mandala or the sphere represented the godhead, the cosmos and the world soul, it gradually developed into an image analogous to the divine and as a symbol of the individual soul or psyche, eventually becoming an image of the "ideal ego"[15] or the "absolute ego" (Schelling) which stood, however, in contrast to the limited empirical ego. The projection of this image outward into "the All" was increasingly withdrawn into the inner world of the individual human being, to that region where Jung, independently and still unaware of these associations, came upon it again. Not that he discovered it; rather it appeared in his dreams, actively revealing itself. Jung, however, had the right feeling for what is important and grasped the fact that something of significance was revealing itself to him.

223   In the lives of certain important medieval mystics, the idea that the individual human being carries a "divine spark" or a likeness of God in the deepest centre of his psyche played a central role,[16] and consequently, self-knowledge, not in the sense of a subjective, egocentric mirroring of the ego but as a recognition of man's "deepest centre," is of great importance in the thought of Meister Eckhart, Johannes Tauler and Heinrich Seuse.[17] Even love for one's neighbour has its sole basis in love for this Self.[18] One comes to the Self through composure and the sacrifice of all ego desires, wilfulness, and intellectual curiosity. (Keep below humbly, and in

---

[14] As formulated in the *Poimandres* of Hermes Trismegistus; cf. Mahnke, p.44.
[15] Mahnke, p. 9.
[16] Cf. Hans Hof, *Scintilla animae*, p. 183.
[17] Cf. Alois M. Haas, *Nim din selbes war*.
[18] Cf. Ibid., p. 51.

your unknowing, go even below your wanting to know.[19]) In this way, one comes to the "innermost man." He is "the noblest god-like innermost hidden man[20]," who consists of "purest soul-substance."[21] This is the kingdom of God, "where God lives and acts."[22] This divine ground of the human psyche, however, is conceived by the medieval mystics as pure spirit and a likeness of the Christian God; the natural creature and matter are not included: on the contrary, it is demanded that one first "alienate" oneself from natural man, as created. In Jung's original experience, on the other hand, the symbol of the psychic ground appears harmoniously embedded in nature.

224   Although in the work of the greater thinkers, such as Plotinus, Augustine, Nikolas von Kues, Pascal, Leibniz, and others, the cosmic mandala-image appears to be harmoniously united with the representation of a more personal God, there is nevertheless a shade of difference between this mathematical symbol of God and the cosmos, and the representation which predominates elsewhere in our culture of a personal God: as womb or matrix of the "psychic ground," the mandala contains more *feminine* features, which in the East are expressed by the image of Buddha's lotus and the golden city, and in our culture by the image of Eden divided into four parts, by the temenos, the fortress, and the round vessel – all feminine symbols. It is a god-image which is more closely related to maternal nature and to the mother-image of matter (*mater-materies!*), which accounts for its first comprehensible emergence in our culture at about the same time as the beginnings of natural science.

225   The feminine factor had a determining influence on Jung's personality and thought. The intellect, the purely masculine spirit of the world of professional scholarship, was alien to him because this world knows nothing of the process of fertilization through the unconscious. "But a larger mind bears the stamp of the feminine; it is endowed with a receptive and fruitful womb which can reshape what is strange and give it a familiar form." That is the "rare gift of a

---

[19] Cf. Ibid., p. 135.
[20] Tauler, ibid., p. 125.
[21] Haas, p. 139.
[22] Ibid., p. 147.

maternal intellect," which was characteristic of Jung, as was said by his friend, Richard Wilhelm.[23] As is often the case with very virile men, Jung's emotional make-up and feelings were highly sensitive and intensely vulnerable, though they were concealed behind his jovial manner and zest for life. Hardly a person has suffered as he did; his great creative work was wrested into the light not only from the hot abyss of passions but also from suffering. Personal injuries, although these could move him deeply, did not affect him as much as the suffering in the contemporary world: the devastation of nature, the overpopulation problem, the war, the rape of still flourishing non-Christian cultures by the brutality of modern technology, all of which kept him constantly and indefatigably on the watch for any possibilities for a healing transformation which might emerge from the depths of the psyche. Perhaps only the people in his immediate surroundings, and those lucky enough to be his patients, were aware of Jung's powers of empathy and his extreme sensitivity, for he concealed his intense vulnerability and only seldom expressed his strongest feelings. The romantic poet which he was, also, breaks out only occasionally in his writings.

226   But the integration of the feminine into the world of masculine Logos to which our culture has been committed up to the present was not simply a personal matter with Jung. He was convinced that, in general, it is required of everyone these days. Well-meaning writers are forever telling us that we must conquer our aggressiveness, if we wish to avoid a world-wide catastrophe.[24] But reason alone has always proven too weak to cope with such a deep primordial urge. A greater power, i.e., *the constellation of an opposing archetype*, is needed to match the one-sidedness of purely aggressive behaviour, and that archetype today is the archetype of the feminine which, so far, has never been adequately integrated into our religious images of the world.

227   In his own life, Jung left a memorial to this fact: over the entrance to his round tower (a mother symbol and a mandala in stone) at

[23] C.G. Jung, "Richard Wilhelm: In Memoriam," CW 15, § 76.
[24] For instance, Konrad Lorenz, *On Aggression*.

Bollingen[25] he chiselled the inscription: "Philemonis Sacrum –
Fausti Poenitentia" (Shrine of Philemon – Repentance of Faust)[26].
This self-incarceration in his own Self, so to speak, forms the
counter-gesture to Faust's drive toward expansiveness, to that will
to power which led him to murder Philemon and Baucis, those two
old people who were the only ones still honouring the gods in a
godless time (Ovid). Thus, Jung consciously sacrificed his own
Faustian drive to the "respect for the eternal rights of man,
recognition of 'the ancient,' and the continuity of culture and
intellectual history," as he said himself[27], for "we have plunged down
a cataract of progress which sweeps us on into the future with ever
wilder violence the farther it takes us from our roots. Once the past
has been breached, it is usually annihilated, and there is no stopping
the forward motion. . . . We rush impetuously into novelty, driven
by a mounting sense of insufficiency, dissatisfaction, and
restlessness. . . . We refuse to recognize that everything better is
purchased at the price of something worse; that, for example, the
hope of greater freedom is cancelled out by increased enslavement
to the state, not to speak of the terrible perils to which the most
brilliant discoveries of science expose us." The masculine drive
toward activity and Faustian aggressiveness – caught in the maternal
womb of the mandala – can only there be transformed into a new
creative form in which the destructive initiative of our existence can
be integrated.

228   One root of our present culture is the Greco-Roman world. The
migrating Indo-Germanic tribes, with their purely patriarchal social
system, settled in Greece, where the previous culture had been more
matriarchal in character. In ancient Greece, the two worlds
coalesced, creating a lasting *tension*, expressed in the dissonant,
conflict-ridden marriage of Zeus and Hera.[28] Something of the sort
also occurred in ancient Rome: the matriarchal principle won its
widest recognition with the flowering of the cult of Isis in the later

---

[25] Cf. *Memories*, p. 250 ff.
[26] Ibid., p. 262, and cf. also p. 260 f.
[27] Ibid., p. 262.
[28] Cf. Charles Seltmann, *The Twelve Olympians and Their Guests;* or Karl Joël, *Der Ursprung der Naturphilosophie aus dem Geiste der Mystik*, passim.

period[29], but this principle was never joined with the patriarchal principle of the Roman state religion.

229   The other root of our culture is the Judaic world. There, too, the patriarchal tribes prevailed over the Canaanite world, with its cult of mother-goddesses, but no real union of the two ever took place. Tehom-Tiamat and the great love-goddesses, down to the "whore of Babylon," remained the rejected counter-principle to the god Yahweh. Thus, the spirit of the early Christian world was also patriarchal. At the same time, however, compensatory trends are noticeable throughout the period. These are first clearly seen in the form of "Wisdom," as she appears in Proverbs and in the probably Greek-influenced apocryphal writings of the Old Testament.[30]

230   The Lord created me at the beginning of his work,
            the first of his acts of old.
    Ages ago I was set up,
            at the first, before the beginning of the earth.
    . . .
    When he marked out the foundations of the earth,
            then I was beside him, like a master workman;
    and I was daily his delight,
            rejoicing before him always. . . .

231 And in the Wisdom of Jesus, the Son of Sirach (24: 3-18):

232   I came out of the mouth of the most High. . . .
    . . .
    He created me from the beginning before the world. . . .
    Likewise in the beloved city[31] he gave me rest. . . .
    . . .
    I was exalted like a cedar in Libanus,
            and as a cypress tree upon the mountains of Hermon.
    I was exalted like a palm tree in En-gaddi. . . .
    I am the mother of fair love,
            and fear, and knowledge, and holy hope. . . .

---

[29] One is reminded of the final chapter of Apuleius' *The Golden Ass.*
[30] Proverbs 8:22-23 (RSV); 29-30. Cf. C.G. Jung, "Answer to Job," CW 11, § 609 ff.
[31] The mandala-shaped heavenly Jerusalem!

233   This figure, as Jung explains in *Answer to Job*[32], "is a feminine numen of the 'metropolis' . . . the mother-beloved, a reflection of Ishtar." The tree metaphor is reminiscent of numerous other Semitic love- and mother-goddesses.

234   In the Wisdom of Solomon, too, this female figure appears as a world-creating *pneuma*, who is kind to man – an understanding divine spirit, who is "conversant with God" and who is "the brightness of the everlasting light, the unspotted mirror of the power of God."[33]

235   Mary, the Mother of Jesus, was regarded as her earthly likeness. She, too, is Wisdom – a mediatrix – and since her Assumption has, as "heavenly bride," the place of the divine Sophia.[34] Another primordial image of the feminine reappears in the Revelation of John, in that "woman clothed with the sun," who bore a son but was caught back into heaven with him.[35] This figure, too, has the attributes of cosmic nature: she is a *feminine Anthropos*, the counterpart of the masculine principle[36], and inasmuch as she completes the latter, she "reconciles nature with spirit"[37] and prepares the way for a new "birth of God."[38]

236   As the final image in the Apocalypse, there appears the motif of the "marriage of the Lamb with his Bride," who is the "new Jerusalem, coming down out of heaven," a city-mandala of precious stones "like a jasper, clear as crystal." This city is another aspect of Sophia, "who was with God before time began, and at the end of time will be reunited with God through the sacred marriage."[39] Jung was enthusiastically interested in the *Declaratio Assumptionis Mariae* of Pope Pius XII; he saw in this declaration a tendency pushing upwards from the depths of the collective unconscious, a "yearning

---

[32] C.G. Jung, "Answer to Job," CW 11, § 612.
[33] Ibid., § 613.
[34] Ibid., § 625. Cf. the *Constitutio Apostolica: Munificentissimus Deus*, § 27. Cf. in this connection Friedrich Heiler, "Das neue Mariendogma im Licht der Geschichte und im Urteil der Ökumene," in "Ökumenische Einheit," *Archiv für ökumenisches und soziales Christentum*, 2, Vol. 2.
[35] Cf. C. G. Jung, 'Answer to Job', CW 11, § 711.
[36] Presumably influenced by the pagan image of the Greek Leto (Ibid., § 711. Italics added by the author).
[37] Ibid., § 711.
[38] Cf. Ibid., §§ 716 – 717.
[39] Cit. Ibid., § 727.

for peace which stirs deep down in the soul', and a compensation to the 'threatening tension between the opposites,'[40] the tension from which every individual suffers today, each in his own way, and the sum total of which must inevitably lead only to war and revolutionary massacres.

237   This same unconscious tendency expresses itself in yet another form: in the singular fantasies that in many places have been woven around the so-called "UFO's" or unidentified flying objects. In his book *Flying Saucers, A Modern Myth*[41], Jung points out that UFO's are most often seen as round objects (plates or saucers!) and that either the salvation or the destruction of our planet is expected from them. In the fantasy of many people, flying saucers have become a symbol of the Self, a redemptive or destructive manifestation of the divine.

238   The mandala differs from a personal god-image not only in its feminine aspect, but also in its unequivocally mathematical-geometrical character. No wonder, therefore, that it was a favourite god-image of the first natural scientists and of the great mathematicians and philosophers, like Nikolaus of Kues, Pascal and Leibniz. The essential characteristic of the mandala is that it points to orientation in chaos, to order and to meaning.

239   When the medieval masculine, spiritual god-image began to lose its vigour at the time of the Renaissance, that great period of cultural transformation, men turned toward the earth and the mother-principle of matter, and it is no accident that it was just at that time – mediated by the *Poimandres* writings in the rediscovered *Corpus Hermeticum* – that the mandala once again began to occupy a special place as a model of the godhead and the cosmos.[42] Marsilio Ficino, for example, recommended the preparation of a circular likeness of the cosmos as a magical means of exerting a positive influence on the constellations.[43] If one contemplates this, one can see through the multiplicity of things in the outer world straight to the images

---

[40] Ibid., § 754
[41] C.G. Jung, "Flying Saucers: A Modern Myth of Things Seen in the Skies," CW 10, §§ 589 – 824.
[42] Cf. Frances Yates, *Giordano Bruno and the Hermetic Tradition*.
[43] Ibid., p. 74 f.

of the higher reality which one bears within oneself. Giordano Bruno recommended a similar construction, as a way of bringing together into a unity all the particular things of the world and all the memory contents of our psyche.[44] Both the Ptolemaic and the Copernican world-systems were for him such a mandala, with deep religious and magical significance,[45] and from Giordano Bruno the tradition moved on to Robert Fludd and Johannes Kepler. On the other hand, Descartes's system of coordinates – also a mandala – appears to be based more on a primordial vision which came up from the unconscious.[46] Not very long ago, this same form was reflected in Niels Bohr's model of the atom, and recently Walter Boehm[47] suggested the infinite sphere with its omnipresent centre as a structural model for the electron.[48] Apparently, whenever man finally confronts something unknown of basic importance, this image is constellated in the outer world as well as in the inner, as a symbol of a final transpersonal *order*.

240   After Jung had discovered the mandala in the depths of his unconscious psyche, he began to observe its appearance and its effects in other people as well. In part three of his paper *A Study in the Process of Individuation*[49], he analyzes a number of such images which illustrate the process of realization of the Self, the "real personality" or the "complete man" or the Anthropos.[50] And in the first part of *Psychology and Alchemy*, he returned to the theme, illustrating how the mandala periodically appeared spontaneously in an individual dream series[51], in quaternity symbols which appear no fewer than 71 times in 400 dreams. These images all seem to symbolize "the god within."[52] The high point in this dream series is a "world clock" which created in the patient an impression of the

---

[44] Ibid., p. 76.
[45] Ibid., p. 155 and Fig. P. 147.
[46] Cf. Marie-Louise von Franz, "The Dream of Descartes," in: *Dreams*.
[47] Walter Boehm, *Die metaphysischen Grundlagen der Naturwissenschaft und Mathematik*. At least he mentions Jung in passing.
[48] Ibid., p. 162.
[49] C.G. Jung, "A Study in the Process of Individuation," CW 9/I, §§ 525-626.
[50] Ibid., § 549. Cf. also "Concerning Mandala Symbolism," CW 9/I, §§ 627-712.
[51] C.G. Jung, *Psychology and Alchemy*, CW 12, §§ 122-331, also summarized in "Psychology and Religion," CW 11, § 91 ff.
[52] Ibid., CW 11, § 101.

most sublime harmony[53]. The centre of this mandala, formed of two intersecting circles, is empty. The space usually occupied by a divine figure is here only an abstract point, but in mandalas drawn by modern men and women, it is often a star, a flower, a cross with arms of equal length, a precious stone, or a human figure, etc., but almost never a god-image. These images are experienced as an *inner psychic centre* and the experience makes it possible to accept oneself.[54] Such a symbol, as Jung says[55], "is an involuntary confession of a peculiar mental condition. There is no deity in the mandala, nor is there any submission or reconciliation to a deity. *The place of the deity seems to be taken by the wholeness of man.*

241 "Modern psychological development leads to a much better understanding as to what man really consists of. The gods at first lived in superhuman power and beauty, on the top of snowclad mountains or in the darkness of caves, woods, and seas. Later on, they drew together into *one* god, and then that god became man. But in our day even the God-man seems to have descended from his throne and to be dissolving himself in the common man."[56] However, this new development, if it occurs unconsciously, brings with it a very great danger for man, namely, that of identifying the god-like power, which has invaded him, with his own limited empirical ego. The individual falls victim in such a case to an inflation (Nietzsche!) and the same inflation takes hold of the collective in the hypertrophy and totalitarian demands of the idealized State. "In the same way that the State has caught the individual, the individual imagines that he has caught the psyche and holds her in the hollow of his hand." The turning-point which differentiates No. 1 from No. 2 has then been missed.

242 Just as the Anthropos, although projected onto the group and thus robbed of its essential function as creator of inner cohesiveness, nevertheless secretly plays a role in the communist myth of redemption, so also does the mandala. The mandala-image bobs up

---

[53] Ibid., §§ 110-111.
[54] Cf. ibid., § 138.
[55] Ibid., § 139.
[56] Cit. ibid., § 141.

repeatedly in the Hegelian and Leninist theory of science as a "circle of circles" or a spiral. Here, too, the archetypal background of the image goes unrecognized, so that it is frozen into a rationalistic formula which individual thinkers, however, are constantly trying to break up.[57]

243   If the process of robbing cosmic nature of its soul – by the withdrawal of the gods or of God into the human being – continues as at present, "then everything of a divine or daemonic character outside us must return to the psyche, to the inside of the unknown man, whence it apparently originated."[58]

244   It was probably unavoidable that this withdrawal of the God-image into the human being should at first meet with a materialistic misinterpretation. Since God could not be found somewhere behind or beyond the stellar constellations, it was thought that he then simply did not exist. Pavel Popovich radioed jokingly to earth from his space-ship that he had found no trace of God in outer space. The next misinterpretation was psychological, namely Freud's notion that the idea of God is merely an illusion, born of repressed sexuality or the will to power of a priestly caste.[59] According to Jung, however, this power is not something known; the idea of God springs from the reality of the unconscious psyche which is much stronger than the ego. It is, namely, *everything within us which compels fear, submission or devotion.* This can be of the most varied nature and can be either good or evil. One man is ruled by a money complex: his god is Mammon; another by a power drive, and still another by an ideological obsession. Hence, man today can *choose* his "god" or "master." "Man is free to decide whether 'God' shall be a 'spirit' or a natural phenomenon like the craving of a morphine addict."[60]

245   Jung "chose" to serve the innermost ultimate centre, the "unknown quantity in the depths of the psyche"[61] which he called the Self and which nowadays is manifested in human beings as the

---

[57] Cf. Wilhelm Raimund Beyer, "Das Sinnbild des Kreises im Denken Hegels und Lenins," *Zeitschrift für Philosophische Forschung,* 26.
[58] Cit. C.G. Jung, "Psychology and Religion," CW 11, § 141.
[59] Cf. ibid., § 142.
[60] Ibid.
[61] Ibid., § 144.

image of a "great, all-embracing human being" (Anthropos) or in the form of a mandala.[62] This Self was never thought of (not even by the alchemists or the Hermetic philosophers, Jung's predecessors) as an essence or a substance identical with the ego, but rather as a "divine nature" differing from the ego and to be found only within, when it can no longer be projected. The protective outer circles, which are so often stressed in mandala-images, signify the isolation of this inner content, which "should not get mixed up with things outside."[63] The inhabitant of the mandala was once a god, but today he appears to be the "great inner man" in the individual human being. "One might also say that man himself, or his innermost soul, is the prisoner or the protected inhabitant of the mandala. Since modern mandalas are amazingly close parallels to the ancient magical circles, which usually have a deity in the centre, it is clear that in the modern mandala man – the deep ground, as it were, of the Self – is not a substitute but a symbol for the deity."[64] Today, "the unconscious produces the idea of a deified or divine man who is imprisoned, concealed, protected, usually depersonalized, and represented by an abstract symbol."[65] Only he who has had this experience, however, knows what this means. "No matter what the world thinks about religious experience, the one who has it possesses a great treasure, a thing that has become for him a source of life, meaning, and beauty, and that has given a new splendour to the world and to mankind. He has *pistis* and peace. . . . Is there, as a matter of fact, any better truth about the ultimate things than the one that helps you to live?"[66]

246   Jung wrote the above nearly 50 years ago and it is astonishing to see how accurately his observations hit the target. When I see cars painted with flower-mandalas by young people, I have to smile and ask myself, "Do they know what they are doing?" A few, especially in hippie circles, appear to sense something – for example, Ronald Steckel, writing in bold type in the periodical *Love*: "And the

---

[62] Cf. ibid., § 150.
[63] Ibid., § 157.
[64] Cit. Ibid.
[65] Ibid., § 158.
[66] Ibid., § 167.

kingdom is within you, and it is outside you, and whoever knows himself will find it."[67] Or when some hippies call to each other, "You are a god; fuck like one." But a great deal of what they feel is still distorted by stupefying drugs and neurotic bad taste. There are those, certainly, who recognize that trips and sex hinder rather than help any recognition of inner truth.[68] What is immediately striking, however, is the fact that most hippie communes were too exclusively oriented toward the "light," "idealistic" side of life, toward "love" without hatred, toward wisdom without seeing their own foolishness, toward spiritual freedom without taking into account the fact that the shadow, in just such a situation, becomes more and more the cynical realist or even the thief. The hippies were too much in the "light," too exclusively introverted, and their opponents, the political reformers were too one-sidedly extraverted, too lost in "destruction" and darkness. Both, however, sensed and in some fashion experienced the presentiment of a new image of the god man somewhere in the depths of the unconscious, but which has not yet, or has only in a very few, reached consciousness.

247   Nevertheless, it seems to me that the hippies are on the track of something better and more real, in their rejection of all Faustian violence (*Philemonis sacrum!*), in their search for creative elements, and especially in their turning inwards; while the progressives have for the most part remained stuck in outdated 19th century Marxist prejudices, in which men naively believe that the basic evils of human nature can be dealt with by force.

248   The religious spirit in the collective unconscious is like a fire; but fire in concrete reality spells destruction. When many people who have experienced this spiritual fire come together, they found an institution; then the spirit dies and the flame is quenched. In this situation, people react differently: some are faithful to the fire, others prefer institutional orderliness. The revolutionaries love the fire but they generally repel rather than attract, even among themselves. When the fire has consumed everything that needs to be consumed

[67] Cf Peter Brügge, "Über die apolitische Jugendbewegung in der Bundesrepublik," *Der Spiegel*, 25:33, p. 48. I owe my acquaintance with this article to the kindness of Manfred Wiele.
[68] Ibid., p. 41

by fire, then come the reasonable, well-balanced people to restrain the fiery ones, who are troublesome. There is therefore a need to find a *container* which can contain the fire. The first such container, in which one can safely handle such fire, is *human relationship*; for even relationship to the collective is rooted first of all in individual relationship.[69] That is why the problem of Eros is of such decisive importance today.

The "progressives" are the "fiery ones" who may indeed have been assigned by fate with the task of destroying everything which is no longer viable. But like all people who play with fire, they will very probably be destroyed themselves, for the future always belongs in the last analysis to those who creatively build new forms of life. Seen in this light, the programmes of certain hippie communes – the cultivation of the land and creative manual work – are worthy of notice.[70] In an interview he gave years ago, Jung emphasized his opinion that the revolutionary unrest of the urban masses could be attributed to the fact that work is despiritualized in technical industry. The work of a peasant or farmer is in itself meaningful and satisfies the human soul; the artisan must indeed relinquish the result of his work but nevertheless he finds satisfaction in the pride of accomplishment it affords. But work on the assembly line means spiritual impoverishment, because creative fantasy is wasted or lies fallow. Jung believed that discontented workers often mistakenly account for their resentments in terms of outer circumstances because they are unable to see that their *soul* is in want.[71] This dissatisfaction is now breaking out in sectors of the society where there is no question of material need (which does not mean, of course, that material need is not still the most urgent question in many parts of the world). The attempt by the hippies to encourage

---

[69] These remarks are summarized from notes taken by Esther Harding at a seminar held by Jung in Polzeath, Cornwall, England, in 1923, with the kind permission of Dr. Harding.
[70] Cf. *Der Spiegel*, op. cit., p. 44. The author of the article is ironical about these activities and implies mockingly that "Robinson" will go back, furtively, to the grocery business. This seems wrong to me because, even though much childishness and neurotic tastelessness are inherent in these attempts, one should nevertheless take seriously the search by these young people for something substantial and real, for such a search does contain the germ of a new attitude which is trying to compensate for the anomalies of our time.
[71] Cf. *C.G. Jung im Gespräch*, William McGuire (Ed.), p. 57 ff. (Talking to Hans Carol, a geologist.)

recognition of what is creative in work, therefore, seems to me to be genuinely significant.

250   The splitting-up of contemporary youth seeking new values into two camps is, in the end, the result of the split in the Self or in the God-image of which we have not become conscious. Its effect is like that of Böhme's God-image, of a mandala in which the light and the dark sides of God stand opposed to each other in two antagonistic semi-circles (instead of being united in one circle).[72] This split has a long and hidden prehistory, which is bound up with the whole history of Christianity.

---

[72] Cf. Victor Weiss, *Die Gnosis Jakob Böhmes.* The mandala reproduced in C.G. Jung, "A Study in the Process of Individuation," CW 9/I, fig. 1, is originally from Böhme's *XL Questions concerning the Soule,* English ed. 1647.

Chapter 8
Coincidentia oppositorum

251 When he was 11 (1887), Jung had a vision which left its stamp on him for the rest of his life. It was an event of such significance that it must be given in his own words:[1]

252 One fine summer day that same year I came out of school at noon and went to the cathedral square. The sky was gloriously blue, the day one of radiant sunshine. The roof of the cathedral glittered, the sun sparkling from the new, brightly glazed tiles. I was overwhelmed by the beauty of the sight, and thought, 'The world is beautiful and the church is beautiful, and God made all this and sits above it far away in the blue sky on a golden throne and. . .' Here came a great hole in my thoughts, and a choking sensation. I felt numbed, and knew only, 'Don't go on thinking now! Something terrible is coming, something I do not want to think, something I dare not even approach. Why not? Because I would be committing the most frightful of sins . . . . the sin against the Holy Ghost. . . . All I need do is not go on thinking.'

253 I reached home in a pretty worked-up state. . . . That night I slept badly. . . . The next two days were sheer torture. . . .

254 On the third night, however, the torment became so unbearable that I no longer knew what to do. I awoke from a restless sleep just in time to catch myself thinking again about the cathedral and God. I had almost continued the thought!

---

[1] *Memories*, p. 52 ff.

... Sweating with fear, I sat up in bed. ....Now it is coming, now it's serious! I *must think*. It must be thought out beforehand. *Why* should I think something I do not know? I don't want to, by God, that's sure. But *who* wants me to? .... Where does this terrible will come from?. . . it has come on me like a bad dream. Where do such things *come from*? This has happened to me without my doing. Why? After all, I didn't create myself. I came into the world the way God made me – that is, the way I was shaped by my parents.

255 He went on thinking then and realized that his parents could not have been responsible, nor their parents. Finally, his thoughts led him back to Adam and Eve, who had been created directly by God himself.

256 They were perfect creatures of God, for He created only perfection, and yet they committed the first sin. . . . How was that possible? They could not have done it if God had not placed in them the possibility of doing it. That was clear, too, from the serpent, whom God had created before them, obviously so that it could induce Adam and Eve to sin. . . . *Therefore, it was God's intention that they should sin.*

257 This thought liberated me instantly from my worst torment, since I now knew that God Himself had placed me in this situation. At first I did not know whether he intended me to commit my sin or not. . . .

258 "What does God want? To act or not to act? I must find out what God wants with me. . . ." Oddly enough, I did not think for a moment that the devil might be playing a trick on me. The devil played little part in my mental world at that time, and in any case I regarded him as powerless compared with God. . . . Hence there was no question in my mind but that God Himself was arranging a decisive test for me, and that everything depended on my understanding Him correctly. . .

259 "Is it possible that God wishes to see whether I am capable of obeying His will even though my faith and my reason raise before me the spectres of death and hell? That might really be the answer! But these are merely my own thoughts. I may be mistaken. . . ."

260 I thought it over again and arrived at the same conclusion. "Obviously God also desires me to show courage," I thought. "If that is so and I go through with it, then He will give me His grace and illumination."

261 I gathered all my courage. . . and let the thought come. I saw before me the cathedral, the blue sky. God sits on His golden throne, high above the world – and from under the throne an enormous turd falls upon the sparkling new roof, shatters it, and breaks the walls of the cathedral asunder.

262 So that was it. I felt an enormous, an indescribable relief. Instead of the expected damnation, grace had come upon me, and with it an unutterable bliss such as I had never known. . . . A great many things I had not previously understood became clear to me. . . . In His trial of human courage God refuses to abide by tradition, no matter how sacred. . . .

263 . . .He could also demand something of me that I would have had to reject on traditional religious grounds. It was obedience which brought me grace. . . . One must be utterly abandoned to God; nothing matters but fulfilling His will. Otherwise all is folly and meaninglessness. From that moment on . . . my true responsibility began. Why did God befoul His cathedral? That, for me, was a terrible thought. But then came the dim understanding that God could be something terrible. I had experienced a dark and terrible secret. It overshadowed my whole life, and I became deeply pensive.

264 The "terrible God" whom Nicholas von Flüe also encountered[2], whom Martin Luther and Jakob Boehme and many others knew,

became for Jung a permanent reality as a result of this experience. All his childish and naïve ideas about a "loving God" as a *Summum Bonum* were outgrown once and for all. Jung's description makes it abundantly clear that it was not a question of an intellectual insight but that a very deep moral conflict was involved.

265   In contrast to the mandala dreams and visions mentioned in the preceding chapter, the unconscious is here *personified* in a God-figure. The Self is symbolized in this case not as a meaningful mathematical order of things but as a God who acts. The advantage of such a personification "lies in making possible a much better objectification of the *vis-à-vis*"[3] and in the fact that emotions, feelings, love, hate, fear, and reverence can thus join in the encounter, as they do not when the more abstract mandala form is constellated. "The whole man is challenged and enters the fray with his total reality. Only then can he become whole and only then can 'God be born,' that is, enter into human reality and associate with man in the form of 'man.'"[4]

266   But here we meet the great difficulty. The God of the Christian world is only good but man – his likeness – is not: thus the "Christian God-image cannot become incarnate in empirical man without contradictions. . . ."[5]

267   Jung wrestled with this problem all his life and expressed his struggle dramatically in *Answer to Job*.[6] In his old age, he once remarked that now that he knew more, he would like to rewrite all of his books except *Answer to Job*, but he would leave that one just as it stands. He wrote it in one burst of energy and with strong emotion, during an illness and after a high fever, and when he had finished it, he felt well again. *Answer to Job* should not be taken as a theological work.[7] It is intended, as Jung himself wrote[8], to show "the way in which a modern man with a Christian education and

---

[3] *Memories*, p. 368 f.
[4] Ibid. P. 369.
[5] Ibid.
[6] C.G. Jung, "Answer to Job," CW 11, §§ 553-758. Cf. also A. Jaffé, *Der Mythos vom Sinn im Werk von C.G. Jung*, p. 115 ff.
[7] Cf. Jung's answer to Josef Rudin in C.G. Jung, *Letters*, vol. 2, p. 553 f.
[8] C.G. Jung, "Answer to Job," CW 11, § 561.

background comes to terms with the divine darkness which is unveiled in the Book of Job. . . . In this way I hope to act as a voice for many who feel the same way as I do, and to give expression to the shattering emotion which the unvarnished spectacle of divine savagery and ruthlessness produces in us."

268   What God, in his cruel game with Satan, inflicts upon his faithful servant Job is frightful. Men and women who innocently lived through Hiroshima, who languished in concentration camps, or who are suffering in detention camps today will best understand this. The greatness of Job lies in the fact that, throughout his afflictions, he never doubts the existence of God, nor does he ever pretend in an inflated way to judge him ("I lay my hand on my mouth"), while at the same time he stands by the dictates of his conscience and his conviction of right and wrong and appeals to Sophia, or to God's omniscience, against the "wrathful" Yahweh. He turns to Sophia, with whom God had shared his life at the beginning of the world, but who had been lost from sight "since the days of the Creation."[9] The principle of divine Eros had thus disappeared into unconsciousness, to be replaced by the ideal of perfection, the attainment of which was demanded of Israel by God.

269   Job's uprightness and his love of God produce a curious change in God himself, for whom Job's behaviour is to a certain extent a moral defeat. This change is the decision to become man in Christ[10], and to turn once again toward the feminine in the form of Mary, Mother of God (who serves as a renewed image of Sophia). Through Mary, a new God-man will be created, since now that he has been surpassed by his creature, God needs to regenerate himself.[11] But the elimination of any taint of sin in both mother and son sets them apart from the rest of mankind. They "are not real human beings at all, but gods"[12], so that the masculine ideal of perfection, in contrast to the feminine ideal of wholeness, is still predominant. However, a so-called ideal state or condition is always threatened with an

---

[9] Ibid., § 620.
[10] Cf. ibid., §§ 625-631.
[11] Cf. ibid., § 640.
[12] Ibid., § 626.

enantiodromia.[13] "No path leads beyond perfection into the future – there is only a turning back, a collapse of the ideal, which could easily have been avoided by paying attention to the feminine ideal of completeness."[14] In ever-sharpening contrast to the "wholly good" images of Mary and Christ, the counter-image of Satan, the Antichrist, stands out, even in Holy Scripture, as the embodiment of God's counter-intention, or shadow; Christ himself saw Satan fall like lightning from heaven (Luke 10:18), thus coming that much closer to our human world.

270   According to legend, Satan, filled with envy, wanted also to be incarnated as a human being, so that the *dark* God might likewise become man. As an incubus, he impregnated a pious virgin without her knowledge. *This was the begetting of Merlin.* The mother's piety, however, prevented Merlin's falling forfeit to evil. Later, however, at the end of the astrologically preordained millennium allotted to the reign of Christ, Satan will succeed in being incarnated in the image of the Antichrist, and will thus bring about the final catastrophe, as described in the Revelation of St. John.[15]

271   At first, God incarnated only his good side in Christ. After the death of Christ, the Holy Ghost began to work its effect, which means both the continuation of God's incarnation in man and the transformation of all men who believe in this"'spirit of truth" into "fellow heirs with Christ," even into "gods," that is, into god-men.[16] Owing to his sinlessness, Christ was not wholly a human being. Job, on the other hand, "was an ordinary human being, and therefore the wrong done to him, and through him to mankind, can, according to divine justice, only be repaired by an incarnation of God in an empirical human being. This act of expiation is performed by the Paraclete; for, just as man must suffer from God, so God must suffer from man. Otherwise there can be no reconciliation between the two."[17]

---

[13] Transformation into its opposite.
[14] C.G. Jung, "Answer to Job," CW 11, § 627.
[15] Ibid., § 654.
[16] Cf. ibid., § 655 f.
[17] Cit. ibid., § 657.

272   The entire drama, as Jung emphasizes, reveals a curious incongruity between God and his creatures, for it is inconceivable that an all-knowing, good, and all-powerful God could get as worked up about his helpless creations, men and women, as he does in Holy Scripture. The disproportion in power is far too great. Rather, it looks as if God were "unconscious" and that he therefore succumbed many a time to his own shadow, Satan. "How then could he expect man with his limited consciousness and imperfect knowledge to do any better?"[18] "To believe that God is the Summum Bonum is impossible for a reflecting consciousness."[19] "A more differentiated consciousness must, sooner or later, find it difficult to love, as a kind father, a God whom on account of his unpredictable fits of wrath, his unreliability, injustice and cruelty, it has every reason to fear."[20] "It is quite right, therefore, that fear of God should be considered the beginning of all wisdom." *God is a coincidentia oppositorum*[21], at the same time the highest love and the greatest good, and dark inhuman cruelty. "The inner instability of Yahweh," however, "is the prime cause not only of the creation of the world, but also of the pleromatic drama for which mankind serves as a tragic chorus. The encounter with the creature changes the creator."[22]

273   The appearance of the Antichrist at the end of the second Christian millennium is to be accompanied by an indescribable world-wide catastrophe, which is described in the darkest colours in the Johannine Revelation. Then, however, unmediated and in the midst of the most utter destruction, there will appear in heaven the *sun-woman*, "with the moon under her feet, and on her head a crown of twelve stars."[23] She is that feminine Anthropos-image who completes the patriarchal, exclusively masculine image of God; "she contains in her darkness the sun of 'masculine' consciousness. . . . She adds the light to the dark, symbolizes the hierogamy of

---

[18] Ibid., §658. Cf. also § 661.
[19] Ibid., § 662.
[20] Ibid., § 664.
[21] Ibid., cf. also § 685 f.
[22] Ibid., § 686.
[23] Cf. on this and on what follows ibid., § 711 ff.

opposites, and reconciles nature with spirit."[24] This woman gives birth to a man-child who, however, is at once taken back to God. Psychologically this means that we are dealing with an image which was still latent (at the beginning of the Christian era) which will not be activated until a later time. This man-child embodies the mythologem of the "divine child," that is, he is *a symbol of the coming into consciousness of the total Self*[25] *as a complexio oppositorum* which, to us, appears dark only when consciousness takes all the light to itself and lays claim to too much moral authority.

274   In his apocalyptic visions, St. John anticipated the insights of the alchemists and of Jakob Boehme: he sensed that the godhead possesses a terrifying dual aspect, "a sea of grace is met by a seething lake of fire, and the light of love glows with a fierce dark heat of which it is said 'ardet non lucet' – it burns but gives no light. That is the eternal, as distinct from the temporal, gospel: *one can love God but must fear him.*"[26]

275   The paradoxical nature of his God-image splits the individual human being and all of Western mankind into similar opposites, thus constellating apparently insoluble conflicts. But today when we observe the individual person, torn apart by inner conflicts, we see that his unconscious produces symbols, such as an Anthropos figure or a mandala, which *unite the opposites*[27] *and symbolize the essence of the individual process.*

276   Viewed psychologically, God's becoming man is a symbol for a process of growth which is set off when one becomes conscious of the tension of the opposites in one's inner wholeness and which wants to force us to harmonize and unite the opposing forces from the unconscious to which our conscious mind is so constantly exposed.[28] "The unconscious wants both: to divide *and* to unite. In his striving for unity, therefore, man may always count on the help of a metaphysical advocate. . . . The unconscious wants to flow into consciousness in order to reach the light, but at the same time, it

---

[24] Cit. ibid., § 711.
[25] Cf. ibid., § 714.
[26] Cit. Ibid., §733.
[27] Cf. ibid., § 738.
[28] Cf. ibid., § 740.

continually thwarts itself, because it would rather remain unconscious. That is to say, God wants to become man, but not quite. The conflict in his nature is so great that the incarnation can only be bought by an expiatory self-sacrifice offered up to the wrath of God's dark side."[29] This self-sacrifice, the deep acceptance of suffering and inner conflict, is symbolized by the cross;[30] for the painful coming into consciousness of the inner opposites brings with it an immediate feeling of redemption, a redemption from a hollow, helpless state of being unredeemed.

277   Jung saw the split within the Christian Church itself and the split in our Western world as the consequences of the fact that we are not conscious of the inner conflict produced in us by the ambivalence of our God-image. The split in our youth, which was discussed in the preceding chapter, is but another reflection of the same thing; one segment of youth identifies itself too closely with the good and the principle of light; the other segment has fallen into the "wrathful-fire" of the dark Antichrist side of God. It is only those few who have enough courage to take up the conflict within themselves and make it conscious who are the creative ones and who can help to avoid the total war which threatens all of us.

278   In the individual, the problem of the opposites appears first and foremost as a conflict of conscience, the severest forms of which do not consist in a choice between a recognized good and a temptation to evil, but rather in cases where *each* alternative has justification and can result in good as well as in evil. In such a case, one must either yield to the conventional code of morality provided by the environment (the Freudian superego), or, on the other hand, wait with a listening attitude for the creative decision to come from the Self[31] and muster the courage to act on it in spite of the danger of error, as the boy Jung did, when he finally decided, after much indecision, to think through to the end the thoughts that came to him from the unconscious about God's unholy behaviour and to allow the shocking image to surface into his consciousness. For

---

[29] Ct. Ibid.
[30] Cf. ibid., § 659.
[31] Explained in C.G. Jung, "A Psychological View of Conscience," CW 10, §§ 825 – 857.

beyond the ambivalence and duality of the unconscious, which pushes us into good as well as into evil, there is the figure of the "advocate," the divine Sophia or the Holy Ghost – that is, the paradoxical *unity* of the Self – which can lead us toward a higher level of consciousness, the gentle but unyielding inner voice of truth which pushes us in the direction of individuation and permits no self-deception.

279   Jung was not happy when Erich Neumann published his book *Depth Psychology and a New Ethic*[32], because he felt that Neumann's attitude was somewhat inflated. We do not need "new Tables of the Law," he said once, "the ethic we have will do if it is really lived. We stand in much greater need of a widening of our reflective consciousness, so that we can be more clearly aware of the opposing forces within us and cease trying to sweep evil out of the way, or denying it or projecting it, as we have done until now." Put still more simply, this means that we should *really* see our shadow, instead of mindlessly living it out. "If God himself should demand from me a murder," Jung once said[33], "I would not commit it; instead, I would throw my tiny human freedom and consciousness onto the scale, and sooner offer myself as a sacrifice."

280   Before he wrote *Answer to Job*, Jung had a dream, reported in his memoirs[34], in the course of which he was led by his father to the centre of a mandala-shaped building and into the "highest presence". "My father knelt down and touched his forehead to the floor. I imitated him, likewise kneeling, with great emotion. For some reason I could not bring my forehead quite down to the floor – there was perhaps a millimetre to spare." After this dream, Jung expected fate to send him severe trials (the death of his wife, for one thing) to which he would have to submit, but he was unable to submit entirely. "Something in me was saying, 'All very well, but not entirely.' Something in me was defiant and determined not to be a dumb fish: and if there were not something of the sort in free men, no *Book of Job* would have been written several hundred years before the birth

---

[32] Erich Neumann, *Depth Psychology and a New Ethic.*
[33] One recalls Abraham's near sacrifice of Isaac.
[34] *Memories*, p. 243 ff.

of Christ. Man always has some mental reservation, even in the face of divine decrees. Otherwise, where would be his freedom?"[35] Today, mortal man is actually in a position to annihilate God's creation. "The dream discloses a thought and a premonition that have long been present in humanity: the idea of the creature that surpasses its creator by a small but decisive factor."[36] *This "small but decisive factor" is consciousness.*

281   The idea of a possible "unconsciousness in God" naturally gave much offense to a number of Jung's contemporaries, and even Erich Neumann was unable to accept it and wrote Jung a long letter of protest.[37] Jung replied in meticulous detail, defending his own point of view,[38] chiefly by reference to the theory of evolution as understood by contemporary natural scientists. "We know," he writes, "that after hundreds of millions of years of far-reaching, accidental transformation of species, man at last entered the plan of creation."[39] "Here the miracle of reflecting consciousness is so great that one cannot help suspecting the element of *meaning* to be concealed somewhere within all the monstrous, apparently senseless biological turmoil, and that the road to its manifestation was ultimately found on the level of warm-blooded vertebrates possessed of a differentiated brain – found as if by chance, unintended and unforeseen, and yet somehow sensed, felt and groped for out of some dark urge."[40]

282   "We simply do not know of what the constructive factor of biological development consists. We know well enough that warm-bloodedness and brain differentiation were necessary for the emergence of consciousness and therewith for the gradual revelation of meaning. . . . Since creation without man's reflecting consciousness has no recognizable meaning,

---

[35] Ibid., p. 246 f.
[36] Ibid., p. 247.
[37] Reprinted in full in an Appendix to Aniela Jaffé, *Der Mythus vom Sinn*, pp. 179-82. This Appendix is not included in the English version of Jaffé's book, *The Myth of Meaning.*
[38] Cf. Jung's letter to Erich Neumann, in: C.G. Jung, *Letters*, vol. 2, pp. 493-496.
[39] Cf. for example, the beautiful presentation by Loren Eiseley, *The Immense Journey*. I am indebted to Dr. René Malamud for acquaintance with this book.
[40] *Memories*, p. 371, and A. Jaffé, *The Myth of Meaning in the Work of C. G. Jung.*

then with the hypothesis of latent meaning a cosmogonic significance for man is intended, a genuine *raison d'être*. *If, however, latent meaning as a conscious plan for creation is ascribed to the Creator, then the question arises: why should the Creator organize this whole phenomenon of the world, since he already knows wherein he can see his reflection? And why should he be reflected, since he is already conscious of himself?* Why should he create a second, inferior consciousness alongside his omniscience – some billions of murky little mirrors which will reflect an image he knows in advance? After all these reflections, I have come to the conclusion that man's likeness to God is a matter which concerns not only man but also his Creator. God's situation is similar or identical to that of man, which is to say that, among other things, he is as unconscious as man, or even more so, since according to the myth of the incarnation, he even felt induced to become man and to offer himself as a sacrifice to man."[41] Creation, or the nature which surrounds us and of which we are a part, is, in Jung's view, probably not entirely meaning-less, but the meaning is *latent*, since the unconscious, which is sheer nature, harbours a *latent meaning* which becomes actual only when it becomes conscious in us. To take simply one small instance: every dream contains a latent meaning but this meaning does not become a part of our objective reality until we consciously understand the dream, which otherwise would simply pass as "meaningless."

283 Full realization of the cosmogonic meaning of consciousness came to Jung during a trip to Africa (1925), when he travelled from Nairobi to the Athi plains, a great game reserve in Kenya. He describes this visit in poetic language[42]:

---

[41] Letter to Erich Neumann, in: C.G. Jung, *Letters*, Vol. 2, p. 493 ff.
[42] *Memories*, p. 284 f.

284 To the very brink of the horizon we saw gigantic herds of animals: gazelle, antelope, gnu, zebra, warthog, and so on. Grazing, heads nodding, the herds moved forward like slow rivers. There was scarcely any sound save the melancholy cry of a bird of prey. This was the stillness of the eternal beginning, the world as it had always been, in the state of non-being; for until then no one had been present to know that it was this world. . . .There the cosmic meaning of consciousness became overwhelmingly clear to me. . . . Man, I, in an invisible act of creation put the stamp of perfection on the world by giving it objective existence. This act we usually ascribe to the Creator alone, without considering that in so doing we view life as a machine calculated own to the last detail, which, along with the human psyche, runs on senselessly, obeying foreknown and predetermined rules. In such a cheerless clockwork fantasy there is no drama of man, world, and God; there is no 'new day' leading to 'new shores', but only the dreariness of calculated processes. . . . man is indispensable for the completion of creation . . . in fact, he himself is the second creator of the world, who alone has given to the world its objective existence – without which, unheard, unseen, silently eating, giving birth, dying, heads nodding through hundreds of millions of years, it would have gone on in the profoundest night of non-being down to its unknown end.

285 When Jung experienced the unutterable beauty of an African sunrise, it became clear to him "that within the soul from its primordial beginnings there has been a desire for light and an irrepressible urge to rise out of the primal darkness. . . . That is why the sun's birth in the morning strikes the natives as so over-whelmingly meaningful. The *moment* in which light comes *is* God. That moment brings redemption, release. . . . In reality, a darkness altogether different from natural night broods over the land. It is the psychic primal night which is the same today as it has been for

countless millions of years. The longing for light is the longing for consciousness."[43]

286   Many people were even more offended by Jung's discussion of the dark side of God and the origin of evil than they were by his view of God as an unconscious being (a bit more unconscious in fact than man).[44] Evidently our infantile side is reluctant to give up the idea of a "loving God" who graciously watches over us, even though the reality is so completely at variance with such a picture. In the attempt to save this precious idea, many people even prefer to believe that man is responsible for all evil, although they are not eager to scrutinize this idea too carefully either. "The horror which the dictator States have of late brought upon mankind is nothing less than the culmination of all those atrocities of which our ancestors made themselves guilty in the not so distant past. Quite apart from the barbarities and blood baths perpetrated by the Christian nations among themselves throughout European history, the European has also to answer for all the crimes he has committed against the coloured races during the process of colonization. In this respect, the white man carries a very heavy burden indeed. It shows us a picture of the common human shadow that could hardly be painted in blacker colours. The evil that comes to light in man . . . is of gigantic proportions. . . .Since it is universally believed that man *is* merely what his consciousness knows of itself, he regards himself as harmless and so adds stupidity to iniquity. He does not deny that terrible things have happened and still go on happening, but it is always 'the others' who do them. . . . In reality, we merely lacked a suitable opportunity to be drawn into the infernal melée. None of us stands outside humanity's black collective shadow."[45]

287   "If we project evil onto 'the others', then we lose the possibility of insight and therewith the ability to deal with evil."[46]

288   We are a part of nature, and our darknesses are those of nature, which God has created. Not all darkness can be ascribed to

---

[43] Ibid., p. 298 f.
[44] Cf. H.L. Philp, *Jung and the Problem of Evil*, and especially Jung's answer in: C.G. Jung, *The Symbolic Life*, CW 18, §§ 1584 – 1690.
[45] Cit. C.G. Jung, "The Undiscovered Self," CW 10, §§ 571 – 72.
[46] Ibid., § 572.

mankind. We learned long ago to forgive some of our fellow human beings their misdeeds, on the grounds that in their youth they were exposed to unprecedented horror by objective circumstances. Thus, the fearful question of the origin of evil in God remains – unless one becomes a dualist, which corresponds to a psychic split. In the first millennium of the Christian era, the idea of God as the Summum bonum prevailed, but not long after the year 1000, signs of restlessness and of the fear of a coming world catastrophe began to increase.[47] Today the Christian world is inescapably confronted with the principle of evil: with open and public injustice, tyranny, lies, slavery, and the restraint of conscience. Honest men can no longer look away from these things or seek excuses for them. "Evil has become a determinant reality. It can no longer be dismissed from the world by a circumlocution. We must learn how to handle it, *since it is here to stay*."

289   What is important is that we give up the illusion that we know for sure what good and evil are and that we can teach such knowledge to others, because with that conviction we have succumbed. "Every form of addiction is bad, no matter whether the narcotic be alcohol or morphine or idealism. We must beware of thinking of good and evil as absolute opposites."[48]

290   When the opposites are consciously recognized, then both good and evil are thereby relativized, although this by no means implies that these categories have therefore become invalid. Wrong that is done, intended, or thought will be revenged in our soul: the thief steals from himself, the murderer murders himself. The relativization of the opposites makes ethical decision more difficult than ever. "Nothing can spare us the torment of ethical decision. Nevertheless, harsh as it may sound, we must have the freedom in some circumstances to avoid the known moral good and do what is considered to be evil, if our ethical decision so requires."[49] For this, thoroughgoing self-knowledge is needed, and this knowledge will reveal to the individual how much there is of light within him, and

---

[47] For this and what follows, see *Memories*, p. 360 ff.
[48] Ibid., p. 361.
[49] Ibid.

also how much of darkness. In general, however, this is exactly what people wish to avoid: they prefer to project evil onto another person or nation or class.

291   This is Jung's view of the psychological situation in the world today: "Some. . . call themselves Christians and imagine that they can trample so-called evil underfoot by merely willing to; others have succumbed to it and no longer see the good. Evil today has become a visible Great Power. One half of humanity fattens and grows strong on a doctrine fabricated by human ratiocination; the other half sickens from the lack of a myth commensurate with the situation. The Christian nations have come to a sorry pass; their Christianity slumbers and has neglected to develop its myth further in the course of the centuries. Those who gave expression to the dark stirrings of growth in mythic ideas were refused a hearing."[50]

292   The question of the origin of evil, which was raised by the Gnostics many centuries ago, has never been answered. When God becomes man, however, and when the God-image is a *complexio oppositorum*, this becomes apparent first and foremost in the form of a conflict within the human being[51] because the God-image, psychologically speaking, is a manifestation of the ground of the psyche. However, along with this cleavage, which is now becoming unavoidably clear, *healing tendencies* are swelling up from this same ground of the psyche, tendencies which are manifested in the form of mandalas or other symbols of the Self, and these symbols signify a *synthesis* of the opposites. Jung therefore understands the myth of God's incarnation in man as "*man's creative confrontation with the opposites and their synthesis in the self, the wholeness of his personality.*"[52] "In the experience of the self it is no longer the opposites 'God' and 'man' that are reconciled, as it was before, but rather the opposites within the God-image itself. That is the meaning of divine service, of the service which man can render to God, that light may emerge from the darkness, that the Creator may become

---

[50] Ibid., p. 361 f.
[51] Ibid., p. 366.
[52] Ibid., p. 370. Italics added by the author. For the way in which Jung lived this confrontation, cf. Barbara Hannah, "Some Glimpses of the Individuation Process in Jung Himself," *Quadrant*, 16, pp. 26 ff.

conscious of His creation, and man conscious of himself."[53] That is the essence of an "explanation myth" which Jung acknowledged toward the end of his life.[54] When Jung spoke of these things, he spoke with deep seriousness, and one realized that behind his cheerful manner there lived another Jung, the real Jung, who never ceased to struggle, passionately and with the greatest suffering, with the problem of God. Everything that happened to him, and everything that happened in the world, he referred to God, and put to him the questions: why, and to what purpose? Like Jacob at the ford, he held fast to this dark, mysterious Other until his grace was revealed. If he had to choose between "the world" and "God," he never hesitated in deciding which to follow; the mystery of the Self was always the decisive factor in his life. "But anyone who attempts to do both, to adjust to his group and at the same time pursue his individual goal, becomes neurotic. Our modern Jacob would be concealing from himself the fact that the angel was after all the stronger of the two – as he certainly was, for no claims were ever made that the angel, too, came away with a limp."[55] Jung knew that God's messenger is the stronger, therefore he never turned away from the struggle. When he was once asked how he could live with the knowledge he had recorded in *Answer to Job*, he replied, "I live in my deepest hell, and from there I cannot fall any further.' And that is why he put the following the epigraph to his German book *Symbolik des Geistes*: 'Spiritus enim omnia scrutatur, etiam profundal Dei' – 'For the Spirit searches everything, even the depths of God' (I Corinthians 2:10)."

293   The profoundly serious thought to which Jung gave expression in *Answer to Job* has shocked many well-meaning but superficial people, and oddly enough theologians, who were primarily concerned, have understood it least. Interestingly, however, *Answer to Job* appeared on certain American best-seller lists. The effect of

---

[53] Ibid., p. 370 f.
[54] Ibid., p. 371. Naturally, human understanding and the human will can never pretend to have fathomed the depths of the divine spirit; any such statements are of course merely human and an "endless approximation" to the concealed. Cf. the Jung's letter to Walter Bernet, in: C.G. Jung, *Letters*, Vol. 2, p. 258.
[55] Ibid., p. 377.

this book was in some ways like that of an underwater nuclear explosion – it reached and shook up many people for Jung had the courage to think and give voice to thoughts that had been germinating in a few other minds, but had not reached the surface. But why is it that, in spite of everything, so many people cannot accept these thoughts? The reason for this is, in my opinion, to be found in a special characteristic of our time, which is the subject of the following chapter.

◆

Chapter 9
Man's Morning Knowledge and Evening Knowledge

294   St. Augustine, The Church father, made a distinction between two kinds of awareness[1]: a morning awareness (*cognitio matutina*) and an evening awareness *(cognitio vespertina)*. The former is self-knowledge *(cognitio sui ipsius)*, a knowledge in which the human being recognizes himself in the image of the Creator; the latter is the knowledge of things created. Self-knowledge, or self-awareness, is not a narcissistic self-mirroring of the ego, but rather the illumination of the latter through the Self[2]. Augustine compares the gradual transformation of morning awareness into evening awareness with the succession of the symbolic days of the Genesis story of creation. On the first day, there is knowledge of the Self in God, then follows knowledge of the firmament, of the earth, of the sea, of plant, water, and air animals, until finally, on the sixth day, "man discovers knowledge of man himself." Thus, his morning knowledge gradually turns into evening knowledge *(vesperascit)* and it loses itself in the innumerable outer things, thereby becoming more and more removed from the inner knowledge of God. The morning light of the *cognitio creatoris* or of the Self is then extinguished. Jung gives the following psychological interpretation of Augustine's formulation: "But the knowledge arising with this first light finally and inevitably becomes the *scientia hominis*, the knowledge of man, who asks himself, 'Who is it that knows and understands everything? Why, it is myself.' That marks the coming

---

[1] *The City of God*, Book XI, Ch. 7. Cf. also Augustine's commentary on I Thessalonians 5:5, and Jung's commentary, in "The Spirit Mercurius," CW 13, §§ 299 ff.

[2] Or, according to Jung, "that . . . of which the ego is the subject." Cf. ibid., § 301.

of darkness, out of which arises the seventh day, the day of rest, 'Sed requies Dei requiem significat eorum qui requiescunt in Deo.'[3] The Sabbath is therefore the day on which man returns to God and receives anew the light of the *cognitio matutina*. And this day has no evening."[4]

295   Meister Eckhart later took up this thought of Augustine. He too made a distinction between an "evening knowledge," in which the creature is known in himself (*in ihrem An-sich-sein*), and a "morning knowledge," in which creature and the human self are known "in the One which is God Himself." This morning knowledge, however, is discovered only by the man who is "detached," who has forgotten his ego and all creatures and who lives in a psychic condition "in which God is nearer the soul than the soul is to itself."[5]

296   In the Indian Vedas, too, we find a similar idea of a gradual darkening of the light of human consciousness, with whose deepening man is forced to turn back to the light of his own innermost self. In the Brihadaranyaka Upanishad, King Janaka asks the wise Yajnavalkya:

297   'Yajnavalkya, what light does a person here have?'

298   'He has the light of the sun, O king,' he said, 'for with the sun, indeed, as his light, one sits, moves around, does his work and returns.'

299   'But when the sun has set, Yajnavalkya, what light does a person here have?'

300   'The moon, indeed, is his light,' said he, 'for with the moon, indeed, as his light, one sits, moves around, does his work, and returns.'

301   'But when the sun has set, and the moon has set, what light does a person here have?'

---

[3] "But the rest of God signifies the rest of those who rest in God."
[4] C.G. Jung, ibid.
[5] Cf. A.M. Haas, *Nim din selbes war*.

302 'Fire, indeed, is his light,' said he, 'for with fire, indeed, as his light, one sits, moves around, does his work, and returns.'

303 'But when the sun has set, Yajnavalkya, and the moon has set, and the fire has gone out, and speech is hushed, what light does a person here have?'

304 'The soul (*atman*), indeed, is his light . . . for with the soul, indeed, as his light, one sits, moves around, does his work, and returns.'

305 'Which (*katama*) is the soul?'

306 'The person here who among the senses is made of knowledge, who is the light in the heart. . . .'

307 'When one goes to sleep, he . . . dreams by his own brightness, by his own light.'[6]

308 The image of a gradual darkening of the light – in psychological terms, of consciousness – expresses the fact, in Jung's interpretation, "that every spiritual truth gradually turns into something material, becoming no more than a tool in the hand of man . . . but modern man is already so darkened that nothing beyond the light of his own intellect illuminates his world – 'occasus Christi, passio Christi.' That surely is why such strange things are happening in our much-lauded civilization more like a *Götterdämmerung* than any normal twilight."[7]

309 This process of a darkening of consciousness has been repeated countless times in human history and must therefore correspond to a profound archetypal structure in us. This basic pattern is symbolized most simply in the world-wide mythological and fairytale motif of the aging, sick, and dying king, who is superseded by a new successor, both child-like and creative. Sometimes this hero-successor is the third, youngest prince[8] who has been derided as a fool, or again he may be a young man of the people, the "son of

---

[6] *The Thirteen Principal Upanishads*, R.E. Hume (Trans.), Brihadaranyaka Upanishad, IV, 3, 2-9.
[7] C.G. Jung, "The Spirit Mercurius," CW 13, § 302.
[8] The *fourth* in the group – the king plus three sons.

a poor widow," a foundling, or a despised blockhead. Usually the old king abdicates voluntarily after the hero has performed his heroic feats and passed successfully through the necessary ordeals, but in other cases the king resists and must be forced to renounce his rule.[9]

310 While myths and fairytales tell of a hero who *supersedes* the old king, from the Egyptian culture, and alchemistic philosophy that was influenced by it, evolved the mythologem of the *transformation* of the old king into his young successor[10]; indeed, the essential theme of alchemistic philosophy revolves around this motif of the transformation of the king.[11] In contrast to the fairytales mentioned, in this setting the consubstantiality of father and son, of the dying old king and his successor, the "new sun-child," is recognized and expressed. The alchemical parables of the mystic death or sacrifice of the old king and of his transformation often express what many fairytales describe: the aging king has become *egocentric*; his attitude has become rigid and therefore his "heart" must be dissolved in water.[12] He is uninhibitedly desirous and aggressive, and this is why he is sick. Since the king represents an earthly likeness of God, he also symbolizes a *God-image which is outworn and in need of renewal*.[13] This latter represents the dominant or governing symbolic conception of the collective consciousness of a culture and of its institutions. Such traditional outlooks or views and such traditional systems "age" unavoidably. They then no longer correspond to the life of the unconscious psyche and its needs and therefore must be renewed, both in the individual and in the collective. Religious dogma has lost its inner life and therefore the psyche wants to produce new forms in order to help psychic wholeness, the Self, to return to life in altered form. [14]

---

[9] For example, in the Grimm fairytale "The Devil's Three Golden Hairs" or in "Ferdinand the Faithful and Ferdinand the Unfaithful."
[10] In ancient Egypt, this motif had a long prehistory in old African ideas and images and in the theology of Kingship in the ancient Orient, for which see Frazer, *The Golden Bough*, Part 4, pp. 331 ff, and C.G. Jung, *Mysterium Coniunctionis*, CW 14, §§ 349 ff, and the literature referred to therein.
[11] Cf. C.G. Jung, ibid., §§ 1-177.
[12] Cf. ibid., § 17.
[13] Cf. ibid., § 170.
[14] Ibid., § 30 f.

311   The distinguished historian Arnold Toynbee, who valued Jung and his work very highly, has clarified and described the typical phases of this eternally reappearing psychic process from a political-historical point of view. A majority of the cultures we know anything about today stand in the relation of a child to an earlier culture, in that the new culture successfully carries out or deals with a task or problem on which the earlier one came to grief. Most cultures may therefore be said to "grow," not in the sense of a geographical expansion, but rather of development to a higher level of spirituality, of which autonomy is the most characteristic feature. The solution of new problems is always first achieved by individuals and is then imitated by others. In this very fact lies the seed of the later downfall, because imitation always brings with it standardization and mechanization. An overvaluation of one's own accomplishments and institutions begins to take place and this is accompanied by a mood of presumption or arrogance. The latter often leads to militarism, and militarism often – although not always – leads to a rapid downfall. In the stage of decline, division occurs, a cleavage, as it were, in society, and in the soul of the individual. Those in power are no longer creative and come to rely only on their power; the masses become an "inner proletariat," that is, a group of men and women who feel that they have been denied their rightful place in society. This group is joined by an "outer proletariat" of primitives who have previously been under the influence of the culture which is now declining. A living culture is a unity; its technical, political, spiritual, and cultural parts are united with one another. In the stage of decline, however, this unity is dissolved. The breakdown of a culture is usually followed by a period of unrest, until a great power brings peace by establishing a universal state; the latter then often brings a second flowering, an Indian summer to the declining culture. Generally, it is through a world-state or a world-church that the declining culture is connected with the new cultures, which are like its children. And creativity conquers once again, precisely in the fall. "Creativity would not be creative, if it did not receive into itself all the things of heaven and of earth, including its own

opposite." Today, we live at a critical time; signs of the decline of our culture are clearly observable.[15] Arnold Toynbee sees a solution only through Christianity, if a solution still is possible at all.

312   Jung fully agreed with Toynbee's ideas about such culture life-cycles, which in Jung's view are determined by archetypal forms. "Toynbee has seen what I mean," he said in a filmed interview, "by historical function of archetypal developments. That is a mighty important determinant of human behaviour, and can span centuries or thousands of years. It expresses itself in symbols. . ."[16]

313   The symbol which represents the archetypal determinant of our culture is the Christ-image, whose historical appearance, trans-formation, growth, aging, and possible renewal Jung deals with in detail in *Aion*.[17] He points out that the historical Christ-image, in the interpretation of the faithful and of the Church fathers, has assimilated to itself all the known symbols of the Anthropos, mainly the cross, mandala, quaternity, and "soul-kernel," and thus has gradually become a representation of the archetype of the Self.[18] It can hardly be judged an accident that it was precisely Jesus, the son of a carpenter, who became the redeemer of the world. "He must have been a person of singular gifts to have been able so completely to express and to represent the general, though unconscious, expectations of his age. . . . In those times the omnipresent, crushing power of Rome . . . had created a world where countless individuals, indeed whole peoples, were robbed of their cultural independence and of their spiritual autonomy."[19] Christ, as symbol of the Self and conqueror of the world, confronted this power. However, he

---

[15] Cf. the Introduction to Arnold Toynbee, *A Study of History*, Vol. I: "Rise and Fall of Cultures," pp. 1 – 50.

[16] Cf. Richard I. Evans, *Conversations with Carl Jung*, p. 115. Jung continues, " . . . sometimes symbols that you would never think of at all. For instance, as you know, Russia, the Soviet Republic, had that symbol of the red star. Now it is a five-rayed red star. America has the five-rayed white star. They are enemies; they can't come together. In the Middle Ages for at least 2000 years the red and white were the couple; they were ultimately destined to marry each other. Now America is a sort of matriarchy, inasmuch as most of the money is in the hands of women, and Russia is the land of the little father; it's a patriarchy. So the two are mother and father. To use the terminology of the Middle Ages, they are the white woman, the 'femina alba', and the red slave, the 'servus rubeus'. The two lovers have quarreled with each other."

[17] C.G. Jung, *Aion*, CW 9/II.

[18] Ibid., § 68 ff.

[19] *Memories*, pp. 237 f.

embodied only the perfect and light side of human wholeness, not its dark side, which was split off and which was represented by the figure of the Antichrist: at the end of the Christian era the Antichrist would seize control. These two figures, Christ and Antichrist, were identified shortly after the beginning of the Christian era, with the two fishes which symbolize the astrological aeon of the Fish (roughly A.D. 1-2000). Thus, the symbol of the Self was understood as a symbol in process of transformation during the course of history.[20] Since about the year 1000 – the beginning of the age of the second fish, therefore – the end of the world and the coming of the Antichrist have been expected and predicted over and over again, and around that time many free-thinking, revolutionary new religious movements sprang up[21], which at first came to a head in the breakthrough called the Reformation and later on paved the way for a rationalism which was at least in part anti-Christian.[22]

314   As has been explained, alchemical symbolism also plays a compensatory role in this general historical process, inasmuch as fish mythologems appear in alchemy which unite the two "hostile" fishes of the Christian aeon in *one* figure.[23] In alchemy, the fish is the mysterious *prima materia*, or initial material, of the work, the *piscis rotundus*, the round fish in the sea, which must be cooked until it begins to shine.[24] (One thinks of Jung's dream of the radiolarian.[25]) Or it is a "hot starfish" in which divine love manifests.[26] According to certain texts, it carries in its body the "dragon's stone," which many seek without knowing it.[27] The fish exerts a magnetic attraction on human beings[28]; it is a living stone out of which the elixir of immortality can be produced. In gnostic speculations about the primordial man there are anticipations of these alchemical interpretations[29], and in both Gnosticism and alchemy there is a

---

[20] *Aion*, CW 9/II, § 127 ff.
[21] Cf. ibid., § 139.
[22] Ibid., § 149.
[23] Cf. ibid., § 193 ff.
[24] Ibid., § 195.
[25] Related by Jung in *Aion* (§ 208) without identifying the dreamer.
[26] Ibid., § 199.
[27] Ibid., § 214.
[28] Ibid., § 239.
[29] Cf. ibid., § 301 ff.

constant recurrence of quaternary symbols of the Self, as well as a *four-way rotation of a quaternary symbol* which makes visual the time-bound aspect of the Self symbol. In this rotation, the Self is periodically renewed and, in psychic transformation processes extending over centuries of history, experiences a gradual development which appears to consist in a spiral path toward greater human consciousness.

315   Like Toynbee, Jung was convinced that we are in a period of cultural decline today and that the survival or disappearance of our culture depends on a renewal of our archetypal myth. Jung's first dream of the royal phallus in the grave, and his fear that it might crawl over him *like a worm*, is to be understood in the light of this myth of the king's renewal. The "old king" – the Christian outlook or the Christian God-image – is dead and buried; that is, he has fallen into the depths of the collective unconscious, into matter, and into everything that would be attributed to his adversary[30], and has been transformed into the worm-like phallus which raises itself up toward the light. The worm or serpent in alchemical symbolism is the first form taken by the bird phoenix and by the old king.[31] It is an initial, primitive archaic life-form out of which the new image of the king develops. The orientation of the phallus toward the light, in Jung's dream, shows that this new content is striving toward the region of consciousness. One could in fact understand Jung's whole life as a struggle to free the "new king" from the depths of the collective unconscious.

316   It is the old king – who has not yet abdicated – who has everywhere stood in the way of acceptance of Jung's work. In the scientific world, to which Jung for the most part addressed his writings, the old king was predominantly represented by 19th century rationalism and materialism, still prevalent among second-rate "competent authorities," which cannot conceive of a non-material reality of the psyche. In compensation to medieval

---

[30] Cf. C.G. Jung, *Mysterium Coniunctionis*, CW 14, § 471: "For these reasons, too, the king constantly needs the renewal that begins with a descent into his own darkness, an immersion in his own depths, and with a reminder that he is related by blood to his adversary."
[31] Cf. Ibid., § 472 ff; § 483.

spirituality, which saw all reality in the father-realm of the spirit, today's materialists find reality in matter (*mater!*) whereas Jung regarded both realms, spirit and matter, as archetypal ideas which, in the last analysis, transcend consciousness. In Jung's view, as has been explained above, they can be described only in terms of the traces they leave in our psyche. The only immediately given reality for us is psychic experience. Certainly, there is nothing in Jung's view against the hypothesis that matter has some form of psychic life. Jung even described the psyche, on occasion, as a qualitative aspect of matter.[32] "The psyche is nothing different from the living being. It is the psychical aspect of the living being. It is even the psychical aspect of matter."[33] "We discover that this matter has another aspect, namely, a psychic aspect. And so it is simply the world ... seen from within. It is just as though you were seeing into another aspect of matter."[34] At present, however, most materialists still believe in "dead" matter, whose purely mechanistic behaviour is exactly determined. As a result of this projection, Jung's purely scientific empirical discoveries, which are easy enough to verify, have been rejected as "mystical" or unclear.[35] This kind of "scientific" rationalism is closely connected with a "religious belief" in the absolute determinism of all observable inner and outer processes – that "stupid clockwork fantasy," as Jung calls it – according to which no new creation, either by man or by nature, is held to be possible.

317   In theoretical physics, there is still much discussion concerning the problem of "determinism" (relativity) versus "indeterminacy" (quantum physics), but the scale inclines increasingly toward indeterminacy, and this creates a new problem, namely the question: does the limited free play provided by the theory of indeterminacy contain only meaningless accidents, or does it include meaningful creative acts as well? This problem will be discussed later. In

---

[32] Richard L. Evans, *Conversations with Carl Jung*, p. 68.
[33] Ibid., p. 83.
[34] Ibid., p. 68.
[35] An unusually clumsy recent example is Shulamith Kreitler's *Symbolschöpfung und Symbolerfassung*, pp. 32 ff.

accordance with the law of the darkening of morning consciousness, contemporary science has gotten lost in the knowledge of the 10,000 things, in the overspecialization about which so many complaints are heard, and in the bewildering accumulation of constantly increasing knowledge of details, but without any adequate comprehensive interpretation. The introduction of computers means at one and the same time apex and end, because the computer forces us to take up once again the creative role reserved for human beings, which the computer cannot replace.

318   It seems to me that this insight can provide an explanation for the contemporary unrest among university students. The "establishment" and the power of some professors which have been under attack by the students are in fact the spirit of the "old king," and student interest in sociology is, in my opinion, nothing but a first attempt to place the human being, the person, in the centre of the focus of attention. However, Jung's outlook is, at least up to a point, opposed to these present trends, for he places greater interest on the individual; we will return to this subject in more detail.

319   Even in areas where materialistic determinism does not get in the way, various philosophers and psychologists reject Jung because they are unable to grasp the fact that the unconscious really is unconscious or, in other words, because, in their very different ways, they regard the unconscious as a kind of phantasmagoria appertaining to the ego, rather than as something autonomous and existing in its own right; in short, they do not see it as psychically objective. Consequently, demands are made that one should cling to a "'metaphysic" beyond the psyche.[36] This kind of resistance, in my experience, cannot be dealt with simply by discussion and argument; in most cases, only a practical analysis will help, an analysis in which the subject is shocked into an experience of the objective reality of his inner world; even this is useful only if the

---

[36] Cf., for instance, Sigmund Biran, *Die ausserpsychologischen Voraussetzungen der Tiefenpsychologie.* Biran does not even mention Jung. Cf. also the book – in itself appealing – by Fritz Jürgen Kaune, *Selbstverwirklichung.*

subject does not try to rationalize away his experience, or simply desert the field and take flight, as occasionally happens.

320   Similar constellations also occur in the narrow field of psychiatry and psychotherapy: the materialistic trend in chemotherapy which Jung himself for the most part – but not altogether – rejected[37], and at the opposite pole all those therapeutic attempts which aim at influencing the patient only on the conscious level. For the most part Jung is simply not mentioned by the "old king," though occasionally he is brushed aside as passé (a projection!) or dismissed with some sort of personal abuse.

321   Another cultural area in which the "old king" will not relinquish his claims to power (we know from Toynbee that his kingdom, in the period of decline, decays a province at a time) can be seen in the attitude of certain theologians of both Catholic and Protestant churches. The virtually stereotyped objection to Jung's discoveries consists in the reproach that in his view all religious contents and statements are regarded as "only psychological" and are thereby robbed of their "metaphysical" reality. In the expression "*only* psychological" there is an implication that psychology is "*only* what man knows of himself"[38] (evening knowledge, therefore, "in which man knows man"), while with Jung psychology means, first and foremost, an empirical investigation of the *unknown* part of the psyche, which is manifested in dreams, slips of the tongue, involuntary fantasies, sudden convictions that come out of the blue. This is an objective psychic realm to which we can set no bounds and which we can never legitimately speak of as "my" unconscious. "You cannot reach the limits of the soul by walking, even if you pace off every street, its meaning is so deep," says Heraclitus.[39] "*The psyche is an autonomous factor,*" Jung emphasizes over and over, "and religious statements are based on unconscious, i.e., on transcendental, processes. These . . . statements are filtered through the medium of human consciousness: that is to say, they are given visible

---

[37] Cf. Evans, *Conversations with Carl Jung,* pp. 108-9.
[38] Cf. on this C.G. Jung, "Psychology and Religion," CW 11, § 3.
[39] Hermann Diels, *Die Fragmente der Vorsokratiker I,* p. 161.

forms which in their turn are subject to manifold influences from within and without. That is why whenever we speak of religious contents we move in a world of images that point to something ineffable. . . . If, for instance, we say 'God', we give expression to an image or verbal concept which has undergone many changes in the course of time. We are, however, unable to say with any degree of certainty – unless it be by faith – whether these changes affect only the images and concepts, or the Unspeakable itself."[40] Jung also considered the statements in Holy Scripture to be "utterances of the soul,"[41] and to this, many theologians raise the objection that this is not the case, that Holy Scripture is a direct revelation of the transcendental.[42] In regard to this objection the psychologist must emphasize that psychic religious experiences are always so impressive that one feels them to be a revelation.

322   "It is, in fact, impossible to demonstrate God's reality to oneself except by using images which have arisen spontaneously or are sanctified by tradition, and whose psychic nature and effects the naïve-minded person has never separated from their unknowable metaphysical background. . . . But if there is occasion for criticism, then it must be remembered that the image and the statement are psychic processes which are different from their transcendental object: *they do not posit it, they merely point to it.*"[43]

323   From these and many of Jung's other statements, it is quite clear that Jung never doubted the trans-psychic existence of God, but for him, It or He is Unspeakable. When statements concerning God are made, they are part of psychic experience and thus are subject to psychological investigation and criticism. Whoever holds fast to trans-psychic dogmatic truths through *faith* will find in Jung's work no criticism of his conviction. "Only heedless fools will wish to

---

[40] C.G. Jung, "Answer to Job," CW 11, § 555. Italics added by the author.
[41] Ibid., § 557.
[42] Cf, for example, Max Frischknecht, *Die Religion in der Psychologie von C.G. Jung*, in which Jung is accused of atheism; and J. Röösli, "Der Gottes- und Religionsbegriff bei C. G. Jung," *Schweizerische Kirchenzeitung*, 112 (1944) pp. 302-304. Cf. the reply of Hans Schär in *Religion and the Cure of Souls in Jung's Psychology.*
[43] C.G. Jung "Answer to Job," § 558. Italics added by the author.

destroy [the Christian dogma]: the lover of the soul, never."[44] "Psychology as the science of the soul has to confine itself to its subject and guard against overstepping its proper boundaries by metaphysical assertions or other professions of faith."[45] The concept of the Self, therefore, by no means takes the place of God but is "rather perhaps a vessel for divine grace." This attitude of Jung's, which is entirely new in the psychology of religion (personally rooted, for him, in the profound change described in Chapter 2), has not been understood by many theologians. However, there have been a number of them from both confessions who have understood him. On the Catholic side, special mention should be made of Father Gebhard Frei, whose religious Eros made it possible for him to understand Jung's point of view and to bring it into harmony with his faith.[46] Others, like the Dominican Wittcut[47], Father Victor White, O.P.[48], in Oxford, the Carmelite Père Bruno, and Josef Rudin, S.J.[49], have tried to bring Jung's thinking, at least to some extent, into line with Catholic teaching, and this is also true of Josef Gold-brunner, S.J.[50] In the work of the latter, however, the "old king" sometimes makes his presence felt, in my opinion, with a power play. Wherever Jung's empirical observations do not accord with tradition, they are twisted into something that is "only psychological," on which the "old king" can pass judgement.[51] In his correspondence, Jung often protested against this sort of thing, usually arguing that if psychology does not presume to trespass in the field of metaphysics, then theology has not the right to trespass

---

[44] Final sentence of "Psychology and Religion," CW 11, § 168.
[45] *Psychology and Alchemy*, CW 12, § 15.
[46] Cf. his essay, "Zur Psychologie des Unterbewussten," *Gloria Die*, 2, Part 3 (1947/48); also Frei, *Imago mundi*,
[47] *Catholic Thought and Modern Psychology*.
[48] *Gott und das Unbewusste* and *Seele und Psyche*.
[49] *Psychotherapie und Religion*. Josef Rudin, *Neurose und Religion* and "C.G. Jung und die Religion," *Psychotherapie und religiöse Erfahrung*.
[50] *Individuation: A Study of the Depth Psychology of Carl Gustav Jung; Realization: The Anthropology of Pastoral Care*; "Dialog zwischen Tiefenpsychologie und katholischer Theologie," *Festschrift für W. Bitter*; *Personale Seelsorge, Tiefenpsychologie und Seelsorge*.
[51] Thus, for example, Raymond Hostie, S.J., *Religion and the Psychology of Jung*. Cf. also Walter Bernet, *Inhalt und Grenze der religiösen Erfahrung*. Cf. also Rudolf Affermann, "Die Frage der Tiefenpsychologie nach der Echtheit des Glaubens," *Evangelische Theologie*, pp. 311 ff.; David Cox, *Jung and St. Paul*; H.L. Philp, *Jung and the Problem of Evil*.

in the field of empirical psychology; the two disciplines can live together in a healthy way only on a basis of mutual respect.

324   Even though a certain opposition on the intellectual level of theory cannot be gainsaid, this opposition rarely interferes in the practice of therapy. On the contrary, a Jungian analysis has helped many "who had played the apostate or cooled off in their faith" to find "a new approach to their old truths,"[52] in that they acquire a new understanding of the traditional symbolism and also because they are forced by their dreams to reflect seriously on religious questions. I have had the experience of seeing a devout traditional Japanese Buddhist find in this way a new dimension of a faith which had become all too intellectual.

325   Among the Protestants, also, individual theologians have taken up Jung's thought with positive results, with real understanding in the case, for example, of Ivar Alm[53] the Swedish theologian. In Germany, Walter Uhsadel,[54] Otto Händler,[55] Adolf Köberle,[56] Bishop Wolfgang Heidland, Gerhard Zacharias,[57] and especially Ulrich Mann have worked toward a positive understanding of Jungian psychology. Ulrich Mann, in his broadly designed work, *Theogonische Tage*, has shown how the God-image in human consciousness has been transformed during the last millennia in which we have some reliable knowledge of cultures and how it may be working once again toward a transformation along the lines of Jung's observations.[58] Of Swiss Protestants, it is especially the theologian Hans Schär who has taken up Jung's ideas and under-

---

[52] *Psychology and Alchemy*, CW 12, § 17. Cf. Felicia Fröböse, *Träume – eine Quelle religiöser Erfahrung?*; J.A. Sanford, *Dreams: God's Forgotten Language*.

[53] "C.G. Jungs Erfahrungen in theologischer Sicht," *Theologische Zeitschrift der Theologischen Fakultät der Universität Basel* 19.

[54] W. Uhsadel, *Der Mensch und die Mächte des Unbewussten*; "Tiefenpsychologie als Hilfswissenschaft der praktischen Theologie," *Wege des Menschen* 21.

[55] *Tiefenpsychologie, Theologie und Seelsorge*; *Das Leib-Seele-Problem in theologischer Sicht*.

[56] "Das Evangelium und das Geheimnis der Seele," *Zeitschrift für systematische Theologie* 21, p. 419 ff.

[57] *Psyche und Mysterium*. Zacharias comes from the Eastern Church.

[58] Ulrich Mann, *Theogonische Tage*. Die Entwicklung des Gottesbewusstseins in der altorientalischen und biblischen Religion; "Symbole und tiefenpsychologische Gestaltungsfaktoren der Religion," *Grenzfragen des Glaubens*, p. 153 f.; "Tiefenpsychologie und Theologie," *Lutherische Monatshefte* 4, p. 188 ff. "Quaternität bei C.G. Jung," *Theologisch-Lutherische Zeitschrift* 92, p. 331 ff. On the transformation of the God-image, cf. Georg von Gynz-Rekowski, *Symbole des Weiblichen im Gottesbild und Kult des Alten Testaments*.

stood them.[59] Paul Tillich knew Jung's work and independently developed similar views of his own.[60]

326 For the Protestant (Jung said that he belonged to "the most extreme left wing of Protestantism"), who is not so dependent on traditional ideas as the Catholic, Jung's approach is easier to accept in that the Protestant has no unambiguously formulated dogma to defend. On the other hand, it is more difficult for him because of the poverty of symbols in his religion. Rudolf Bultmann's "demythologizing" initiated this work of spiritual destruction[61], and it is being carried further every day, so that before long there will be no Protestant theology aside from a collection of rationalistic subjective opinions. Ulrich Mann is justified, therefore, when he asserts that Bultmann's demythologizing programme is a remnant of 19th century positivism[62] with no genuine understanding of what a myth is and that it is therefore philosophically impoverished. Ulrich Mann continues, "If God really entered the flesh, then he is visible, he has even become 'touchable', and therefore one can and must speak of God in a 'worldly' and 'human' way, just as the myth does." Jung stresses the fact that no science "will ever replace a myth, and a myth cannot be made out of any science. For it is not that 'God' is a myth, but that myth is the revelation of a divine life in man. It is not we who invent myth, rather it speaks to us as a Word of God. The Word of God comes to us, and we have no way of distinguishing whether and to what extent it is different from God."[63]

327 In a certain sense, Jung's discoveries have more to offer to Catholic theologians, whose convictions are still deeply rooted in the great symbolic images of dogma and ritual[64], and I know that some Catholics who were no longer able to participate in the Mass

---

[59] *Religion and the Cure of Souls in Jung's Psychology; Seelsorge und Psychotherapie.*
[60] Cf. his address on Jung at the Memorial Meeting, December 1961, in the Memorial volume of the Analytical Psychology Club of New York, pp. 28 ff. Cf. also Aniela Jaffé, *The Myth of Meaning*, pp. 104-5.
[61] Cf. in this connection Ulrich Mann, "Hermeneutische Entsagung," in: 'Seelsorge als Lebenshilfe', *Uhsadel-Festschrift.*
[62] *Theogonische Tage*, p. 64 ff., 646.
[63] *Memories*, p. 373.
[64] Cf. Hugo Rahner's beautiful interpretation of Christian symbolism, *Greek Myths and Christian Mystery.*

with wholehearted conviction came to a renewed sense of its impenetrable, deeper meaning [65]through reading Jung's essay "Transformation Symbolism in the Mass."[66] Catholicism is also a step ahead of Protestantism in the recognition of the feminine principle, since Protestantism has been, up to the present time, a one-sidedly masculine religion, apart from a few small rudiments of a Sophia mysticism.

328   Jung remained outside both confessions; he understood too deeply the legitimacy of *both* standpoints. Christian doctrine itself is split, he writes, and every Christian is exposed to this split, a fact which we dare not try to evade.[67] This decision not to belong to a Church did not denote an anti-Christian attitude on Jung's part; rather it was a "re-considering of the kingdom of God in the human heart"[68] and therewith an acceptance of the conflict in his own soul. Jung intentionally put himself with those people who stand outside the Church[69], with those who "know," that is, with those who must actually have had the experience if they are to be able to "believe." He could not live with "metaphysical" convictions that have simply been handed down by tradition.[70]

329   The same conflict as the conflict with certain "dogmatically" inclined scientists and theologians – the representatives of the "old king" – also exists in still a third area: in relation to Jung's psychological interpretation of alchemical symbolism. There are circles of Freemasons, Rosicrucians, and Hermetic philosophers for whom the alchemistic world of images and ideas is still very much alive, but as a secret doctrine of initiation which, following historic models, claims absolute "metaphysical" validity. These circles also reject Jung's approach, at least in part, as "only psychological,"

---

[65] It seems to me the more regrettable that rationalistic currents are becoming conspicuous in contemporary Catholicism, currents which undermine the highest value, namely the symbolism of the ritual. The spiritual desolation wrought by the demythologizing tendencies in Protestantism should have taught them better!

[66] CW 11, §§ 296 – 448.

[67] Cf. C.G. Jung, "Psychology of the Transference," CW 16, § 392.

[68] Ibid., § 397.

[69] Letter of April 29th, 1944, to Gebhard Frei, quoted in *Glorie Dei*, p. 249.

[70] Cf. "Psychotherapists or the Clergy," CW 11, §§ 516 ff. In a BBC interview with John Freeman ("Face to Face"), Jung said, 'I don't have to believe, I *know*.' (In *C.G. Jung Speaking*.) Cf. also his letter to Gerhard Zacharias, 24th August, 1953, in *C.G. Jung: Letters*, vol. 2, p. 120 f.

although on the other hand they welcome the rehabilitation of their symbols.[71] Even Mircea Eliade, surprisingly, was converted to a similar point of view[72], at first hesitantly[73], then later openly[74] – the "old king" refuses to be melted down for his rebirth, lest he lose his omnipotence!

330   There are exponents of Eastern wisdom, too, who apply the same criticism to Jung. Whereas they themselves preach the absolute metaphysical truth of the branch of Eastern wisdom they represent, Jung's approach seems to them to be simply a natural first step on the way to enlightenment, a first step still burdened with the chthonic shadow of the only-natural, above which one should rise by a kind of voluntary spiritual leap.[75] Hans Jacobs in particular, in his book *Indische Weisheit und westliche Psychotherapie*[76], delivers a sharp attack against Jung from this point of view. Jung's religious experiences could only have been, in the last resort, simply profane because they were not metaphysically heralded. It is interesting that a number of Indians have defended Jung on this point[77], rather than attacking him, and have shown conspicuous understanding of his ideas in other ways as well.[78] It is mainly those Westerners infected with Eastern ideas who have attacked Jung so fanatically, an attack which points to unconscious doubts.

331   Seen in a certain perspective, it is striking that the criticisms discussed above, although coming from such different directions, nevertheless all come back to the same point: to Jung's unwillingness to espouse absolute metaphysical truths. Jung always preserved a quite unambiguous attitude against this demand: "...it seems to me advisable . . . in view of the limitations of human knowledge to assume from the start that our metaphysical concepts are simply

---

[71] J. Evola, *La Tradizione ermetica*.
[72] Eliade goes so far as to express the absurd opinion that the psychological evidence consists in unconscious imitations of the metaphysical reality of the alchemical opus. He does not say how this could possibly be demonstrated.
[73] "Note sur Jung et l'Alchimie," *Le Disque vert*, p. 107.
[74] *Schmiede und Alchemisten*, p. 234 ff.
[75] Cf. for example Eleanore Lauterborn, *Swami Omkaranananda und C. G. Jung*.
[76] Particularly, p. 139 ff.
[77] Cf. A.V. Vasavada, "The Place of Psychology in Philosophy," *Indian Philosophical Congress*.
[78] Cf. Samiran Banerjee, "Prof. Dr. C.G. Jung," *The Psychotherapy* I, No. 14, and particularly, Padma Agrawal, *Symbolism. A psychological study*.

anthropomorphic images and opinions which express transcendental facts either not at all or only in a very hypothetical manner."[79] We have often enough had the experience of discovering that our assertions about the physical world turn out to be inadequate. Moreover, the question arises: Who is right in respect to the almost infinite number of different "metaphysical truths"? Nothing demonstrates the extreme uncertainty of such assertions better than their diversity. And yet, people still feel the need to make statements of this kind[80] because they have experienced the numinosity of an archetype. Such "inspired" testimony, however, can affect the multitude either as though it were spoken from the heart or as pure nonsense. As we know, lunatics also proclaim the absolute truth. "In metaphysical matters what is 'authoritative' is 'true,' hence metaphysical assertions are invariably bound up with an unusually strong claim to recognition and authority."[81] But such claims are not proof of truth. It seems wiser therefore, on a conservative estimate, to approach the question more modestly and give our serious consideration to an unconscious psychic or psychoid[82] factor.[83] "Our hypotheses are uncertain and groping, and nothing offers us the assurance that they may ultimately prove correct. That the world inside and outside ourselves rests on a transcendental background is as certain as our own existence, but it is equally certain that the direct perception of the archetypal world inside us is just as doubtfully correct as that of the physical world outside us. If we are convinced that we know ultimate truth concerning metaphysical things, this means nothing more than that archetypal images have taken possession of our powers of thought and feeling. "[84] Thus, Jung was ready to stand surety for an ultimate human *freedom*, for a freedom from outer *and* inner coercion. Inner experience forfeits nothing of its reality nor of its living quality for him who has it, but he will remain *tolerant* and will not attempt to force his experience or his convictions on others.

---

[79] C.G. Jung, *Mysterium Coniunctionis*, CW 14, § 436.
[80] Cf. ibid., § 437.
[81] Ibid., § 439.
[82] Psychic-like.
[83] Ibid., § 441.
[84] Ibid., § 442.

332   It follows, of course, that there would be no point whatever in fostering a conflict situation between the representatives of ideas or systems with claims to metaphysical authority and the psychological view as developed by Jung. When such people distorted and misrepresented his thought, Jung's own reaction was simply one of annoyance. In the last analysis, the father-king and his son are consubstantial in the alchemical transformation process[85], and it is up to the individual to believe in either principle, as long as his own soul is content. A problem exists only in the case of those who are no longer able to "believe" in their own "truth" and hence – because they are undermined by doubt – become aggressive; exactly as in a number of fairytales the old king turns wicked and tries to kill the new hero while he is still a child, because he suspects that the youth will supersede him[86]; in the myths, however, he never succeeds. The child-hero on the other hand usually does not resist him forcibly (or only seldom, in self-defence) because *he* – in contrast to the father-king – bears his own antithesis, his own shadow, in himself; only in this way can he express a genuine inner wholeness.

333   The new image of wholeness coming to life on the threshold of the collective unconscious during the present period, that was glimpsed in the Apocalypse of John but was then "caught up to heaven" again, meaning it disappeared into the unconscious, is that youth to whom the sun-woman gives birth.[87] "That higher and 'complete' (teleios) man is begotten by the 'unknown' father and born from Wisdom, and it is he who, in the figure of the *puer aeternus – vultu mutabilis albus et ater* (of changeful countenance, both white and black) – represents our totality, which transcends consciousness.

---

[85] The essay by James Hillman, "Psychology: Monotheistic or Polytheistic," *Spring* 1971, pp. 193 ff., on this subject seems to me to be unsuccessful. Hillman's conclusions are based on the erroneous assumption that monotheism equals Self equals old king, and polytheism equals animus and anima equals son, which historically is not justified. The early stages of Israelite monotheism, for example, is anything but a senex psychology, and the same is true of Akhnaton's monotheistic reform in Egypt or of early Stoic monotheism. On the other hand, late Roman polytheism as a state religion is a purely senex affair. Any religion can at any time find itself in either stage, that of superannuated rigidity or that of the youthful upward impulse. Everything that Hillman proceeds to develop on the basis of this thesis is therefore, in my opinion, beside the points.

[86] Cf. for example the Grimm fairytale "The Devil's Three Golden Hairs."

[87] Cf. C.G. Jung, "Answer to Job," CW 11, § 710 ff; Quote § 742. Inverted commas have been added by the author.

It was this boy into whom Faust had to change, abandoning his inflated one-sidedness which *saw the devil only outside.*"

334   Elsewhere, I have tried to show that today's generation gap grows from this archetypal background.[88] The young identify themselves to a considerable extent with the "divine youth," the older generations with the "old king," and the result is a bitter and unnecessary struggle. The transformation of the king into his son, the youth, is *always impossible when the feminine principle is missing,* or is too weak, that is to say, when the *Eros principle* is missing. Speaking practically, this is the case when a man's anima is undifferentiated and unconscious, and when a woman is possessed by the animus, which weakens her natural femininity. Only then do the old king and the young king, in the man and woman, and in their environment, fall into conflict.

335   This was never as clear to me as on the occasion, in 1968, when I happened to be in Paris at the time of the largest student revolt there. At heart, I was basically on the side of the students, but then I saw the "flics" standing by their armoured cars, simple fellows who were watching the action disconsolately and who obviously would have been so much happier at home with their Yvette or their Madeleine. No – nothing is accomplished with force and on the level of masculine Logos alone! That is why Jung turned his back on all Faustian pressures and drives, "which see the devil only outside," retired to his tower, Philemon's sanctuary, and remained an unyielding defender of eternal and inalienable human rights. There was nothing of martyrdom or of lamb-like sentimentality in his attitude; he would have considered such characteristics dis-honourable, as he once remarked[89]. He defended himself when he was attacked, but he never used force or intrigue to promote his views. He was fond of quoting an old Chinese proverb: "In a meeting, the wise man speaks once, and if he is not listened to, then he retires to his estate in the country." Jung had no country estate, but he went back to the simple, frugal life in his stone tower on the Lake of Zurich.

[88] Marie-Louise von Franz, "On the Religious Background of the *puer aeternus* Problem," in: *Psychotherapy*; *Puer aeternus*; see also my commentary on "Reich ohne Raum," in: *Puer aeternus*.
[89] Cf. Jung's seminar in Polzeath, Cornwall, p. 16.

Chapter 10
Mercurius

³³⁶ "Christianity slumbers and has neglected to develop its myth in the course of the centuries. Those who gave expression to the dark stirrings of growth in mythic ideas were refused a hearing."[1] "Those" were spirits like Gioacchino da Fiori, Meister Eckhart, Jakob Boehme, Pope Pius XII – but especially the *alchemists* who, occasionally with considerable awareness but more often quite naively and unsuspectingly, gave form in their unconscious projections to the stirrings of growth in the Christian myth.[2]

³³⁷ The first late-Greek Egyptian alchemists whose writings are extant are known as gnostic, some of them Christian gnostic, natural philosophers (Zosimos, Komarios, Stefanos, and others), for whom there was no distinction between religion and natural science, or between philosophy and experimental science. They had a philosophic-religious view of the world and sought to reinforce their premises by means of "chemical" experiments. Very probably, it was the happy combination of the speculative philosophical spirit of the Greeks with the highly developed Babylonian science of metallurgy and the Egyptian techno-chemistry, especially the Egyptian embalming process (which was thoroughly imbued with magico-religious meaning), which resulted in this creative new impulse toward a real natural science in the Alexandrian period and in the first centuries of Christianity.[3] Central to the work of almost all the important alchemists is an Anthropos-image, a divine or greater man, who must be freed from his imprisonment in matter and in

---

[1] *Memories*, p.363.
[2] Cf. C.G. Jung, "Introduction to the Religious and Psychological Problems of Alchemy," CW 12, §§ 1 – 43.
[3] Cf. Jack Lindsay, *The Origins of Alchemy in Graeco-Roman Egypt.*

darkness, work through which the human liberator achieved immortality at the same time. On the one hand, the ideas contained in the Egyptian liturgy of embalming played a conspicuous role in this work, because in this ritual, the corpse is transformed by concrete material operations into the god Osiris and thereby identified with him;[4] on the other hand, certain gnostic myths were also important, myths which taught that the "divine great man" or "light man," either because he had been seduced by some evil power or other, or because he had been drawn down by his own reflection into the depths, had fallen into the darkness of the material world, whence he was calling for help and from which it was the adept's task to free him.[5] Seen psychologically, this myth expresses the *projection of an unconscious content.* Sojourning at first in the *pleroma* – that is, in a spiritual realm transcending consciousness – the Anthropos falls into matter – that is, his image is constellated there and man now senses that that is where it is and seeks it there. Something similar to this process, which happened in late antiquity, recurred in our own culture in recent centuries. For many, the metaphysical Christian God-image lost its meaning more and more, and as it did so, the fascination with material nature seemed to increase. When Albert Einstein, in opposition to Niels Bohr, declared, "God does not play with dice" (as an objection to the indeterminism of quantum physics), or when Wolfgang Pauli exclaimed, after hearing of the breakthrough of the parity principles, "So, God is left-handed after all!" – it is clear from these emotional utterances that not a few important physicists, avowedly or not avowedly, are still today seeking "God's secret" in their investigation of matter. For them, as for the alchemists, that is where "the numinous" is now to be felt.

338   Inasmuch as the early chemists knew almost nothing about matter as we today understand it and were groping their way in the dark, it is understandable that they filled this darkness with fantasies and with hypothetical models which – as has been the history of

---

[4] In my opinion, Lindsay has almost entirely missed the meaning of precisely this aspect. The corpse was bathed in natron. *Natron:* ntr means "God."
[5] Cf. C.G. Jung, *Psychology and Alchemy,* CW 12, § 447 ff.

every branch of science – later proved to be inadequate or mistaken. Since – right up to Jung's day – alchemy was looked upon merely as a precursor of chemistry, these fantasies were accordingly dismissed as "confused superstitions" or "unscientific fantasies."[6] It is one of Jung's greatest achievements, the significance of which, in my opinion, has not yet been adequately recognized, that he rediscovered the projected religious myth of alchemy and showed unmistakably *where* it originated and where it is still at work today: not in matter but in the *objective unconscious psyche* of Western man.

339 A parallel development seems to have taken place in the Far East: while some religious movements and teachings pointed toward a direct way to a transcendental experience of the spirit, there developed in certain forms of Indian yoga and in Chinese Taoism, which was shaped by a feminine spirit (Tao equals mother), a kind of alchemy which, as in the West, sought to liberate the "higher, nobler man" from matter, though in the East this was almost exclusively from the physical matter of the body.[7]

340 Long before Jung knew anything about alchemical symbolism, when he was still a student in the Gymnasium, he would shorten the way home from school by indulging in an ongoing fantasy. He imagined a castle where he was the possessor of a well-guarded secret. In the castle, there was a copper column which ramified at the top into a kind of branch-work of rootlets. These little roots drew from the air an undefinable something which was then transformed into gold in an apparatus in the cellar. He felt this as "a venerable and vitally important secret" which he had to keep to himself.[8] Many years later, in 1926, he had a curious dream which he recognized

[6] By, for example, Julius Ruska, who, influenced by such prejudices, even gave erroneous dates and textual misinterpretations. On the other hand, many of these alchemistic fantasies, detached from the investigation into matter, remain alive among certain Freemasons, Rosicrucians, etc., as moralizing secret teachings, without their empirical basis, however, and thinned down to metaphysical speculations.
[7] Cf. for example Jung and Wilhelm, *The Secret of the Golden Flower; Alchemy, Medicine and Religion in the China of A.D. 320,* the Nei P'ien of Ko Hung (= Pao-p'u-tzu), translated by J. R. Ware; Lu-ch'iang Wu and Tenney L. Davis, "Ancient Chinese Treatise entitled Ts'an T-ung Ch'I by Wei Po-yang," *Isis,* 18 (1932), pp. 237 ff; Mircea Eliade, *The Forge and the Crucible,* pp. 109 ff. and the literature cited therein. There were also alchemists who at the same time worked with outer matter, for example, Wei Po-yang. Cf. A. Waley, "Notes on Chinese Alchemy," *Bulletin of the Oriental School of London,* 6 (1930), pp. 1 – 24, esp. p. 11.
[8] Cf. *Memories,* p. 101.

was calling his attention to alchemy.[9] In this dream he was trapped in a castle and his coachman exclaimed, "Now we are caught in the 17th century." Later, he understood that the 17th century was the period in which alchemy had died out and therefore he had to dig it up again from that period. Two years after this dream he became acquainted with Taoist alchemy through Richard Wilhelm. This stimulated him to investigate Western alchemy as well, and he ordered the compilation called *Artis auriferae, quam Chemiam vocant, Volumina duo* (1593). The night before the book arrived, he had a dream. He recounts how, in a previous series of dreams, there had always been a wing or annex beside "his house" which was strange to him; now he finally reached the other wing: "I discovered there a wonderful library, dating largely from the sixteenth and seventeenth centuries. Large, fat folio volumes, bound in pigskin, stood along the walls. Among them were a number of books embellished with copper engravings of a strange character, and illustrations containing curious symbols such as I had never seen before."

341   The next day the above-mentioned compilation of alchemical writings was delivered and Jung saw in it an indication that alchemy must belong to those historical substrata of his personality which he would have to investigate. Jung was not conversant during his youth, as Goethe had been, with the still-living remnants of alchemical philosophy – he knew nothing about them, except for a couple of obscure allusions in *Faust*. He became alert to them, however, as he noticed that he and his patients had dreams which appeared to contain motifs parallel to alchemy.[10] His dreams, which he reports in *Memories*[11], now forced him to concern himself with these writings more deeply.[12] For years thereafter he made detailed synoptic collections of excerpts from the numerous texts and thus, from a wilderness of material, gradually sorted out those leading symbols and ideas which constantly recur and which therefore

---

[9] Cf. ibid., p. 229.

[10] He knew Herbert Silberer's *Problems of Mysticism and Its Symbolism*.

[11] *Memories*, 239 ff.

[12] For the way in which he set about this task, cf. Marie-Louise von Franz, "C.G. Jung's Library," *Spring* 1970; and Aniela Jaffé, *From the Life and Work of C. G. Jung*, pp. 46 ff.

seemed to be the most important. These might be summarized as follows:

342   The Western alchemists experienced their own unconscious projected into matter. Since their experiments were dangerous[13] and were attended by rumours of black magic, they usually had to work in isolation and concealment, and since they often had no idea how to set about extracting the secret of matter, they followed their dreams and visions[14] in an attempt to penetrate into the un-explorable. Thus, they found themselves in a situation parallel to our contemporary dilemma when we attempt to investigate the darkness of the unconscious psyche. In their day, the alchemists were the "empiricists in experience of God," in contrast to the denominational representatives of the different creeds, whose aim was not experience but the consolidation and exegesis of a historically revealed truth.

343   As we know, Greek alchemy, like the mathematics and the natural sciences of antiquity, was continued by the Arabs. In the Islamic world, the alchemists were much closer in spirit to the Shi'ites, who were also "empiricists in experience of God," than they were to the more orthodox circles. Muhammed ibn Umail (10th century) for example, who became famous in the West as "Senior" (the Sheikh), was a Shi'ite and his work, *Book of the Silvery Water and Starry Earth* clearly bears the stamp of his own mystical experience.[15] (Similarly, in a later period, it was the Kabbalists in Judaism who characteristically took up alchemy, rather than the orthodox circles.[16]) The alchemists were always associated with those religious undercurrents in a particular cultural setting that were of an introverted cast and that were in search of direct experience.

344   This continued to be the case when alchemy returned to Christendom as a result of the Crusades and through the mediation especially of the Spaniards and the Sicilian Arabs and Jews. It was

---

[13] Lead poisoning and explosions were not unusual.
[14] Cf. "The Visions of Zosimos" that Jung interpreted in detail, CW 13, §§ 85 – 144.
[15] Cf. Marie-Louise von Franz, *Aurora Consurgens*, Ein dem Thomas von Aquin zugeschriebenes Dokument der alchemistischen Gegensatzproblematik = C. G. Jung, *Mysterium Coniunctionis*, GW 14/III, § 22 ff (in German edition only).
[16] Cf. especially the large collection of Kabbalistic-alchemistic works in Knorr von Rosenroth, *Kabbala Denudata*.

then taken up by individual clerics, among whom Albertus Magnus, Vincent de Beauvais, Roger Bacon, Alain de Lille, Raymund Lully, and probably Thomas Aquinas were conspicuous.[17] They were in search, as in recent years Albert Einstein and Wolfgang Pauli have been, of traces of the Creator's hand in his creation, even of God himself, who appeared to be active in matter as a hidden god.

345   In the first part of *Psychology and Alchemy*, Jung illustrates, by means of a series of dreams of a modern natural scientist, how very much alive the myth of alchemy still is in the unconscious. For the alchemists, inorganic matter was not "dead" but something unknown and alive, which was not to be merely manipulated technically but with which one must establish a *relationship* in order to investigate it. The alchemists sought to attain to this relationship through their dreams, their exercises in meditation, and a disciplined fantasying which they named "phantasia vera et not phantastica"[18] and which is very much the same as the "active imagination" rediscovered by Jung.[19]

346   The "spirit of matter" which they sought went more often by the name of *Mercurius* than by any other. In accordance with an identification that was widespread in late antiquity, *Mercurius* was, for the alchemists also, identical with Hermes, the god of revelation and with the gnostic Hermes-Thoth.[20] He is the same gnostic god referred to in our amplification of Jung's first dream: the pneumatic Adam or spiritual man, sunk in matter, who was pictured as a *phallus* – a divine-human creative spirit hidden in the depths of matter (in Jung's dream in the grave in the meadow). Mercurius was thought of as a kind of god in the earth. It is the *numinosum* which, for modern man, appears to have moved into the depths of the earth but in actuality lives in the depths of his own psyche; this is true not only for certain individuals, but for very many people.

---

[17] Cf. Marie-Louise von Franz, *Auror Consurgens*, passim.

[18] Cf. C.G. Jung, *Psychology and Alchemy*, CW 12, § 360, FN 36, *Artis Auriferae* II, p. 214 f.: "Et hoc imaginare per veram imaginationem et non phantasicam."

[19] Cf. above Ch. 5. Cf. also "Dialogus Mercurii Alchemistae et Naturae," *Theatrum Chemicum* IV, Zetzner (Ed.), p. 509 ff.

[20] For this and the following, cf. Jung, "The Spirit Mercurius," CW 13 §§ 239 ff. "In East and West alike, alchemy contains as its core the Gnostic doctrine of the Anthropos and by its very nature has the character of a peculiar doctrine of redemption" (§ 252).

347   The motif of the god hidden in the earth may be illustrated by the dream of a modern student. She had lost her Christian faith and inclined to the materialistic picture of the world offered by modern natural science. In its flat, rationalistic way, however, this image could not give her any psychological satisfaction. On the Christmas Eve before her 19th birthday, she had the following dream:

348   I am kindling a sort of Yule fire in front of the University. I jump over it, to find myself suddenly standing on the edge of the sea, where a fish tries to swallow me. I manage to escape from him and walk landwards away from the sea. There I meet a painter who is standing perplexed in front of his easel. He says that he can no longer paint and does not know why. Offering to find out for him, I climb into the landscape he has painted, which had suddenly become real. At first, I come to a half-dark underground passage, into which some light still falls through an arcade. Standing there is an enormous round stone table, on which is lying a red-clad child about four meters long, a boy, chained. Revolted, I ask a woman standing nearby why he is chained. She says, 'Sh-h – it is dangerous – he is a nascent god!'

349   Then I suddenly find myself still deeper down in the earth, in complete darkness, in a labyrinthine maze of passages. Everywhere I hear the groaning and the cursing of those imprisoned there. I know that I must direct myself leftwards and to the center, in order to avoid getting lost. I come into a barely lighted room; in it crouches the 'primal family', a couple, clothed in hides, and a child. But I have to go on and deeper down. An inexplicable fear comes up in me because I know that something terribly dangerous lies ahead. 'It' is in a chamber in the center of the earth. I know somehow that at the other end of the room there is a pole, set in the earth at head-level, and that the people who go in and see 'it' are taken with such panic that they start to run away, run into the pole and perish. I impress on myself over and over again,

"Four steps – then look – then stoop." I go in and look. I see the countenance of God, which expresses such terrible sadness that nobody can bear it. Beside myself with terror I run away; but I remember to stoop and so I escape.

350   Then I am in a small room. On the wall hangs a painting by the painter whom I had met and under it is a legend, "Anathema and death to Artist P., because he failed to honor the fiery child who comes out of the water, and that is why he will smash his palette." Now I know what I had promised to look for. I try to get out again onto the other side of the earth. I come into an enormous room where dead warriors and sailing folk of all the ages are sojourning. They are dining merrily at long tables. I know that I may not make any sort of contact with them or I shall have to stay in the Land of the Dead forever. I creep quietly along the wall and through the room. But when I am nearly away from it a warrior lifts his wine glass and calls out to me, "Ah, there's a girl who cannot go back among the living any more, unless she finds the water which is made from the Virgin." With one movement I am outside. I find myself suddenly on the earth's surface again, on the other side of the sphere of earth. I am deadly tired and aged and broken from shock. I see a sort of apothecary's shop and go in. But I am so exhausted that I faint. As I am coming to, after a while, I see straight in front of me a shelf with a small flask of clear water. I know, "There it is! The water that is sought after!" I take it, I give all the money I have to the apothecary, who says scornfully that it is nothing but ordinary water, and leave the shop. There is radiant light, the sun is at its midday zenith, and a man is standing near me. I know that I have always been married to him. We walk arm in arm to the shore of the sea and look out at the water. From the depths of the water comes a double team of black horses drawing a chariot on which something unrecognizable, numinous and covered with sea-foam is lying. It occurs to me, as I awaken. "That is the birth of Aphrodite."

351 This dream contains nearly all the motifs that have been commented upon here: the symbolism of the transformation of the old image of God which has fallen into matter, into the new "divine boy," and the famous alchemistic motif of the mercurial water of life, of which one old text says, literally, that it is "virginal" and another text that it is "to be found at apothecary's shops, and it is cheap in price; for the people of this world despise it."

352 At the end of the dream there appears "the sun at its mid-day zenith" which in the teachings of the alchemist Zosimos means the completion of the work. The appearance of the Self at the end is the birth of a feminine goddess, because it is the dream of a woman. At the time of the dream the dreamer knew nothing of alchemy; yet the dream exhibits the spontaneous manifestation of the same archetypal images as in the alchemistic tradition, images that have been constellated by the questions of our age.

353 Mercurius, the god in matter, was for the alchemists not only quicksilver but a "philosophical" substance, a water "that does not wet the hands," a "dry water" or a "divine water." As such, it was taken to be the basic substance of the universe. Mercurius was at the same time fire and light, actually the "light of nature, which carries the heavenly spirit within it."[21] He is a hidden "hell-fire" in the centre of the earth, and at the same time "the fire in which God himself burns in divine love." In this sense, he is always *a paradox containing within himself the most incompatible possible opposites.* The alchemists at least suspected the psychic origin of this symbol and therefore defined Mercurius as "spirit" and "soul."[22] He is described as "pneuma," "the stone uplifted by the wind," or "the spirit of the world become body within the earth."[23]

354 *As pneumatic stone, he unites spirit and matter* and is at the same time that mysterious, secret something which animates and brings to life everything in the world[24], a sort of *world-soul,* of whom Avicenna wrote, "He is the spirit of the Lord which fills the whole

[21] Cf. C.G. Jung, "The Spirit of Mercurius," CW 13, §§ 254 – 258.
[22] Ibid., § 260.
[23] Ibid., § 261.
[24] Ibid., § 263.

world and in the beginning swam upon the waters. They call him also the spirit of Truth, which is hidden from the world."[25] Certain older texts equate him with God, without circumlocution.[26] But this divinity is not only good, like the Christian God, he is "double" (*duplex*); he can be deceitful and changeable and he "enjoys equally the company of the good and the wicked,"[27] he is "good with the good and evil with the evil."[28] Above all, he consists of all possible opposites, and whoever does not understand this "destroys himself" as well as those who "fasten their soul to the perishable gold" instead of incubating in piety and modesty this "egg of nature" and from it bringing forth the microcosm (man and woman).[29]

355   Mercurius is also hermaphroditic; the texts call him "the true Hermaphroditic Adam" and he contains the four elements within himself.[30] As the "high man," *homo altus*, as he is also called, he is obviously a human-divine masculine-feminine Anthropos, or in other words a representation of the Self.[31] When he first appears, he is often *senex* and *puer* at the same time, that is, the "old king" and the "new king," as this set of opposites was described in the foregoing chapter. In the course of the alchemical process, however, the "old king" aspect dies off and is replaced by the "royal youth."

356   Because of certain resemblances to the trinitarian God of Christianity, Mercurius is often described as triune[32] and represents now the counterpart of Christ and now the whole Trinity – indeed he is even "the Logos become world."[33] Sometimes, however, he is identified with Lucifer and the devil. His relation to the feminine principle is especially worth noting. He is the son of the great mother, Nature: "The mother bore me and is herself begotten of me[34]," and he has a particular connection with the goddess Venus and with the moon and is himself sometimes described as "the most

---

[25] "Aquarium Sapientium," *Musaeum Hermeticum,* p. 85, quoted in Jung, op. cit.
[26] Cf. ibid., § 264.
[27] Cf. ibid., § 267.
[28] Cf. ibid., § 276.
[29] Cf. ibid., § 267.
[30] Cf. ibid., § 268.
[31] Cf. ibid.
[32] For examples, cf. ibid., §§ 270 – 272.
[33] Cf. ibid., § 271.
[34] Cf. ibid., § 272.

chaste virgin[35]." The alchemist Michael Maier equates him with the Arcadian Hermes Kyllenios, who was worshipped as *phallus*, as *god of love and fertility*.[36] And in Christian Rosencreutz's *Chymical Wedding* he appears as Cupid, with an arrow (the "dart of passion" – *telum passionis*). He cultivates connections with the dark underworld and with the kingdom of the dead, and is at once the dark initial condition and the highest achievement, an "earthly God" who unifies everything in himself.[37] The aspect of all-embracing unity was usually symbolized by the dragon or the snake which takes the form of a ring and bites its own tail (Uroboros), or by fabulous beings who combined in themselves the attributes of earth, water, and air.

357   In all of these symbolic projections of the alchemists we encounter, as Jung explains[38], the phenomenology of an "objective" spirit, "a true matrix of psychic experience, the most appropriate symbol for which is matter. Nowhere and never has man controlled matter without closely observing its behaviour and paying heed to its laws. . . . The same is true of that objective spirit which today we call the unconscious: it is refractory-like matter, mysterious and elusive, and obeys laws which are so non-human or superhuman that they seem to us like a *crimen laesae maiestatis humanae*."

358   In contrast to the light, spiritual Christ-symbol, Mercurius is a dark and hidden god, embodying the *complexion oppositorum* and compensating the one-sidedness of the God-image in collective consciousness.[39] "Hesitatingly, as in a dream, the introspective brooding of the centuries" gradually put together the figure of Mercurius, which is not meant to take the place of Christ but to stand "in a compensatory relation to him."

359   Jung became aware of this fact with special acuteness through one of his own visions[40]. As he reports in *Memories*[41]:

---

[35] Cf. ibid., § 273.
[36] Cf. ibid., § 278.
[37] Ibid.
[38] Cf. ibid., § 286.
[39] Cf. ibid., § 295.
[40] In the year 1939, just as he was giving a seminar on the Spiritual Exercises of Ignatius Loyola, at the Federal Institute of Technology (ETH) in Zurich.
[41] *Memories*, p. 236 f.

360   One night I awoke and saw, bathed in bright light at the foot of my bed, the figure of Christ on the Cross. It was not quite life-size, but extremely distinct; I saw that his body was made of greenish gold. The vision was marvellously beautiful, and yet I was profoundly shaken by it. . . .

361   . . . The vision came to me as if to point out that I had overlooked something in my reflections: the analogy of Christ with the *aurum non vulgi* [a gold which is not the ordinary gold] and the *viriditas* of the alchemists. When I realized that the vision pointed to this central alchemical symbol . . . I felt comforted.

362   The green gold is the living quality which the alchemists saw not only in man but also in inorganic nature. It is an expression of the life-spirit, the *anima mundi* or *filius macrocosmi, the Anthropos who animates the whole cosmos.*[42] This spirit has poured himself out into everything, even into inorganic matter; he is present in metal and stone.

363   Mercurius is the son of the macrocosm; he is also extolled by the masters of the art as "*benedicta viridit* – blessed greenness."[43] (In ecclesiastical symbolism, the colour green is an attribute of the Holy Spirit.) Greenness, in the opinion of the alchemist Mylius, is "a kind of germination" which "God has breathed into created things" and from which they receive their life. Thus, Jung's vision combined the Christ-image with the figure of Mercurius into a *unity*. "Seen in historical retrospect," he wrote[44], "it was a moment of the utmost significance when the humanist Patrizi proposed to Pope Gregory XIV that Hermetic philosophy [which was supposed to be the teachings of Hermes, that is, of Mercurius-Thoth[45]] should take the place of Aristotle in ecclesiastical doctrine. At that moment two worlds came into contact which – after heaven knows what happenings – must yet be united in the future."

---

[42] Italics added by the author.
[43] Cf. C.G. Jung, *Psychology and Religion*, CW 11, §§ 118 and 151.
[44] C.G. Jung, "The Spirit of Mercurius," CW 13, § 303.
[45] Added by the author.

364 The dream of a modern woman illustrates the fact that a widespread contemporary tendency in the collective unconscious, rather than some personal problem, was being expressed in Jung's vision.[46] She dreamed:

365 I enter my house at dusk. The hall is twilit and quite empty, but there is a heap of straw on the stone floor and on it the figure of a man, clothed like a vagabond, of middle years. With deep emotion, I realize that it is 'Christ'. His body, however, does not consist of flesh and blood, but of brightly shining, hotly glowing metal. He says, 'You could do me a favour. Take a basin of water and pour it over me, *to soften my radiance*'. I do it. The water evaporates with a hiss and the body changes to dark metal without losing its mobility or its life. The stranger smiles and says softly, 'Thank you.'

366 The alchemists say of Mercurius that he is "shining bright and burning hot, heavier than metal and lighter than air."[47] He wants to soften or dull his radiance in the dream above, in order to remain hidden as the secret in the life of the individual and not be visible from outside. Today it looks as if there were a tendency in the collective unconscious to annex the Mercurius aspect to the Christ figure, as if to unite the spirit of the unconscious with consciousness, but not in order to eliminate the Christ figure; for the attainments of the Christian ethic must on no account be lost once again, a fact which certain regressions into pre-Christian paganism have in recent years convincingly underscored.

367 Jung saw in the figure of Mephistopheles in *Faust* a much closer parallel to the Mercurius of alchemy than to the Christian devil. Faust encounters him as an unknown visitor (at first as a poodle), then Mephistopheles makes himself known as a tempter, offering love and the joy of living. If Faust had not met him, he would have killed himself, or else withered away as a bookworm. But Faust could

---

[46] Cf. my paper, "The Cosmic Man as Image of the Goal of the Individuation Process and Human Development," in: *Archetypal Dimensions of the Psyche*, pp. 113 – 157.
[47] Cf. C.G. Jung, "Flying Saucers: A Modern Myth," CW 10, § 727.

not stand up to Mephistopheles – he fell victim to an inflation and, at the end of the tragedy, to the lust for power. *That* is how Mephistopheles became his destroyer. Jung was disgusted, therefore, when Mephistopheles was disposed of at the end and relegated to hell, through the angel's cheap trick.[48] Faust's fate shows what happens when the constellated archetypal image of Mercurius meets a weak and morally childish consciousness which cannot defend its ethical integrity; he seduces it into betrayal and murder. For Faust – in order to wrest more land from the sea – disposed of that old couple, Philemon and Baucis, who, according to legend, were the only ones still worshipping the gods Jupiter and Mercury in a time of general decay and immorality. The arrogant, hybris-filled way in which we are today destroying the natural environment and whose evil consequences we are just beginning to recognize, corresponds to this Faustian inflation.

368   Jung therefore emphasizes[49]: "Mercurius, that two-faced god, comes as the *lumen naturae* . . . only to those whose reason strives towards the highest light ever received by man, and who do not trust exclusively to the *cognition vespertina* [the evening consciousness]. For those who are unmindful of this light, the *lumen naturae* turns into a perilous *ignus fatuus*, and the psychopomp into a diabolical seducer. Lucifer, who could have brought light, becomes the father of lies whose voice in our time, supported by press and radio, revels in orgies of propaganda and leads untold millions to ruin."

369   Fundamentally Mercurius is also the continuation of certain compensatory personifications of the god-man which have traditionally also manifested themselves in folklore in other forms. In Judaism and in Islamic legend, a related figure turns up in the form of Elijah and El-Khidr, and in the medieval Grail saga in the form of Merlin[50]. In the so-called *Pirkê de Rabbi Eliezer* 31, for example, the prophet Elijah is described as the "incarnation of an eternal soul-substance," with the same nature as that of the angel[51],

---

[48] Cf. *Memories*, p.77 ff and p. 99.
[49] C.G. Jung, "The Spirit of Mercurius," CW 13, p. 303.
[50] Merlin was also associated with Elijah.
[51] Cf. Jung's letter to Père Bruno O.C.D., CW 18/II, §§ 1518 – 1531.

and according to a number of legends it is *he* who will awaken the dead at the resurrection. After his ascent to heaven in a fiery chariot, he sojourns with the angels or soars as an eagle over the earth spying out the secrets of human beings. Elijah is, as Jung points out, a morally darker figure than Christ. Like Moses, he once killed a man, and in several legends, he appears as a knave and a trickster. On one occasion he even transforms himself into a courtesan, in order to rescue the pious Rabbi Meir from persecution. Even at his birth he possessed two souls (*Mercurius duplex*!). He had hair all over his body, he was wrapped in fiery wrappings and nourished by flames. According to another legend, his body came from the Tree of Life.[52]

370   In Islamic legend, Elijah is usually replaced by El-Khidr, the "first angel of God," who also appears as an unknown wanderer on the earth in the guise of trickster and tester of men (especially in the 18th sura, 64ff. of the Koran). Elijah is also identified with Enoch and Idris (who equals Hermes-Thoth) and later with St. George. Popular fantasy was forever busy with his ascent to heaven; he was, after all, one of but four human beings who had attained to immortality *with* his body.[53] It is not surprising, therefore, that he also finally appears in alchemistic literature as "Helyas Artista," Helyas "in whose time all that is hidden will be revealed."[54] Elijah, like Mercury, is a symbol of the Self. "He is a personification of the god-man type, but he is more human than Christ, since he was begotten and born in original sin, and he is more universal, inasmuch as he also incorporates pre-Yahwistic heathen divinities like Baal, El-Elyon, Mithras, Mercurius and the personification of Allah and El-Khidr."[55] He was even identified with the sun-god Helios (from which the world "Elijah" was supposedly derived).

371   Elijah and El-Khidr like to wander freely around in the world of human beings as unrecognized strangers, revealing themselves through a miracle just before they depart, after having put mankind or a man to some test or other. Many popular European fairytales

---

[52] Cf. ibid., § 1521 f.
[53] Elijah, Enoch, Christ, Mary.
[54] Gerhard Dorn, "De Transmutatione metallorum," *Theatrum chemicum*, I, p. 610; quoted by C.G. Jung, CW 18, § 1528.
[55] Ibid., § 1529.

also begin with the formula, "In the days when Our Lord still wandered the earth…" Psychologically this shows that the official god-image was felt to be too "metaphysical" and too removed to the heavenly realm. One was no longer able to meet God himself in the here and the now. The god Mercurius or Elijah or Khidr, the messenger of God, on the other hand, wanders around in the guise of a stranger who confronts the individual directly. Similar motifs are also frequently found in the dreams of contemporary men and women. A 43-year-old graphic artist, for example, had the following dream:[56]

372   I dream that I go into a Catholic Church [the dreamer is Protestant but often visits churches out of an interest in art]. A service is in progress, so I slip into a pew in the rear, inconspicuously. Then a simply clad, somewhat tramp-like stranger, surrounded with an air of mystery, comes and sits quietly next to me. In spite of his homely appearance he is somehow numinous. Suddenly I realize, with deep emotion, that he is Christ. I jump up and turn toward him. The stranger puts his finger to his mouth and smiles. It dawns on me how shocked and incredulous the reaction of the praying congregation and the priest would be if I said to them that Christ is here. So I hold my peace, sit down again and the stranger and I smile at each other in secret understanding.

373   This dream illustrates the enormous difference between the collectively worshipped Christ-image, as image of the Self, and a personal numinous experience of the same image. It was the alchemists who, in the past, sought the latter; hence they were the precursors of these contemporary seekers who are also looking for immediate religious experience.

374   The most varied representatives of that outlook which claims absolute metaphysical validity for its particular religion or doctrine

---

[56] Cf., my paper, "The Cosmic Man as Image of the Goal of the Individuation Process and Human Development," in: *Archetypal Dimensions of the Psyche*, pp. 133 – 157.

have found a stumbling-block, and have sometimes taken offense, at the objectivity with which Jung regarded the religion-creating archetypal representations. This objectivity seems to them like a relativization of their "absolute" truth. The object-oriented (extraverted) "Western attitude . . . tends to fix the ideal – Christ – in its outward aspect and thus to rob it of its mysterious relation to the inner man."[57] Jung's response to this attitude was: "Anyone who can square it with his conscience is free to decide this question as he pleases, though he may be unconsciously setting himself up as an *arbiter mundi*. I for my part prefer the precious gift of doubt, for the reason that it does not violate the virginity of things beyond our ken."[58]

375   In his introduction to *Psychology and Alchemy*[59], Jung has given a description that cannot be bettered of the relation between the two worlds, that of official Christianity and that of alchemistic thinking:

376   Alchemy is rather like an undercurrent to the Christianity that ruled on the surface. It is to this surface as the dream is to consciousness, and just as the dream compensates the conflicts of the conscious mind, so alchemy endeavours to fill in the gaps left open by the Christian tension of opposites. Perhaps the most pregnant expression of this is the axiom of Maria Prophetissa ['One becomes two, two becomes three, and out of the third comes the one as fourth...'] . . . which runs like a *leitmotiv* throughout almost the whole of the lifetime of alchemy, extending over more than seventeen centuries. In this aphorism, the even numbers which signify the feminine principle, earth, the regions under the earth, and evil itself are interpolated between the uneven numbers of the Christian dogma. They are personified by the *serpens mercurii*, the dragon that creates and destroys itself and represents the *prima materia*. This fundamental idea of alchemy points back to the Tehom (Genesis I), to Tiâmat

---

[57] C.G. Jung, *Psychology and Alchemy*, CW 12, § 8.
[58] Ibid. (arbiter mundi = world judge)
[59] Ibid., § 26 ff.

with her dragon attribute, and thus to the primordial matriarchal world. . . . The historical shift in the world's consciousness towards the masculine is compensated at first by the chthonic femininity of the unconscious. . . . Were the unconscious merely complementary, this shift in consciousness would have been accompanied by the production of a mother and daughter [in contrast to the Father-Son-Holy Ghost of Christianity[60]] for which the necessary material lay ready to hand in the myth of Demeter and Persephone. But, as alchemy shows, the unconscious chose rather the Cybele-Attis type in the form of the *prima materia*[61] and the *filius macrocosmi* [that is, Mercurius]. . . .This goes to show that the unconscious does not simply act *contrary* to the conscious mind, but *modifies* it more in the manner of an opponent or partner. The son type does not call up a daughter as a complementary image from the depths of the 'chthonic' unconscious – it calls up another son. This remarkable fact would seem to be connected with the incarnation in our earthly human nature of a purely spiritual God, brought about by the Holy Ghost impregnating the womb of the Blessed Virgin. *Thus the higher, the spiritual, the masculine inclines to the lower, the earthly, the feminine; and accordingly, the mother, who was anterior to the world of the father, accommodates herself to the masculine principle and, with the aid of the human spirit (alchemy or "the philosophy"), produces a son – not the antithesis of Christ but rather his chthonic counterpart, not a divine man but a fabulous being conforming to the nature of the primordial mother.*[62] And just as the redemption of man the microcosm is the task of the 'upper' son, so the 'lower' son has the function of a *salvator marocosmi*.

---

[60] Added by the author.
[61] The initial material of the alchemical opus (this footnote has been added by the author)
[62] Italics added by the author.

377 This formulation sounds like the presentation of a myth, but "myth is the primordial language natural to these psychic processes, and no intellectual formulation comes anywhere near the richness and expressiveness of mythical imagery."[63] This is because myth is the language of the psyche, and our rational consciousness does not embrace the psyche and it "is therefore ridiculous to speak of the things of the soul in a patronizing or depreciatory manner."[64] "I have been accused of "deifying the soul", Jung says, by 'Not I but God himself has deified it.'"[65]

378 There have always been great individuals who knew about this divine aspect of the soul: St. Augustine, Meister Eckhart, Ruysbroeck, Tauler, and numerous others – even Giordano Bruno called the soul "God's light."[66] In the East, on the other hand, this outlook has always been common property. For the Indian, everything highest and lowest is contained in the transcendental subject. Accordingly, the significance of the Atman, the Self, is heightened beyond all bounds[67], while with us an equally boundless undervaluation of the soul prevents its growth and development. We find all our values in the outside world; the inner world remains barbaric and underdeveloped and liable to overwhelm us at any moment with states of possession unless we succeed in understanding its contents and connecting them with our conscious life.

379 The experience of the unconscious has, however, an *isolating* effect[68], and there are many people who cannot bear this. Yet to be alone with the Self is the highest and the most decisive human experience, since one "must be alone if he is to find out what it is that supports him when he can no longer support himself. Only this experience can give him an indestructible foundation."[69]

---

[63] Quoted in *Psychology and Alchemy*, CW 12, §§ 26, 28.
[64] Ibid., § 11.
[65] Ibid., § 14.
[66] Cf. Frances Yates, *Giordano Bruno and the Hermetic Tradition*, p. 271 f., 282.
[67] Cf. *Psychology and Alchemy*, CW 12, 9, 12.
[68] Cf. Ibid., § 61.
[69] Quoted in ibid., § 32.

Chapter 11
The Philosopher's Stone

380   When Jung was a schoolboy, he liked to play outdoors. Along the garden wall of his parents' house there was a slope in which was embedded a stone, "my stone," as he called it[1].

381   Often when I was alone, I sat down on this stone, and then began an imaginary game that went something like this: "I am sitting on top of this stone and it is underneath." But the stone could also say "I" and think, "I am lying here on this slope and he is sitting on top of me." The question then arose, "Am I the one who is sitting on the stone, or am I the stone on which *he* is sitting?" This question always perplexed me, and I would stand up, wondering who was what now?

382   When he carved and hid the little black man mentioned earlier, while he was a pupil in primary school, he gave the manikin a pebble from the Rhine, painted with colours and divided into an upper half and a lower half. That was "his" stone[2], his store of vitality. Jung felt safe after he had done this, and the feeling of being inwardly at odds with himself, which often tormented him at that time, was relieved. It was not until much later that he learned that Stone Age men had also possessed such stones and kept them in special hiding-places which were, so to speak, the repositories of their strength. This is still the case with indigenous Australians.[3] The stone, therefore, appears to be an age-old symbol for the eternal, the enduring in man,

---

[1] For this and for the quotations that follow, cf. *Memories*, p. 35.
[2] Ibid., p. 37.
[3] Their *churingas* are either stones or pieces of wood; their magic life force resides in them. Cf. Jung, "The Visions of Zosimos," CW 13, § 128.

from which he draws the strength he needs for life. The stones which many different peoples pile up on graves have the same meaning: they symbolize that which, in human beings, survives death. The ancient Germans for example arranged such stones on their graves, so-called Bautar stones, and there presented sacrifices. They believed that the souls of their dead ancestors lived in the stones and migrated from them into new-born children.[4] The Swiss saint, Brother Klaus of Flüe, testified that in his mother's womb, before his birth, he had a vision of a star, of a great stone and of the chrism. The stone signified his steadfastness, in which he should remain and never relinquish his goal.[5] He who possesses this stone cannot be "dissolved" by collective influences or by inner problems, whence comes the feeling that it is a part of the person which can outlast everything else. From the time of the earliest alchemical texts, one meets again and again the theme of the stone (*lapis philosophorum*) as an equivalent of the sought-after gold. The "stone sent by God" was the starting-point and the goal of the alchemistic *opus*, the stone which can transform any metal into gold and which, according to some authors, is hidden in the human body and is to be extracted from it. It is god's mystery in matter and is even described as the "stone that hath a spirit [pneuma]" which must be extracted from it.[6] In Far Eastern alchemy, the diamond body corresponds to this stone; the alchemist creates this body through his meditative exercises, thereby attaining immortality during his lifetime.[7]

383   In Western alchemy, too, several masters suspected that it was a question of a meditative development of one's own inner personality which, it was hoped, would then complete itself in the outer world. The "stone" was for them, as for the Eastern meditators, a kind of immortal body. In an early Egyptian burial ritual, the moment of resurrection was represented in the grave by the erection of the so-called *djed* pillar, a stone column, and one of the oldest Greek alchemical texts, "Kommarios to Cleopatra," celebrates the

---

[4] Cf. P. Hermann, *Das altgermanische Priesterwesen,* Jena 1929, p. 52-54.
[5] Cf. Marie-Louise von Franz, *Die Visionen des Niklaus von Flüe,* p. 16 ff. (English version?)
[6] Cf. C.G. Jung, "Psychology and Religion," CW 11, § 151.
[7] Cf. Richard Wilhelm, *The Secret of the Golden Flower,* passim; M. Eliade, *The Forge and the Crucible: The Origins and Structure of Alchemy; Lu K'uan Yü, Taoist Yoga: Alchemy and Immortality.*

production of the stone, in lofty language, as a resurrection mystery in which a "statue" comes forth from the fire reborn.[8]

384   When the alchemical tradition later moved into the sphere of Arabian culture, the *lapis* (stone) was equated with the Ka'aba in Mecca, and when it moved back again to the West, the authors found a parallel to "their" stone in the "stone the builders rejected [which] has become the head of the corner" (Matthew 21, 42; Ephesians 2, 20/21), thereby identifying it with Christ, who is otherwise always taken as the rejected cornerstone.[9] The alchemical stone, according to some authors, is also identical with Mercurius and with the mercurial water, discussed in the previous chapter. It frequently appears as the companion of the lonely searcher and as a divine four-fold Anthropos figure.[10] Petrus Bonus, a 14th century writer, says of the alchemical *opus*[11]:

385   But as regards the fixation and permanence of the soul and spirit at the end of the sublimation, this takes place when the secret stone is added, which cannot be grasped by the senses, but only by the intellect[12], through inspiration or divine revelation, or through the teaching of an initiate. . . . This secret stone is a gift of God. There could be no alchemy without this stone. It is the heart and tincture of the gold, regarding which Hermes says: "It is needful that at the end of the world heaven and earth be united: which is the philosophic Word."

386   Petrus Bonus then further describes the stone as the *resurrecting body* which is spiritual as well as corporeal and of such subtlety that it can penetrate and pervade anything. "The old philosophers discerned the Last Judgment in this art, namely in the germination

---

[8] Cf. "Komarios an Kleopatra," M. Berthelot, *Collection des anciens Alchimistes Grecs*, Paris 1887/88, IV, XX, 8, cited in C.G. Jung, *Psychology and Alchemy*, CW 12, § 406; cf. Marie-Louise von Franz, *On Dreams and Death*, p. 118 f.
[9] Cf. C. G. Jung, *Psychology and Alchemy*, CW 12, § 451 f.
[10] Ibid. § 454 ff.
[11] Ibid., § 462.
[12] In the sense of spirit.

and birth of this stone, for in it the soul to be beatified [*beatificandae*] unites with its original body, to eternal glory."[13] This association of the stone with the idea of corporeal immortality is a motif which constantly recurs in numerous places. Thus, in an ancient Mexican cycle of sagas, Quetzalcoatl, the god and bringer of salvation, is begotten by a green jewel which penetrated his mother; a precious stone was also put into the mouths of the dead to revive them after death.[14] Stone statues of the gods were tended and worshipped in Egypt because they were expected to preserve the imperishable nature of the Pharaoh's life-principle (Ka), and in the Apocalypse of Elijah it is said of the saints who escape the persecution of the Antichrist that their flesh will be turned to stone, so that it shall remain uninjured until the end of time.[15]

387   Although the alchemistic texts show many variations, a synoptic scrutiny will nonetheless uncover certain basic motifs. According to this, the philosopher's stone is produced in three typical stages: the *nigredo* (blackness), the *albedo* (whiteness or whitening) and the *rubedo* or *citrinitas* (reddening or the colour of gold).

388   In the first phase, the *nigredo*, the initial material (*prima materia*) is dissolved, calcinated, pulverized and washed, a dangerous stage in which poisonous vapours often develop, lead or quicksilver poisonings are generated, or explosions occur. According to old texts, there lives in lead "an impudent demon who can cause a sickness of the spirit, or lunacy." The operator feels bewildered, disoriented, succumbs to a deep melancholy, or feels that he has been transported to the deepest layer of hell. The *nigredo* has its parallels in the individuation process, in the confrontation with the shadow. Everything that one has criticized with moral indignation in others, is "served up" in dreams as a part of one's own being. Envy, jealousy, lies, sexual drives, desire for power, ambition, greed for money, irritability, all kinds of childishness suddenly stare implacably at one, out of one's dreams. Illusions about oneself and the world fall apart, ideals are revealed as desire for power in

[13] Ibid.
[14] Cf. C.G. Jung, "The Visions of Zosimos," CW 13, § 133 and many other instances.
[15] Ibid.

disguise, "sacred" convictions as hollow. Should there be a latent psychosis, then the lead-demon, Nietzsche's "Spirit of Gravity," can cause actual mental illness. The ego feels robbed of its illusory omnipotence and confronted with the dark and bewildering power of the unconscious. This condition can last for a long time, even for years, until every bit of darkness has been made conscious, all autonomous partial personalities (autonomous complexes) have been recognized and morally subdued or domesticated.

389   In the alchemical work, this phase is followed by the *albedo*. This phase corresponds in the individuation process to the integration of the inner contra-sexual components, the anima in the case of a man, the animus with a woman. (Since almost all the alchemical texts were written by men, the *albedo* is usually described as a stage "in which the woman rules and the light of the moon comes out.") Of course, the washing, calcination, etc. of the *nigredo* continues throughout this second phase, because, like the Hydra of Lerna that Hercules fought, the shadow keeps growing new heads from time to time. The operation of the *albedo*, however, is otherwise not so violent or strenuous as that of the *nigredo*. It consists chiefly in regulating the fire with wisdom: too much fire destroys, too little allows the process to "cool down." Psychologically, it is a question of the transference problem, the constellation of a love relation between doctor and patient, or else the problem of a great and passionate love which is just as often constellated outside the therapeutic situation.[16] In alchemical symbolism, the projected problem is represented by the "mystic marriage" of the elements in all kinds of variations. In its early stages, a great and passionate love relationship is almost always recognizable (in any case usually visible only to the observer) as a projection of the animus, alternatively the anima, onto another person[17], so that there often arises a relationship founded on mutual unconsciousness[18] in which all possible opposites – trust and

---

[16] Cf. principally C.G. Jung, "Psychology of the Transference," CW 16, §§ 353 ff.

[17] Ibid., §§ 358 ff.

[18] Ibid., § 364. As Freud correctly saw, this generally has an incestuous character (§ 368), which is an indirect hint that quite a bit of what is seen in the beloved partner should really belong to the subject.

anxiety, hope and doubt, attraction and repulsion – counter-balance one another.[19]

390   The old alchemists often worked together with a female friend (*soror mystica*) or with their wives, and their anima and animus components were projected into the matter with which and upon which they were working, which means that they sought to produce the "royal marriage" of these components in the retort. In a love situation in therapy or in life, four figures are also always constellated: the man and his anima, and the woman with her animus. Among these four factors, every conceivable phenomenon of psychic attraction and repulsion is possible.[20] For us, this situation is new to the extent that animus and anima were previously contained in the dogma as religious symbols: the animus in the figure of Christ (the heavenly bridegroom of many women), the anima in the figure of Mary, or in the Church. These projections have today, however, to a very large extent unconsciously left the religious figures and entered into the human sphere, a fact which causes the relation between man and woman to seem enormously more important but also much more difficult and which, in Jung's opinion, ruins many a marriage.[21] The advantage of this recently created difficulty lies in the fact that it forces us at last to give our attention to the unconscious psyche. Partners in the chemical marriage are usually described as brother and sister, mother and son, or father and daughter. Their union is incestuous. The purpose of this incestuous aspect of such a love-configuration is to make us conscious of the projection, that is, it constrains us to realize that in the end it is a question of the inner union of the components of the personality in ourselves, of a "spiritual marriage" as an unprojected inner experience.[22] A unification of the inner opposites in the Self is, as it were, intended.[23] The old alchemists had an easier time of it than we have, since for them, the problem lay in matter, in the retort,

---

[19] Ibid., § 375.
[20] For details, cf. ibid., §§ 309 ff and especially § 407 ff. This constellation has its historical prototype in the so-called cross-cousin marriage of various primitive peoples. Cf. §§ 433 ff.
[21] Ibid., § 442.
[22] Ibid.
[23] Ibid.

where they sought to produce the philosopher's stone by means of the "chymical marriage." We, however, must bring the process to completion in ourselves; that task hits us right in the centre of our being, and goes deeper.

391   Because of the present population explosion and the closer contact between people brought about by technology, the social primordial order of the so-called marriage-classes has been shattered, as it was originally a social order suitable for smaller communities. The instinctual energy which is always seeking social cohesion shifted, in the higher cultures, mostly toward religious and political areas[24], but nowadays these areas of life are also infected with the general dissolution, so that we are currently in danger of falling into a chaotic mass psyche. A saving counter-trend, therefore, is constellated in the people of our time in the form of a drive toward an inner consolidation of the individual and toward a differentiation of his capacity for relating to his fellow man.

392   If we do not become conscious of this fact, then this tendency will express itself in reality all the same, but in a negative way, leading to an inner *hardheartedness* between people, as we know from the background of so many current crimes. Collective man "becomes a soulless herd animal governed only by panic and lust: his soul, which can live only in and from human relationships, is irretrievably lost."[25]

393   Because the animus and anima often conflict with one another (the cause of many modern marital crises!), their activation creates a relation between a man and a woman which is characterized at once by the strongest attraction and by bitter hostility. The intensity of the bond is meaningful because without it the partners might well leave each other at the first quarrel: the bond forces them to work through the animus-anima problem. The maintenance of a "moderate fire" which "does not scorch the King and Queen," as recommended by the alchemists, is in the highest degree difficult, for it means keeping to a middle way between the physical and spiritual components.[26] The withdrawal of the projection seldom

---

[24] Cf. ibid., § 443.
[25] Ibid., § 444.
[26] Cf. "Transference" § 448. There are two typical dangers: "The first is the danger of the patient's using

results in an end to the relationship. Normally, a human connection remains, "for without the conscious acknowledgement and acceptance of our kinship with those around us there can be no synthesis of personality. . . . The inner consolidation of the individual is not just the hardness of collective man on a higher plane, in the form of spiritual aloofness and inaccessibility, it emphatically includes our fellow man."[27] This explains why Jung, in contrast to therapists of many other schools, cultivated private personal contact with many of his patients; many of them later became his students.

394   The clash between animus and anima means, first and foremost, conflict and severe suffering because the merely natural man, i.e., the unconscious man, has, as it were, to die during his own lifetime. Whoever gets into this situation will without fail be confronted with that "other" who will oppose and thwart his ego-will from within, namely his own shadow, as well as the individual reality of the "You" which does not correspond to his expectations, and finally that psychic "Not-I," the archetype of the collective unconscious with their fate-forming power.[28] Therefore, says Jung[29], the crucified one is an "eternal" truth, for whoever finds himself on the path of individuation cannot evade that suspension between the opposites which is symbolized by the crucifixion. But just at the deepest point of suffering, the content of the next stage appears, the "birth of the . . . inner man,"[30] that is, the Self[31], or the stone of the wise.

395   In the alchemical procedure, the *rubedo* or *citrinitas* (reddening or gold colour) follows the *albedo*. In this phase, the work comes to an end, the retort is opened, and the philosopher's stone begins to radiate a cosmically healing effect. He unites all the opposites in

---

the opportunities for spiritual development arising out of the analysis of the unconscious as a pretext for evading the deeper human responsibilities, and for affecting a certain 'spirituality' which cannot stand up to moral criticism; the second is the danger that atavistic tendencies may gain the ascendancy and drag the relationship down to a primitive level. Between this Scylla and that Charybdis there is a narrow passage, and both medieval Christian mysticism and alchemy have contributed much to its discovery." Cf. in this connection, see Jung's letter to John Trinick in: C.G. Jung, *Letters*, Vol. 2, p. 392 ff.

[27] C.G. Jung, "The Psychology of the Transference," CW 16, § 444.
[28] Cf. ibid., § 470.
[29] Ibid.
[30] Ibid., § 482.
[31] That is why, as early as Augustine, the crucifixion was understood as a "sacred marriage."

himself and binds together the four elements of the world.[32] The Self, too, which is brought into reality in the individuation process, is the wider, inner man who reaches toward eternity, the Anthropos who is described as spherical and bisexual and who "stands for the mutual integration of conscious and unconscious."[33]

396   The meeting of the opposites within oneself always means *intensive suffering*, and this also appears unambiguously in alchemical symbolism. The motif of torment is very much in evidence in the dream-visions of the famous early alchemist, Zosimos of Panoplis, who lived in the third century A.D.[34] In these visions, Zosimos beholds a priest who appears on a bowl-shaped altar and announces to him that he will show him a process of spiritualizing the body. The priest tells Zosimos that he was overpowered by one who came "in haste in early morning and pierced him through with a sword, dismembering him, scalped him and burned him until his body was transformed and became spirit." Thereupon the priest spews forth his own flesh, "changed into the opposite of himself," a small manikin. The latter tears his flesh with his own teeth, and sinks back into himself. In a second vision, the homunculus appears to watch over men who are boiled in torment in boiling water on the bowl-shaped altar. They, too, are suffering a spiritualization process. The priest, however, is the one who "sacrifices and is sacrificed." Later, the *opus* consists in building a temple out of *one* white stone, in whose interior flows a spring of the purest water, from which a light "sparkling like the sun" shines forth. There sits the priest, who from a brazen man has now been transformed into gold. The motif of torment is repeated several times, and in the end the comely figure of a man bearing the name "Meridian of the Sun" is sacrificed, boiled, and delivered over to "the place of punishment."

397   The temple, a monolith, represents the *lapis*, the philosopher's stone, in which, and on whose account, the entire sacrificial

---

[32] Cf. "The Psychology of the Transference," CW 16, § 529.
[33] Ibid., §531.
[34] Reproduced in full and interpreted in Jung, "The Visions of Zosimos," CW 13, §§ 85 ff.

operation takes place.[35] This dramatic representation of the alchemical *opus* shows "how the divine process of change manifests itself to our human understanding and how man experiences it – as punishment, torment, death and transfiguration." Zosimos describes "how a man would act and what he would have to suffer if he were drawn into the cycle of the death and rebirth of the gods, and what effect the *deus absconditus*[36] would have" if a mortal man should allow the spirit of the unconscious to be activated and attract his attention.[37]

398   In the visions of Zosimos, an archetypal transformation and a sacrifice mystery are symbolized which also form the underlying basis of the liturgy of the Mass, transmuted into its most highly spiritual form.[38] For this reason, Jung made a thoroughgoing psychological study of the Mass, which cannot be cited here, but which includes a summary of the psychological meaning of sacrifice, which is also the heart of the alchemical transformation mystery.[39]

399   The act of sacrifice means that I am giving up something which belongs to *me*; the more valuable the gift and the more the sacrifice is made without any thought of receiving something in return, the more it becomes a gift of myself, since we are unconsciously identified with possessions which are important to us.[40] "*If you can give yourself, it proves that you possess yourself.* . . . So anyone who can sacrifice himself and forgo his claim must have had it; in other words, he must have been conscious of the claim. This presupposes an act of considerable self-knowledge. . .."[41] In the act of sacrifice, therefore, the ego, with its natural egotistical claims, decides against itself, to the extent that it subordinates itself to an authority which is *higher* than itself. This authority is the principle of individuation, or the Self, which emerges in the act of sacrifice because it forces the ego from within to a subordinate position. The central significance

---

[35] Ibid., § 112.
[36] The hidden god.
[37] Ibid., § 139.
[38] Cf. C.G. Jung, "Transformation Symbolism in the Mass," CW 11, §§ 296 ff.
[39] Ibid., §§ 387 ff.
[40] Ibid., § 389.
[41] Ibid., § 390.

of the sacrifice for the ego now becomes clear: it is *the* possibility for the ego to experience the superior presence and reality of the Self. Does it also have a meaning for the Self? For the Self, it is the moment in time when it can enter into us and so pass from a condition of unconsciousness into consciousness, from potentiality into actuality.[42] It is, so to speak, the moment when the "unknown god" in us becomes conscious, thereby becoming at the same time human.[43] From the diffuse state of unconsciousness, the Self collects itself in the action of self-reflection on man's part and emerges as a unity. Inasmuch as the Self existed prior to the ego, it is the ego's father, but inasmuch as it can become manifest only through the work done by the ego, it is our son – hence the identity of *senex* and *puer* in the Mercurius symbolism. The self-reflection of the human being or the urge toward individuation, which is the same thing, gathers together the diffuse inner being into a unity, so that it can come into effective life in the figure of the One, the Anthropos. In this way, the circle of consciousness is widened and the sources of conflict dry up because the paradoxes in the Self have been made conscious.[44] Since something "eternal" and indestructible is inherent in the Self, the ego, too, experiences an approximation of such a state. But the Self seems to have as strong an inclination to become conscious in us, as we have to find our redemption in the Self. In the apocryphal Acts of John (probably the second century A.D.), Christ says to his disciples[45], "As you dance[46], ponder what I do, *for yours is this human suffering which I will to suffer.*[47] For you would be powerless to understand your suffering had I not been sent to you as the Logos by the Father. . . . If you had understood suffering, you would have non-suffering. . . . Understand the Word of Wisdom in me." Through suffering, the ego becomes conscious of the Self. "You no longer see yourself as an isolated point on the periphery, but as the One in the centre. Only subjective consciousness is isolated,

[42] Ibid., §§ 397-398.
[43] Ibid., § 398.
[44] Ibid., § 401.
[45] Ibid., § 415.
[46] Christ dances a round dance with his disciples.
[47] Italics added by the author.

when it relates to its centre, it is integrated into wholeness' and finds in the midst of suffering a quiet place beyond all involvements."[48]

400   In the gnostic interpretations of the Christ-symbol, as well as those of the alchemical stone and the Mercurius and Anthropos images, the Self emerges as a *natural* symbol of wholeness that is in contrast to the dogmatic Christ-image, in that the latter contains nothing – or scarcely anything – of the dark, the feminine, the material.[49] It is therefore understandable that the medieval theologians should have occupied themselves with the *body* of Christ, and that the medieval Grail legends revolve around the idea of Christ's blood in the Grail vessel, because the image of the resurrection-body did not satisfy them. That is why the whole discussion was taken up again at the time of the announcement of the dogma of the Assumption of Mary. Through Mary's assumption and coronation, the masculine triad in heaven is completed by a fourth, feminine being. Thus, a quaternity is constituted, representing a genuine totality symbol, not merely a postulated one. "The totality of the Trinity is a mere postulate, for outside it stands the autonomous and eternal adversary with his choirs of fallen angels and the denizens of hell. Natural symbols of totality such as occur in our dreams and visions, and in the East take the form of mandalas, are quaternities or multiples of four, or the squared circles."[50]

401   It is no accident that the alchemists selected the symbol of the *stone* for their god-image because this symbol emphasizes the principle of matter, because it is to be found everywhere, it is "cheap," and its fabrication lies within the reach of every man.[51] All these qualities compensate certain defects in the official ecclesiastical Christ-image: "an air too rarefied for human needs, too great a remoteness, a place left vacant in the human heart. Men felt the absence of the 'inner' Christ who belonged to every man. Christ's

---

[48] Cf. "Transformation Symbolism in the Mass," CW 11, § 427 f.
[49] Ibid., § 435.
[50] C.G. Jung, "The Visions of Zosimos," CW 13, § 127. Jung devoted a special study to the problem of the Trinity and the fourth in "A Psychological Approach to the Dogma of the Trinity," CW 11 §§ 169 ff. Cf. also Jung's foreword to Zwi Werblowsky, *Lucifer and Prometheus*, CW 11, §§ 468-473.
[51] Cf. "The Visions of Zosimos," CW 13, § 126.

spirituality was too high and man's naturalness was too low."[52] In the image of the stone, however, the "flesh" is glorified, but not by being transformed into spirit; instead the spirit appears to be condensed or "fixed" in matter. The stone is thus a symbol of the inner god in man and is not, like Christ, the "son of man" but rather a "son of the universe" (*filius macrocosmi*), because it did not come from the conscious mind of man but "from the border regions of the psyche that open out into the mystery of cosmic matter."[53] The figure of Christ is only light and perfect: this one-sidedness was necessary in order to make possible a broadening and intensification of consciousness; but this led in the course of time to a split and to an almost unbearable moral conflict in man.[54] In addition, the *anima rationalis* has been exalted to such an extent that it has broken and become an irreligious scientific rationalism, attempting to repress everything dark and irrational.[55] The symbol of the stone, however, signifies a compensation: it contains the opposites in an undivided state of nature.[56] Thus, there are really two symbols of the Self which anticipate the duality in man of conscious and unconscious[57] and today it is our task to reconcile these two powers in ourselves, as the modern dreams cited in the preceding chapter appeared to be trying to do.

402   The philosopher's stone is not only, like Christ, man's redeemer, but is also and at the same time a god who must be redeemed by man.[58] The alchemist imitates Christ to such an extent that, like him, he acquires a power to redeem, which he then exercises in the interest of the god hidden in matter. In fact, it is really an unconscious, more deeply pervasive continuation of Christian mysticism, a continuation of which the adept himself, however, never becomes clearly conscious. "Had the alchemist succeeded in forming any concrete idea in place of Christ – or, to be more exact,

---

[52] Ibid., § 127.
[53] C. G. Jung, "The Philosophical Tree," CW 13, § 384.
[54] C. G. Jung, "The Spirit Mercurius," CW 13, §§ 291 – 293.
[55] Ibid., § 293 f.
[56] Ibid., § 295.
[57] Ibid., § 297.
[58] On this point, cf. *Psychology and Alchemy*, CW 12, § 451.

that he, regarded not as ego but as self, had taken over the work of redeeming not man but God. He would then have had to recognize not only himself as the equivalent of Christ, but Christ as a symbol of the self. This tremendous conclusion failed to dawn on the medieval mind."[59] For the Indian mentality, on the other hand, this insight is so self-evident that sometimes it appears to us as delusory. Nevertheless, the enormous attraction which the Indian spirit exerts on so many Westerners these days is to be explained on the basis of this constellation. This spirit could form a bridge for us – a bridge whose approach has already been prepared by alchemy – for bringing our own unconscious contents into consciousness.

403   The Gnostics, in their way, had already come to a similar deep understanding of Christ as symbol of the Self, but they were caught in an inflation.[60] They felt themselves to be superior to the "blind multitude," in possession of a mystery which set them apart. "This overweening attitude arose from an inflation caused by the fact that the enlightened [one] has identified with his own light and confused his ego with the self. . . . He forgets that light only has a meaning when it illuminates something dark and that his enlightenment is no good to him unless it helps him to recognize his own darkness."[61] The Church realized the danger of the gnostic unrealism and therefore insisted on the practical, concrete aspects of the symbol. Are we today, after 2,000 years, mature enough to understand and realize man's divinity without forgetting our smallness and darkness? The phenomenon of the Self, in which all the opposites are united, is, as Jung constantly stressed, simply inconceivable, a mystery with which one had better not identify, as long as one is in possession of one's normal faculties. Man himself cannot master the uncanny polarity within his own nature; instead he must learn to understand it as an objective psychic content within himself[62], as a numinous experience which in the past was reserved for the few, but which takes hold of more and more people in the contemporary world.[63]

[59] Ibid., § 452, cf. § 412 f.
[60] Cf. C.G. Jung, "Transformation Symbolism in the Mass," CW 11, §§ 435 – 439.
[61] Ibid., §§ 438, 446.
[62] Ibid., § 446.
[63] Ibid., § 448.

The stone *is* an experience within us, but it is not the ego. Hence Jung's question, when as a boy he sat on the stone, "Am I the one who is sitting on the stone, or am I the stone on which *he* is sitting?" A good deal of wisdom is needed to bear this paradox.

404   In 1950, when Jung, who was a skilled mason, was working on an addition to his holiday home, a workman brought him a cubic cornerstone which had been incorrectly measured and could not be used for building – the "stone that the builders had rejected." He knew at once that *this* was the stone that he should transform into a reminder of the *lapis*.[64] On the front face he carved a circle and in it a *Kabir*, the Telesphoros of Asklepios, with a lantern in his hand; around him he carved the inscription in Greek,

405   Time is a child – playing like a child – playing a board game – the kingdom of the child. This is Telesphoros, who roams through the dark regions of this cosmos and glows like a star out of the depths. He points the way to the gates of the sun and to the land of dreams.

406 And on the other two visible sides of the stone Jung carved alchemical sayings about the philosopher's stone. One of them runs as follows:

407   I am an orphan, alone: nevertheless, I am found everywhere. I am one, but opposed to myself. I am youth and old man at one and the same time. I have known neither father nor mother, because I have had to be fetched out of the deep like a fish, or fell like a white stone from heaven. In woods and mountains I roam, but I am hidden in the innermost soul of man. I am mortal for everyone, yet I am not touched by the cycle of aeons.

---

[64] Cf. C.G. Jung, *Memories*, pp. 253 – 255. Jung was 75 years old at the time. He understood very well how to handle stone and tools. A couple of years ago the son of a stone mason from the neighbourhood said to me, "These days, masons don't know how to work with natural stone any more. But old Jung, down there by the lake, he knew all right. He knew the right way to take a stone in your hand." Cf. also Fowler McCormick, in *Carl Gustav Jung: A Memorial Meeting*, p. 10 ff.

408 In this stone Jung created a memorial to his tower on the upper lake, and to its real occupant, the Self – and to that mysterious life which he called the unconscious, of which so little is as yet really understood.

Chapter 12
Breakthrough to the *Unus Mundus*

409   In the early stages of the alchemical work, the symbol of the hermaphrodite often appears, a monstrous being who represents a union of the opposites which has taken place *too early*. He has to be cut up with the sword and boiled, so that his inner opposites can later be united in the "chymical marriage" as a complete man and a complete woman. In certain respects, the hermaphrodite symbolizes the fate of alchemy itself. In alchemy there was also too early a marriage between knowledge of the nature of matter and of the unconscious psyche – or if not a marriage, then at least a mixture. The separation of the two aspects began in the 17th century with the growth of a more rationalistic outlook; since that time, chemistry – in its tempestuous further development – and physics have got rid of almost all psychological mythologems and symbols in order to understand the real nature of matter in an increasingly unbiased and objective way. Jung, on the other hand, took up the rejected masculine-spiritual half of the hermaphrodite and went to work to demonstrate that alchemical symbolism is an expression of the collective unconscious. He also attempted, quite intentionally, to leave out of account any possible connection between psychic and biological, physiological and, finally, microphysical processes, although he was in fact convinced of such a connection.[1] The disadvantage of such a procedure, as Jung pointed out, lies in the fact that in this case the psychic is explained in terms of the psychic – what is lacking is the possibility of reconstruction in another medium, as is done by the physicist, for example, when he

---

[1] Cf. C.G. Jung's remarks on this subject in "Analytical Psychology and Education," CW 17, § 157.

reconstructs an atomic process in his psychic "theory,"[2] although his work, too, is handicapped by an uncertainty factor, since observation alters the object observed. "As physics has to relate its measurements to objects, it is obliged to distinguish the observing medium from the thing observed, with the result that the categories of space, time and causality become relative."[3]

410   The microphysical world of the atom, however, exhibits certain features whose affinities with the behaviour of the psyche is striking, and thus, it may someday be possible after all to reconstruct psychic processes in another medium outside the psyche, namely in the world of the basic particles. This is probably going on all the time without our knowledge, as the psyche perceives the physical world.[4] Without at first being aware of the parallelism, Jung developed concepts and models that show an astonishing similarity to those of modern physics. Outstanding among these is the concept of complementarity in quantum physics between particles or quanta and waves, but in depth psychology between the contents of consciousness and those of the unconscious. The view of all processes as energetic, as processes of energy, is another such model, as is the discovery of a certain relativity of time and space both in the realm of elementary particles and in that of the deeper layers of the unconscious. Finally, as already mentioned, there is the fact that in both disciplines, account must be taken of the effect of the "observer" on the observed.

411   But this parallelism in thought-models is not all. There are indications that physical energy and psychic energy may be but two aspects of one and the same underlying reality. If this turns out to be the case, the world of matter will then appear as, so to speak, a mirror-image of the world of spirit or of the psyche, and vice versa.[5] From 1929 on, Jung observed a class of events that appear to point to a direct relation between psyche and matter. If one observes a series of dreams and unconscious processes in an individual over a

[2] Ibid., § 162.
[3] Cf. ibid., § 163.
[4] Cf. ibid., § 164.
[5] Cf. C.G. Jung, *Mysterium Coniunctionis*, CW 14, § 768 f.

considerable period of time, one sees that with some frequency, but sporadically and irregularly, a dream motif or an unexpected fantasy will appear in the material environment also, as an outer event, either in very similar form (which is recognized by parapsychology and explained as telepathy) or in a symbolical way, for instance if one sees a black-clad person in a dream and the next day receives news of a death.

412   Jung described such a combination of events as a *phenomenon of synchronicity*. The connection between the inner event (dream, fantasy), and the outer event appears not to be a causal one, that of cause and effect, but rather one of a relative simultaneity and of the same *meaning* for the individual who has the experience.[6] Such synchronistic phenomena appear with special frequency in certain situations in which an archetype is activated in the unconscious of the individual concerned (that is, when he is "in an excited state," as the physicist would say).[7] In such a moment it may seem that the constellated archetype also appears outside the psyche. Jung called this the "transgressive" aspect of the archetype, the aspect which extends into the world of matter, and also the psychoid aspect of the archetype, to the extent that the latter manifests psychically but not exclusively psychically.

413   The difficulty of formulating such synchronistic phenomena scientifically is that they are irregular and hence unpredictable happenings. They elude the statistical and frequency-probability calculations which have been the methods used up to the present time.[8] Jung himself came up against this difficulty when he finally decided to formulate a scientific interpretation of these phenomena which he had long been observing. In order to make it credible, he needed to find a way of giving statistical formulation to an already familiar phenomenon of archetypal constellations with concretely determinable events of similar meaning. He chose the traditional astrological correspondences to marriage, that is, the sun-moon and

---

[6] Cf. as fundamental for the above and for the rest of the chapter, "Synchronicity: An Acausal Connecting Principle," CW 8, §§ 816 – 958, especially §§ 870, 898, 905.

[7] Cf. ibid., § 955 f.; cf. also M.–L. von Franz, *Number and Time*, p.7.

[8] For a more detailed explanation of why the probability calculation is not adequate, cf. ibid., pp. 218 ff.

Mars-Venus conjunctions, because this correspondence is an example, in projected form, of the belief that marriage is connected with an archetypal constellation in the psychic background (which is projected onto heaven). That two people have married is an indisputable fact. The first statistical analysis showed an almost incredibly significant result.[9]

414   On obtaining this positive result, Jung was, however, not quite comfortable and as he sat in front of his tower in Bollingen one afternoon, he suddenly saw, through the interplay of light and shadow, a mischievous face laughing out at him from the masonry of the wall. (Later, with chisel and hammer, he brought this face out of the stone and perpetuated it as the trickster Mercurius.) The thought struck him: had Mercurius, the spirit of nature, played a trick on him? In a soberer and more sceptical frame of mind, he repeated the experiment with a second batch of horoscopes and this time the result was substantially less improbable. In all probability, then, the first result had itself been a meaningful coincidence, in other words, a synchronistic phenomenon! The archetype of the *coniunctio,* or marriage, (in this case, of psyche and matter) had been activated in Jung's psyche – it had been in an "excited state"; he had been emotionally interested to an unusual degree and the trickster had slipped into his hands a correspondingly supernatural, positive, statistical result! The reality of the synchronicity phenomenon, therefore, had once again been manifested, but the statistical "proof" was naturally entirely questionable.[10]

415   Jung then decided to lay the whole story before the reader, exactly as it had happened. As he reviewed the facts, he came back to a criticism of the absolute validity of acausality, which is on very shaky ground in atomic physics in any case, and suggested using as a model, along with causality, a principle which he called that of "acausal orderedness." There are, in fact, ordered "just-so" arrangements in nature for which we can find no *causal* explanations. One of the best known of these in microphysics is the

---

[9] Cf. C.G. Jung, "Synchronicity: An Acausal Connecting Principle," CW 8, § 897, and C. G. Jung, "An Astrological Experiment," CW 18, §§ 1174 ff.
[10] Cf. "Synchronicity," CW 8, § 896 ff.

radioactive period, which obviously manifests a certain "order," even though we cannot determine the time of disintegration of the single particle. There are similar phenomena in the psyche, as well; for example, our idea of natural numbers. All human beings are simply forced, by the very structure of their innate capacity to think, to acknowledge that the number 6 is a so-called "whole" number, that is, it consists of the sum of its parts, 1, 2 and 3, but no one could advance a causal psychological explanation for this. For us, it is simply evident; our psyche is apparently so structured that we have to look at it that way and not in any other way. All of the natural numbers, in Jung's opinion, are especially "primitive," that is, they are archetypal structures which reach farther into the depths of the unconscious than most. They demonstrate an "acausal orderedness" in the psyche. The synchronicity phenomena described above are also just-so correspondences of something inner and outer and cannot be causally explained, but they do not occur with regularity. For this reason, Jung called them *border phenomena* of acausal orderedness. He says[11],

416   The question now arises whether our definition of synchronicity with reference to the equivalence of psychic and physical processes is capable of expansion, or rather, requires expansion. This requirement seems to force itself on us when we consider the above, wider conception of synchronicity as an 'acausal orderedness.' Into this category come all 'acts of creation,' *a priori* factors such as the properties of natural numbers, the discontinuities of modern physics, etc. . . . I incline in fact to the view that *synchronicity in the narrower sense is only a particular instance of general acausal orderedness* – that, namely, of the equivalence of psychic and physical processes where the observer is in the fortunate position of being able to recognize the *tertium comparationis*.

---

[11] Ibid., § 955.

417   In the synchronicity phenomena, or instances of meaningful orderedness[12], images appear in the inner field of vision which stand in analogous, that is, in meaningful, relation to objective outer events, even when a causal relation between the two classes of events cannot be demonstrated.[13] This postulates an *a priori* meaning in nature itself, existing prior to human consciousness[14], a *formal factor* in nature which cannot be explained causally but, on the contrary, is prior to any attempt at explanation on the part of human consciousness. This formal factor of meaning Jung called "absolute knowledge," absolute because independent of our conscious knowledge. It is as if something somewhere were "known" in the form of images – but not by us.

418   The "intelligent" behaviour of lower organisms which are without a brain is probably connected with this "absolute knowledge";[15] it appears also to be independent of any knowledge mediated by the sense organs and points to the existence of a self-subsistent meaning in nature.[16] "Such a form of existence can only be *transcendental*, since, as the knowledge of future or spatially distant events shows, it is contained in a psychically relative space and time, that is to say in an irrepresentable space-time continuum."[17] In contrast to acausal orderedness (for example, the properties of natural numbers, or the discontinuities of physics) which occurs regularly, synchronicity phenomena are *acts of creation in time*.[18] This means nothing more or less than that creation is still continuing today, in the sense of "continuing creation," or *creatio continua*.[19] These acts of creation take place on the one hand within the pattern of an orderedness existing from all eternity, and on the other hand of a sporadically repeated orderedness. The recognition of such an orderedness affects us as *meaning*[20], which is why synchronistic phenomena in earlier

---

[12] Cf. ibid., § 938.
[13] Cf. ibid., § 856.
[14] Ibid., § 932.
[15] Cf. ibid., § 937.
[16] Ibid., § 938.
[17] Cited in ibid.
[18] Cf. ibid., § 955.
[19] Cf. ibid., § 957.
[20] A small mistake in Aniela Jaffé's *Myth of Meaning* (p. 150) should be corrected here. Jaffé says that meaning does not exist apart from human beings but is "created" by them, instead of saying that

times were always taken to be manifestations of divinity[21], or in China as a sign of Tao, of universal meaning. In 1967, I discovered that the number order of the *I Ching* is identical to that of the genetic code. This would seem to indicate that number is, in fact, a basic manifestation of the *unus mundus*. [22]

419   Apart from the eminent physicist Wolfgang Pauli, author of the essay "The Influence of Archetypal Ideas on the Scientific Theories of Kepler" (published originally in the same volume with Jung's paper on synchronicity), I know of no physicist who has made serious use of the suggested model of the principle of synchronicity in an attempt to explain certain contingent events in nature.[23] The subject, however, has awakened the interest of a few philosophically-oriented authors. Thus, Ernst Anrich, in *Moderne Physik und Tiefenpsychologie*[24], has dealt rewardingly with the idea of a final unity of all existence, in the delineation of which depth psychology and physics come together. Oddly, however, Anrich does not elaborate the theme of synchronicity, which he mentions only briefly, and he ends his book with a philosophically oriented confession in which the "fourth," the unique empirical manifestation of the *unus mundus*, on which Jung laid so much emphasis, is missing. Peter Urban, on the other hand, evidences more understanding of Jung's concern in his essay "Philosophische und empirische Aspekte der Synchronizitätstheorie."[25] He writes[26] that "the synchronicity model makes possible an adequate perspective in which to deal with several empirically proven parapsychological phenomena," which does not mean, however, that all the problems of parapsychology are thereby resolved. But, according to Urban, it does make possible a "specific characterization of the time-emotion relationship." Synchronistic

---

meaning is not *recognizable* apart from people. She is referring to the impossibility of establishing "objective" meaning, but that is the case with all knowledge of nature.

[21] Or of the devil, or of good or bad "spirits."

[22] Cf. my essay "Symbols of the *Unus Mundus*," in: *Psyche and Matter,* p. 39 – 62.

[23] It has, of course, been accepted by many of Jung's pupils. Cf. M.–L. von Franz, "The Synchronicity Principle of C. G. Jung," in: *Psyche and Matter,* p. 203 – 228; and "A Contribution to the Discussion of C.G. Jung's Synchronicity Hypothesis," ibid., p. 229 – 244. Cf. also M.–L. von Franz, *Number and Time,* op cit., p. 72, 96.

[24] Klett, Stuttgart 1963.

[25] *Grenzgebiete der Wissenschaft* 17, No. 4, J. Kral, Abensberg 1968, p. 347 ff.

[26] Ibid., p. 356 f. Jean Gebser's idea of the "invisible origin" or "lost primordial origin" has many points in common with Jung's concept of a *unus mundus*. Cf. Gebser, *Der unsichtbare Ursprung.*

phenomena are actually, as Jung emphasizes, of a parapsychological nature, so that it is not surprising that it is a professional parapsychologist, Hans Bender, who, together with John Mischo, has followed up Jung's attempt at an explanation objectively and in all seriousness. He investigated a series of dreams of a woman who had had an unusually large number of synchronistic experiences, particularly from the point of view that her experiences could be a question of telepathy or of synchronistic phenomena[27], and he drew the conclusion: "The coincidences between the dreams and the reality situations appear, as a category of occurrences, to correspond to the 'power of attraction of related things.' Some seem to be more readily apprehended by using the model of synchronicity (the extraordinary lies in the event itself) than with the model of Psi-capacity, in which the future event is regarded merely as the object of extrasensory perception."[28] The two points of view do not exclude one another but could be complementary.

420   Synchronistic thinking has always been more congenial to the eastern spirit than to western causal thinking. It was natural, therefore, that Manfred Porkert should be quick to make use of Jung's ideas in explaining Chinese science[29], and other Sinologists are in sympathy with them.[30] Nevertheless, it is still not possible to say that Jung's idea of synchronicity has been really acknowledged by Sinologists in general. Unexpectedly, though, something quite different is happening: American hippies, and recently a few hippie circles here in Europe, have rediscovered the *I Ching*, the Chinese *Book of Changes*, and often use its oracular technique. Thus, a new generation is growing up that is familiar with the principle of synchronicity on a *practical* level. Perhaps a few individuals of this generation will later on take an interest in scientific work which will bring this principle into our picture of the world. In any case in my experience it has been easy to discuss the problem of synchronicity

[27] "Praekognition in Traumserien," *Zeitschrift für Parapsychologie und Grenzgebiete der Psychologie* 4, No. 2/3, 1960/61; 5, No. 1, 1961; cf. also 4, No. 1, 1960 Francke, Bern-München.
[28] *Zeitschrift für Parapsychologie und Grenzgebiete der Psychologie* 5, No. 1, p. 45 f.
[29] "Wissenschaftliches Denken im alten China," *Antaios* II, Stuttgart 1961.
[30] Hermann Köster, Erwin Rousselle, Carl Hentze. Cf. also A. Rump, *Die Verwundung des Hellen als Aspekt des Bösen im I Ging*, diss. Zurich 1967.

in the circles of these young people without arousing emotional resistance, which still happens when the subject is raised with most scientists of the older generation. The Chinese, in their culture, have always aimed rather at an intuitive grasp of the world as a whole than at a clear rational understanding of details[31], and in respect to the former they discovered in the *I Ching* a kind of technical aid whose depths of meaning we are only now beginning to fathom.[32] The great commentators of the *I Ching* sought to explain the simultaneity of the psychic condition of the questioner with a synchronistic physical process[33] by means of *equivalence of meaning*[34], and to order it in images of 64 typical situations. In the West there is a parallel method, that of so-called geomancy which, however, has remained on a level of primitive magic and, so far as I know, has received a more serious philosophical interpretation only in Africa, in West Nigeria.[35] The Chinese philosopher Wang Fu Ch'I (1619-1692) attempted an "explanation" of the *I Ching* which is worth noting.[36] According to Wang, all existence is grounded in an all-embracing *continuum which contains its own laws within itself.* This continuum, however, dispenses with concrete appearance and is not directly accessible to sense perception. It forms, one might say, something like a latent psychophysical background to the world. From this continuum are differentiated, through its own inherent dynamic, certain images which, in their structure and their position, participate in the ordered lawfulness of the continuum. As a result of their lawfulness, or orderedness, these images also form a part of the world of number and can therefore be grasped by means of a numerical procedure. Wang Fu Ch'i's "images" are what Jung would call archetypal images. The *I Ching*, says Jung, "is a formidable psychological system that endeavours to organize the play of

---

[31] Cf. C.G. Jung, "Synchronicity: An Acausal Connecting Principle," CW 8, § 863.

[32] In spite of newer and supposedly better editions, the Diederichs 1923 version (often reprinted since), in Richard Wilhelm's translation, seems to me to be the best because it leads the reader into a deeper *understanding*. This is the version translated into English by C. F. Baynes.

[33] The fall of the coins or the distribution of the yarrow stalks.

[34] Cf. C.G. Jung, "Synchronicity," CW 8, § 865.

[35] Cf. B. Maupoil, *La Géomancie à l'Ancienne Côte des Esclaves*, Institut Ethnologique, Paris 1943; M.–L. von Franz, *Number and Time*, pp. 265 ff.

[36] Discovered by Hellmut Wilhelm, "The Concept of Time in the Book of Changes," *Man and Time*, pp. 219 f; M.–L. von Franz, *Number and Time*, pp.10 f.

archetypes . . . into a certain pattern, so that a "reading" becomes possible. The role of mediator between the happening in the outer world and the inner situation is then assigned to *number*."[37] The method best suited to the nature of change is, namely, that of counting. "Since the remotest times men have used numbers to establish meaningful coincidences, that is, coincidences that can be interpreted. There is something peculiar, one might even say mysterious, about numbers. They have never been entirely robbed of their numinous aura. . . . The sequence of natural numbers turns out to be unexpectedly more than a mere stringing together of identical units: it contains the whole of mathematics and everything yet to be discovered in this field. Number . . . and synchronicity . . . were . . . always brought into connection with one another . . . both possess numinosity and mystery as their common characteristics. . . . Number helps more than anything else to bring order into the chaos of appearances. It is the predestined instrument for creating order, or for apprehending an already existing, but still unknown, regular arrangement of 'orderedness.' It may well be the most primitive element of order in the human mind. . . . Hence it is not such an audacious conclusion after all if we define number psychologically as *an archetype of order* which has become conscious.[38] Remarkably enough, the psychic images of wholeness which are spontaneously produced by the unconscious, the symbols of the self in mandala form, also have a mathematical structure. . . . These structures not only express order, they create it." From this it follows irrefutably that the unconscious uses number as an ordering factor.

421   Inasmuch as synchronistic phenomena are *acts of creation in time*[39], the moment in time plays a significant role, as Jung's choice of the term "synchronistic"[40] indicates. It should therefore be possible to formulate a relation between number, the instrument we can use to comprehend synchronicity, and time. This relation did indeed attract a certain amount of attention in western speculation

---

[37] C.G. Jung, *Mysterium Coniunctionis*, CW 14, § 401.
[38] Cited in C.G. Jung, "Synchronicity," CW 8, § 870.
[39] Cf. ibid., § 955.
[40] From *chronos* – time.

about numbers for a long period, but this interest has lapsed in more recent times.[41] In Chinese culture, on the other hand, this relation was rather differently understood from the very beginning and was developed into a remarkable form. To the Chinese, time is by no means an empty context in which events take place; it is instead a continuing flow with a form whose contents can be qualitatively determined. All the events which occur in a given moment in time share the same quality, because they are exponents of one and the same momentary situation, from which fact one assumes that a picture is there, which can be "read" or understood.[42] Time becomes a "concrete continuum which possesses qualities or basic conditions capable of manifesting themselves simultaneously in different places by means of an acausal parallelism, such as we find, for instance, in the simultaneous occurrence of identical thoughts, symbols, or psychic states"[43] and other synchronistic phenomena. According to the Chinese view, the different aspects of the *unity of all existence* become manifest in certain typical "phases" of the process of change and these phases are indicated by numbers, or in other words, number in China characterizes *time-variable patterns* or "ensembles" of inner and outer factors within the "world-all." It represents methods of grouping which reflect a ground-plan of the whole cosmos which is, in the end, mathematical.[44] Proceeding from this fundamental attitude toward number, the Chinese used it for an intuitive understanding of the principle of synchronicity.

422   Towards the end of his life, Jung planned to concentrate his research on the nature of natural numbers in which he saw archetypal structures and a primordial, very primitive expression of the spirit, that is, of psychic dynamics. He made notes of the individual mathematical characteristics of the first numbers but was unable to carry out his plan. In my book *Number and Time*, I have tried to go a bit farther in this direction, to show how numbers can

---

[41] For details, cf. M.–L. von Franz, *Number and Time*, pp. 248 ff; C.J. Whitrow, *The Natural Philosophy of Time*, p. 29 ff.

[42] Cf. C.G. Jung's Foreword to the English edition of Wilhelm's translation of the *I Ching*, p. iv (and in CW 11).

[43] Cited in C.G. Jung, "Richard Wilhelm: In Memoriam," CW 15 § 81.

[44] Cf. M.–L. von Franz, *Number and Time*, pp. 42 ff. Cf. Marcel Granet, *Das Chinesische Denken*, p. 215.

be understood as archetypal configurations of motion common to both psychic and physical energy, through which an isomorphism of psychic and physical facts is expressed. This is only a tentative start, however, and it should be pursued by more qualified investigators.

423   Jung assumed that in the deepest level of the collective unconscious we come up against a bit of unknown Nature: "Nature which contains *everything*, also, therefore, what is unknown, *including* matter." The foreknown aspect of things is found there, on an "animal" or "instinctive layer of the psyche," and it is when *this* level is activated in people that synchronistic events are most often observed.[45] On this level, the psyche appears as a quality of matter or matter as a concrete aspect of the psyche, but owing to the inevitability of the psychic phenomenon "there cannot be only *one* approach to the mystery of existence, there have to be at least two: namely, the material occurrence on the one hand and the psychic reflection on the other,"[46] and a decision as to which is mirroring which is scarcely possible.

424   The most essential and certainly the most impressive thing about synchronistic occurrences, the thing which really constitutes their numinosity, is the fact that in them the duality of soul and matter seems to be eliminated. They are therefore an *empirical* indication of an ultimate unity of all existence, which Jung, using the terminology of medieval natural philosophy, called the *unus mundus*.[47] In medieval philosophy this concept designates the *potential pre-existent model of creation in the mind of God*, in accordance with which God later produced the creation. It is, according to John Scotus Erigena, "God's vital or seminal power which changes from a Nothing which is beyond all existence and non-existence into countless forms." God accomplishes this

---

[45] Cf. C.G. Jung, "Ein Brief zur Frage der Synchronizität," *Zeitschrift für Parapsychologie und Grenzgebiete der Psychologie 5*, No. 1, p. 4.

[46] Cf. ibid., p. 5. Cf. also M.-L. von Franz, *Number and Time*, p. 17; A. Jaffé, *From the Life and Work of C.G. Jung*; A. Jaffé, *The Myth of Meaning*.

[47] C.G. Jung, *Mysterium Coniunctionis*, CW 14, § 659 ff. The term *unus mundus* must not be confused with Erich Neumann's concept of *Einheitswirklichkeit*; Neumann means the fusion of the individual with his environment – "Die Psyche und die Wandlung der Wirklichkeitsebenen," *Eranos Jahrbuch 21*, pp. 169 f – while Jung means an irrepresentable "potential" background to the world.

transition into creation through his Son or through the Wisdom, the *Sapientia Dei*, "through which He knows Himself." God creates the All in her, that is, in the primary causes which are not only *in* God but *are* God himself. The *Sapientia Dei* is a homogeneous, or uniform, image which proliferates into a multitude of primordial forms, but nevertheless remains always one. The primordial forms are "ideas" or "prototypes" of all existing things.[48] Hugh St. Victor also calls the *Sapientia Dei* the "exemplar" of the universe, or the *archetypus mundus* in the mind of God, the model for his creation of the universe.[49] This *archetypus mundus* is not only an absolute unity, it is also *timeless*; in it "things which are not simultaneous in time exist simultaneously outside time." "Temporal succession is without time in the eternal wisdom of God."[50] Gerhard Dorn, a pupil of Paracelsus, saw the completion of the alchemical work in a union of the individual with this *unus mundus* in the mind of God[51], for the Mercurius of the alchemists *is* actually himself this *unus mundus*, "the original non-differentiated unity of the world or of Being."[52] Jung saw an anticipation of the concept of the *collective unconscious* in these medieval speculations. In the collective unconscious, too, experience shows that everything appears to be more or less connected with everything else in a unity, although certain archetypes emerge with relative distinctness, round which individual images cluster. The way in which the multiplicity of the collective unconscious is ordered in a unity is revealed with especial clarity in mandala symbolism.[53] "The mandala symbolizes, by its central point, the ultimate unity of all archetypes as well as of the multiplicity of the phenomenal world, and is therefore the empirical equivalent of the metaphysical concept of a *unus mundus*."[54] The

---

[48] "De divis naturae" I, 5; III, 8, 8, 19; II, 20, 31. Migne, *Patrologia Latina* (tom.) CXXII. Cf. M.–L. von Franz, *Number and Time*, pp. 172 ff.

[49] Cf. M.–L. von Franz, *Number and Time*, p. 172.

[50] The last two citations are from Prosper Aquiranus, "Sententiae ex Augustino delibatae" XLI and LVII, cited in C.G. Jung, "Synchronicity," CW 8, § 957, footnote 149.

[51] Cf. C.G. Jung, *Mysterium Coniunctionis*, GW 14, § 659ff, esp. § 663 and § 767 ff.

[52] Ibid., § 660.

[53] Ibid.

[54] Ibid., § 661.

alchemical equivalent is the lapis and its synonyms, in particular the microcosm.[55]

425   In the Chinese psychic world of the *I Ching*, two levels of existence underlie the oracle: the mandala of the "Order of Earlier Heaven," which is timeless, and the mandala-wheel of the "inner-worldly Order of Later Heaven," which brings forth (cyclic) time. Such double mandalas are also found elsewhere and they illustrate the timelessness of the *unus mundus* and its intrusions into time in synchronistic occurrences.[56] The wheels do not, however, encroach upon one another, which is an expression of the incommensurability of the timeless with the temporal world. Such double mandalas would seem to have been especially designed to demonstrate the principle of synchronicity. They indicate that it is a question of a threshold or borderline phenomenon between consciousness and the deeper levels of the unconscious.

426   While the mandala represents a psychological analogy to the *unus mundus,* synchronistic phenomena represent a *para-psychological* analogy which points *empirically* to an ultimate *unity of the world*. In the end, everything that happens happens in one and the same world and is part of it. "Undoubtedly the idea of the *unus mundus* is founded on the assumption that the multiplicity of the empirical world rests on an underlying unity, and that not two or more fundamentally different worlds exist side by side or are mingled with one another. Rather, everything divided and different belongs to one and the same world, which is not the world of sense but a postulate whose probability is vouched for by the fact that until now no one has been able to discover a world in which the known laws of nature are invalid. . . . All that *is* is not encompassed by our knowledge, so that we are not in a position to make any statements about its total nature. Microphysics is feeling its way into the unknown side of matter, just as complex psychology is pushing forward into the unknown side of the psyche. . . . But this much we do know beyond all doubt, that empirical reality has a transcen-

---

[55] Ibid. Cf. also M.-L. von Franz, "The Idea of the Macro- and Microcosmos in the Light of Jungian Psychology," *Psyche and Matter*, p. 180 ff.
[56] Cf. a more detailed account in M.-L. von Franz, *Number and Time*, pp. 235 ff.

dental background. The common background of microphysics and depth psychology is as much physical as psychic and therefore neither, but rather a third thing, a neutral nature which can at most be grasped in hints since its essence is transcendental.[57] . . .

427   The transcendental psychophysical background corresponds to a "potential world" in so far as all those conditions which determine the form of empirical phenomena are inherent in it."[58]

Dorn describes the experience of the *unus mundus* as the opening of a "window on eternity" or of an "air-hole" into the eternal world. And in fact an experience of the Self helps a person to extricate himself from the stifling prison of a conscious image of the world that is too narrow, so that he can be open to the transcendental and so that, at the same time, the transcendental can touch him and move him. It can be compared with the *sartori* experience of Zen Buddhism or with the *samadi* of certain Eastern teachings or with awakening to the Tao in China. Our finite human life has meaning only when it is related to the infinite through the "window on eternity." This is why Jung writes in his memoirs[59], "Only if we know that the thing which truly matters is the infinite can we avoid fixing our interest upon futilities, and upon all kinds of goals which are not of real importance. . . . If we understand and feel that here in this life we already have a link with the infinite, desires and attitudes change. *In the final analysis, we count for something only because of the essential we embody, and if we do not embody that, life is wasted.* In our relationships to other men, too, the crucial question is whether an element of boundlessness is expressed in the relationship.

428   The feeling for the infinite, however, can be attained only if we are bounded to the utmost. The greatest limitation for man is the 'self'; it is manifested in the experience: 'I am *only* that!' Only consciousness of our narrow confinement in the self forms the link to the limitlessness of the unconscious. In such awareness we experience ourselves concurrently as limited and eternal, as both the

---

[57] Cf. C.G. Jung, *Mysterium Coniunctionis*, CW 14, § 767 – 769.
[58] Ibid.
[59] *Memories*, p. 357. Italics are by the author.

one and the other." That is why the experience of the Self, for Dorn, means a glimpse through the "window of eternity," but is at the same time a concentration of one's own being in the "stone," at one and the same time a boundless enlargement and the narrowest of limitations.

429   While in the image of the Anthropos, as symbol of the Self, the underlying unity of all human beings is emphasized, the unity of all cosmic existence is more to the fore in the symbolism of mandalas and of the philosophers' stone – as an irrepresentable background to the world. A genuine experience of this *unus mundus* was in the past almost always hoped for as an event which would happen only at the time of death or after death. Certain ancient Egyptian liturgies for the dead, for example, depict in moving language the way in which the deceased becomes one with all the gods and all the matter of the World-All and is thus finally united with the primordial father Nun, the primordial ocean itself, from which the world was created. The one who has died can then pass effortlessly through all crude material objects and "go into and out of all forms." In Chinese Taoism, this happens to he who has become one with the *unus mundus*: "He walks on air and clouds; he rides on sun and moon and travels beyond the world. Life and death cannot change his self." He understands how "to make the innermost essence of nature his own, and to let himself be moved by the changing primordial powers, to wander there, where there are no boundaries."[60]

430   Jung himself once had a similar experience when he hovered between life and death for a week, after an accident which resulted in a heart and lung infarct. He had ecstatic visions, which he describes in his memoirs.[61] As he hovered high in space above the globe of the earth he saw a stone floating in space (the "pneumatic stone" of the alchemists!), a temple made of a monolith. As he approached the temple, he "had the feeling that everything was being sloughed away; everything I aimed at or wished for or thought, the whole phantasmagoria of earthly existence, fell away or was stripped

---

[60] Chuang Dsi, *Das Wahre Buch von südlichen Blütenland*, pp. 19, 4.
[61] *Memories*, p. 320 ff.

from me. . . . There was no longer anything I wanted or desired. I existed in an objective form; I was what I had been and lived." In the temple all those people "to whom I belonged in reality" were waiting for him. In other visions he experienced the "sacred wedding" of the gods. "I do not know exactly what part I played in it. At bottom it was I myself: I was the marriage. And my beatitude was that of a blissful wedding." It was only with the greatest reluctance and suffering that Jung was able to return to the confinement of earthly existence.[62] What he describes in these visions is a feeling experience of the *unus mundus*, in which everything happening in time is experienced as if gathered up into a timeless objective oneness.

---

[62] Ibid., p. 325 f.

⬥

Chapter 13
Individual and Society

431   Through his investigations into the principle of synchronicity Jung prepared the way for an eventual alliance between depth psychology and microphysics, and therewith for the use of his ideas by contemporary natural science. The concept of psychoid archetypes, especially of the archetype of number, will presumably form a bridge to the meeting with biology, physiology, and microphysics. In principle there are no longer any obstacles to the acceptance of Jung's thought. In other fields, such as anthropology, historical research, mythology, Sinology, theology, and parapsychology, tentative discussion has already begun, and every year more and more serious scholars and scientists are taking notice of his views. Still, it cannot be predicted with any certainty that Jung's discoveries will be widely recognized in the years ahead. There is *one* obstacle to such recognition, as I see it, and that is a political and sociological tendency to see and look for ultimate values in collective factors and goals. Although the coming generation shows a heightened interest in the human being and the human situation, and although young people are taking up psychology and sociology in ever greater numbers, these two disciplines give far more attention at present to statistically calculable, collective human behaviour than they do to the understanding of the individual. Jung is either virtually ignored by those who take this view of the world or he is deprecated as a representative of outdated "bourgeois individualism."[1] This superficial equation of "individualism" with "individuation" needs no

---

[1] Even Peter Hofstaetter quotes only one sentence from Jung in "Gruppendynamik," *Rowohlts deutsche Enzyklopädie*, and that is torn from its context. He mentions Jung only incidentally in his *Einführung in die Sozialpsychologie*, and on p. 369 of that volume confuses archetypes with consciously dominant collective images.

comment, since it reveals complete ignorance of what Jung understood by the word "individuation." All the same, there is a genuine
opposition which seems to me to be worth closer consideration. The
fundamental question concerns the psychological validity of the
statistical methods generally used at present. Jung regarded
statistical statements in the fields of psychology and sociology in the
same way modern physics has come to understand them, namely as
a *mental abstraction*. If I say, for instance, that the stones in this pile
have an average size of 5 square inches, that may be true in theory
but in reality, I would have to look around for a long time before I
found even *one* stone of exactly that size. The actual stones are all of
different sizes and *they are the reality*; the other is a detached idea
about reality in the mind of the observer. The same thing is true of
all general statements about human nature and behaviour: only the
individual is the true carrier of life. One cannot speak of the "life"
of millions of people, because millions of different people are the
carriers of life; *they* are the ultimate reality.[2]

432   Theories based on statistics formulate an ideal average, in which
all exceptions at either end of the scale are abolished and replaced
by an abstract mean. In this way a psychology or an anthropology
is developed which is "generally valid," it is true, but which gives us
an abstract picture of the average man, from which all individual
traits have been erased. This method leads to scientific *knowledge*
but not to *understanding* of the actual human being.[3] The result is
an increasingly *unrealistic, rational picture of the world* in which the
individual figures only as a sort of marginal phenomenon.[4] Jung
writes[5], "We ought not to underestimate the psychological effect of
the statistical world-picture; it thrusts aside the individual in favour
of anonymous units that pile up into mass formations. Instead of the
concrete individual, you have the names of organizations and, at the
highest point, the abstract idea of the State as the principle of
political reality. The moral responsibility of the individual is then

---

[2] Cf. C.G. Jung, "The Undiscovered Self," CW 10, §§ 488 – 588.
[3] Ibid., § 494 f.
[4] Ibid., § 498.
[5] Ibid., § 499.

inevitably replaced by the policy of the State *(raison d'état)*. Instead of moral and mental differentiation of the individual, you have public welfare and the raising of the living standard. The goal and meaning of individual life (which is the only *real* life) no longer lie in individual development but in the policy of the State, which is thrust upon the individual from outside and consists in the execution of an abstract idea which ultimately tends to attract all life to itself. The individual is increasingly deprived of the moral decision as to how he should live his own life, and instead is ruled, fed, clothed and educated as a social unit, and amused in accordance with the standards that give pleasure and satisfaction to the masses.[6] . . . But if the individual, overwhelmed by the sense of his own puniness and impotence, should feel that his life has lost its meaning – which, after all, is not identical with public welfare and higher standards of living – then he is already on the road to State slavery and without knowing or wanting it, has become its proselyte."[7] The idea of the State, or of society, becomes an almost quasianimate reality, from which everything is expected. "In reality it is only a camouflage for those individuals who know how to manipulate it. Thus, the constitutional State drifts into the situation of a primitive form of society – the communism of a primitive tribe where everybody is subject to the autocratic rule of a chief or an oligarchy."[8] The individual, for all practical purposes, is eliminated and is no longer in a position to realize the meaning of his life.

433   Admittedly, individual deviations from social norms *can* make a thoroughly abnormal and antisocial person, but just as often there are deviations which could be fruitful. Adolf Portmann has shown that even among animals there are unusual individuals who lead the way to positive alterations in the behaviour of the group. It sometimes happens that a bird, for example, instead of migrating southwards will try to stay in the spot where it has summered. If the experiment fails, the bird disappears without a trace, but if it succeeds, then the following year a few other birds will follow his

---

[6] Ibid.
[7] Ibid., § 503.
[8] Ibid., § 504.

example; if this continues, it can lead to an alteration in the behaviour of the whole group. It is always the individual, however, who tries out the new adaptation form. On the animal level, a genuine polarity between individual and group is, then, already apparent.[9]

434   Current sociological literature is constantly stressing the fact that the "we-interest" must come ahead of the "I-interest," but in doing so it does not distinguish between conscious and unconscious. "We-interest" is simply a content of collective *consciousness*, not of the group unconscious, and "I-interest" is only a very small part of what goes to make an individual; these labels fail to take into account the individual's unconscious. The fact that historically collective consciousness is probably older and more important than ego-consciousness is relevant here; the ego-consciousness of the individual appears to be a late acquisition and even today is a very labile factor in a great many people. The person with a weak ego usually makes up for his defective ego-consciousness with an obstinate infantile egoism which cannot be abolished until his ego has been strengthened and has thereby matured to the point of a certain degree of social awareness.

435   But what is it, in fact, which holds the group together prior to the emergence of ego-consciousness? Obviously, the same forces that also unite animal groups, namely certain social instincts and, in the case of human beings, archetypal behavioural patterns that are realized in symbolic customs, practices, rituals, totemistic symbols, and religious symbols, that is, in the spiritual or psychological *forms* of the instincts.

436   On the primitive level, the systems of marriage classes, especially, play a part. Jung makes a distinction, at this level, between an exogamous energy, which apparently aims at breaking up groups and family clans that are too narrow, from an endogamous (incest) tendency which works against the disintegration of the group. The social order based on marriage class systems, however, was dissolved long ago, except in the cases of a few very primitive peoples. The

---

[9] For a detailed discussion, see M.–L. von Franz, 'On Group Psychology', *Psychotherapy*.

exogamous order has spread until, with the passage of time, it has swept away all barriers. By way of reaction, the endogamous tendency (which might be called the tendency toward social cohesion) has shifted to the fields of religion and politics[10], where at first religious societies and sects grew up – one is reminded of the brotherhoods and the Christian ideal of "brotherly love" – and later the national state developed. But the increase of international interaction among men and women of all levels and the weakening of the confessional religions bid fair to wipe away or to bridge even these borders, so that mankind is in danger of sinking into an amorphous mass without any visible sign of social order. There is only one possible way of preventing a massive regression to "totemistic" groups (one thinks of the many youth groups, or of revolutionary ideological cliques), and that is by a withdrawal of the endogamous tendency into the individual, which would make it possible for him to *consolidate the fragmented pieces of his own personality, and thereby to become an individual who is secure within himself.*[11] That is why the archetypal motif of the Anthropos and the mandala is constellated with such intensity today in the collective unconscious: to control the otherwise unavoidable dissolution into the mass psyche. And *that* is why the problem of love, or of transference, as discussed above, is of such great importance, for it is the basis of the capacity for human relationship. It is vitally important not only for the individual but also for society, and indeed for the moral and spiritual progress of mankind.[12]

437   In the final analysis, only the symbol of the Self has the power to bind human beings to one another in the sense of a loving community, because it is "the point of reference not only of the individual ego but of all those who are of like mind or who are bound together by fate."[13] Since the Self in its deeper layers is of a collective nature, it represents and makes possible the *participation mystique* of all human beings, "the unity of many, the *one* man in all

[10] Cf. C.G. Jung, "The Psychology of the Transference," CW 16, § 443.
[11] Ibid.
[12] Ibid., § 449.
[13] Cf. C.G. Jung, "Transformation Symbolism in the Mass," CW 10, § 419.

men." That is why it becomes visible in the image of a cosmic man, the *homo maximus*, the *vir unus*, or the Indian purusha, who is at one and the same time the innermost being of the single individual and of all humanity.[14] It is only through the Self that human beings can relate to each other without the admixture of egotistical motivation, while ego-feelings are almost always darkened by all sorts of conscious or unconscious egocentric motivations. The freedom and dignity of the individual, therefore, are rooted only in the transcendental Anthropos.[15]

438 However small and unimportant such an effort may seem to be, nevertheless when one of us concerns himself with the integration of his shadow and of the animus or anima, then this work is carried out in a field onto which "the whole weight of mankind's problems has settled" in our day.[16] If we do not give our full attention to these inner powers, they overwhelm us from within and stifle consciousness; nothing is then left into which the contents of the unconscious can be integrated.[17] "Mass-degeneration does not come only from without: it also comes from within, from the collective unconscious. Against the outside, some protection was offered by the *droits de l'homme* which at present are lost to the greater part of Europe, and even where they are not actually lost, we see political parties, as naïve as they are powerful, doing their best to abolish them in favour of the slave state, with the bait of social security."[18] Our freedom is threatened in equal measure from within by politico-social trends, whose "eternal truths" – that is, whose archetypal images – overwhelm the conscious ego with a state of possession which has a political appearance. In this case, we are contaminated or identical with the archetype of the Anthropos, in primitive *participation mystique*, and cannot distinguish it from our finite empirical ego. This means inflation, with all its consequences of human unrelatedness, loss of soul and inner hardening.[19] Jung writes in a letter[20],

---

[14] Ibid.
[15] Ibid., § 444.
[16] C.G. Jung, "The Psychology of the Transference," CW 16, § 449.
[17] Ibid., § 502.
[18] Ibid.
[19] Ibid., §§ 443 f.

"Even a small group is ruled by a suggestive group-spirit which, if it is good, can have very favourable social effects, although at the cost of the spiritual and moral independence of the individual. The group enhances the ego, which is to say that one becomes bolder, more adapted, more secure, more impudent and less prudent while the *self* is diminished and shoved into the background in favor of the average. . . . Group therapy, in my opinion, educates or trains only social man. In our time, which attaches so much importance to the socialization of the individual, because a special capacity for adaptation is required, psychologically oriented group education certainly has increased importance." "I am fully aware that the individual must adapt himself to society, but I must stand up for the inalienable rights of the individual, because he alone is the carrier of life and because today he is perilously threatened by the levelling-off process. Even in the smallest group only that is acceptable which is accepted by the majority. It must be accepted with resignation. But resignation alone is not enough. On the contrary, resignation encourages self-doubt, from which an isolated individual, who has to stand for something, will in certain circumstances suffer severely. Unless one is something oneself, social relations are meaningless."

439   Seen historically, it has always been the religions which have offered mankind a standpoint *outside* the merely material conditions of existence and their problems, a standpoint from which these needs could be coped with psychologically, or spiritually.[21] Only from a religious standpoint can an individual freely make judgements and decisions. Religion "builds up a reserve, as it were, against the obvious and inevitable force of circumstances to which everyone is exposed who lives only in the outer world and has no other ground under his feet except the pavement."[22] But most religions have compromised with the world and with the State to such an extent that they have become creeds, that is, collective institutions with general convictions instead of a subjective relation to the irrational inner powers. Only the latter can guarantee truly

---

[20] Cf. C.G. Jung, *Letters*, Vol. 2, p. 450 ff.
[21] Cf. C.G. Jung, "Religion as the Counterbalance to Mass-Mindedness," CW 10. § 505 ff.
[22] Ibid., § 506.

ethical behaviour, while ethics without individual responsibility before God is simply conventional morality.

440 The creeds even combat the individual relation to God and describe it as pietism, sectarianism, confused spiritualism, etc. They have become established churches and public institutions to which the majority of people pay mere lip service. The individual, however, requires an inner experience of the transcendental, if he is to hold his own against the physical and moral power of the world; otherwise he succumbs to it. Today the totalitarian states even claim authority in religious matters. "The State takes the place of God; that is why, seen from this angle, the socialist dictatorships are religions and State slavery is a form of worship. . . . Free opinion is stifled and moral decision ruthlessly suppressed, on the plea that the end justifies the means, even the vilest. . . . Only the party boss, who holds the political power in his hands, can interpret the State doctrine authentically, and he does so just as suits him."[23] "The ethical decision of the individual human being no longer counts – what alone matters is the blind movement of the masses, and the *lie* thus becomes the operative principle of political action."[24]

441 "Both the dictator State and denominational religion lay quite particular emphasis on the idea of *community*. This is the basic ideal of 'communism', and it is thrust down the throats of the people so much that it has the exact opposite of the desired effect: it inspires divisive mistrust. . . . As can easily be seen, 'community' is an indispensable aid in the organization of masses and is therefore a two-edged weapon.[25] . . . For this reason one cannot expect from the community any effect that would outweigh the suggestive influence of the environment; . . *a real and fundamental change in individuals . . . can come only from the personal encounter between man and man.*"

442 Western man, however, has fallen under the spell of the ideal of community, and for some time now the churches have been making every effort to encourage "group experience" and to attract the

[23] Ibid., § 511.
[24] Ibid., § 515.
[25] Ibid., § 516, in which what follows is summarized.

public to every sort of social "come-on," from marriage and job bureaus to pop concerts, instead of doing their job, which is to speak to the 'true man' within."[26] Responsible church authorities run from this task, preferring to give in to their own power complex, where they play what Jung used to call "the game of shepherd and sheep."[27]

443   This same tendency has also become rampant as a trend in the narrower field of psychotherapy, in so-called self-experience groups and similar kinds of group therapy. Jung never tired of emphasizing, however, that any healing transformation can occur only in the single individual. "Surgery is performed on the *individual*. I mention this fact because of the modern tendency to treat the psyche by group analysis, as if it were a collective phenomenon. The psyche as an individual factor is thereby eliminated."[28] As Jung also emphasizes in the aforementioned letter, the group spirit threatens the spiritual and moral independence of the individual. "In view, however, of the notorious human inclination to cling to other people and to -isms, instead of finding security and independence in oneself, which is what is needed, the danger exists that the individual will make the group into a father and mother and therefore remain as dependent, insecure and infantile as before."[29]

444   Furthermore, group therapy obviously needs a leader, whose role should be looked at a bit more closely. Viewed historically the role of the priest as well as that of the doctor and the psychotherapist goes back to those of the shaman and medicine man with primitive peoples, among whom the one was more the guardian of traditional ritual and the other more the protector of the life of the soul, especially in connection with the right way of dying and the further journey of the soul after death.[30] Curing the soul of individual and collective states of possession is really the principal task of the shaman. If an ordinary man meets a demon or a spirit – that is, psychologically, an archetypal content of the unconscious – he will

---

[26] Cf. M.–L. von Franz, "On Group Psychology," *Psychotherapy*, p. 295.
[27] Ibid.
[28] Cf. C.G. Jung, *Mysterium Coniunctionis*, CW 14, § 124, FN 58.
[29] Cf. C.G. Jung, *Letters*, Vol. 2, p. 219 f; cf also C. G. Jung, "Analytical Psychology and Education," CW 17, § 159; M.–L. von Franz, "On Group Psychology," *Psychotherapy*, pp. 283 – 296.
[30] Cf. M. Eliade, *Shamanism*.

be possessed by it and will therefore fall ill. The same thing often happens to a shaman during his period of initiation, but he knows how to free and cure himself by means of the right kind of behaviour in relation to the spirit-world. Later on, this enables him to help ordinary sufferers who cannot help themselves.[31] The symbolic inner experiences which the shaman lives through during his period of initiation *are identical with the symbolic experiences the man of today lives through during the individuation process.* One may therefore say that the shaman or the medicine man was the most individuated, that is, the most conscious, person of the group to which he belonged. This fact gave him a natural authority which came from within himself, with other members of his group. From the very beginning, however, even in this early stage, the shaman's *shadow* appeared, namely the *psychopathic black magician,* who misused his inner experience (the experience of the spirit-world) for personal power aims. The real shaman has an unintended power in that the spirits, especially the archetype of the Self, stand behind him, but the black magician claims collective power with his ego and consequently is psychically ill. Modern examples of this are Rasputin and Hitler, and similar figures. *The individuation process, however, is incompatible with any sort of social power claim,* and that is also true when such a person pretends to be a well-meaning, moderate liberal leader or a "fatherly shepherd of souls."

445   When, as a consequence of the development of the denominational and established churches, the suppression of individual symbol-formation in the unconscious began, the authority of the official representatives of the churches became more pervasive and emphatic, if it was no longer rooted in the "natural" authority possessed by those who were more conscious. The expression "shepherd of souls" and the comparison of the faithful with a "herd of sheep" speaks volumes. No one took into account the fact that the dependence and willingness to follow shown by the congregations also represented a great danger, because these same "sheep," who have become accustomed to following, will at any time

---

[31] Cf. M.–L. von Franz, "On Group Psychology," *Psychotherapy,* p. 294.

follow another, possibly destructive, authority just as willingly. Jung reproached Protestantism with not having gone far enough along its own way, namely to the point where the individual would take up the *whole* burden of responsibility for his inner life, so that the old game of "sheep and shepherd" could once and for all be discarded.[32] There is no other way of finding that "inner man," the Anthropos, who is similar to the Christ figure but not identical with it.[33] This inner Anthropos will never play the game of sheep and shepherd," "because he has enough to do to be a shepherd to himself." He is and shows himself to be autonomous in respect to dogma, and therewith to the collective.

446   The collective organizations of the totalitarian states, like those of the denominational churches, interpret all of the individual impulses and movements of the psyche as egoistic willfullness. Science depreciates them as "subjectivism," and the denominations as heresy and spiritual pride[34], which is ironical when one recalls that "Christianity holds up before us a symbol whose content is the individual way of life of a man, the Son of Man, and that it even regards this individual process as the incarnation and revelation of God himself."[35] "Are not Jesus and Paul prototypes of those who, trusting their inner experience, have gone their individual ways in defiance of the world?"[36]

447   Naturally there is also an egotistical, asocial individualism, and society has the right to protect itself against "arrant subjectivisms,"[37] but the more society is composed of de-individualized human beings, the more defenceless it becomes against a power grab by ruthless individualists. It is precisely the suggestive influence of a favourable environment which strengthens the human tendency "to expect everything from outside and to put on a front that simulates the thing that has not happened, namely a genuine far-reaching

---

[32] I am repeating here what I have written in my essays on group therapy!
[33] Cf. C.G. Jung, *Mysterium Coniunctionis*, CW 14, § 488 ff.
[34] Cf. C.G. Jung, 'The Undiscovered Self', CW 10, § 529.
[35] Ibid.
[36] Ibid., § 536.
[37] Ibid., § 535.

change of the inner man"[38] – which is of the greatest urgency today. For "*Resistance to the organized mass can be effected only by the man who is as well organized in his individuality as the mass itself*,"[39] that is, by the one who has had the experience of an inner synthesis in the symbol of the Self.

448   The contemporary division of society into a "right" wing and a "left" wing is nothing but a neurotic dissociation, reflecting on the world stage what is happening in the individual modern man: a division within himself, which causes the shadow – that is, what is unacceptable to consciousness – to be projected onto an opponent, while he identifies with a fictitious self-image and with the abstract picture of the world offered by scientific rationalism[40], which leads to a constantly greater loss of instinct[41] and especially to the loss of *caritas*, the love of one's neighbour so sorely needed in the contemporary world.[42] "In the West it was chiefly the mass factor, and in the East technics, that undermined the old hierarchies. The cause of this development lay principally in the economic and psychological uprootedness of the industrial masses, which in turn was caused by the rapid advance in technics. But technics, it is obvious, are based on a specifically rationalistic differentiation of consciousness which tends to repress all irrational psychic factors. Hence there arises, in the individual and nation alike an unconscious counter-position which in time grows strong enough to burst out into open conflict."[43] Since Jung wrote those words in 1954, the outbreak of the irrational counter-reaction has come to the surface, in the revolt of contemporary youth against technology and industry and academic rationalism: "Destroy what is destroying you!" But this revolt is exhausting itself, for the time being, in a sort of passion for destruction and in outbursts of shadow elements from which no solution can come into being.

---

[38] Ibid., § 537.
[39] Ibid., § 540.
[40] Ibid., § 559.
[41] Ibid., § 562.
[42] Ibid., § 580.
[43] Cf. C.G. Jung, "Transformation Symbolism in the Mass," CW 11, § 443.

449   Today, more than 30 years after Jung's death, signs of the shadow are even more apparent than in his time. Violence, blackmail, lies, and coercion of the individual are everywhere in evidence, and the state or "society" are expected to make good everything that the individual has neglected, through stupidity. But although the situation becomes darker and more threatening, it contains *one* germ of hope, namely that it may have the effect of a shock treatment and that as a result contemporary man, with his lamentable childishness and weakness, may be replaced by a man of the future who will know himself and know he himself is responsible for his own fate and that the state is his servant, not his master.[44] Jung cherished a slight hope for a possible change in the Soviet Union because state slavery there had reached such an extreme that a reaction seemed almost inevitable. The Prague uprisings of 1968, the Sacharow memorandum, and the revolt of other courageous men have shown that the flame of freedom has not been extinguished in Eastern Europe and that decent and honest individuals who hate tyranny and lies will speak out from time to time, there as elsewhere. The Gulf War, the insidious wars in the Balkans and in the Third World, and the catastrophe on Tiananmen Square remind us that the fight for freedom is far from over. But will we have enough sense to protect those freedoms still left to us? In spite of the creeping danger of chaotic individualism, the respect for human rights and recognition of the irrational, hence the creative ground of being, is at present guaranteed nowhere save in those states where the democratic freedoms are still more or less alive.

450   In a genuine democracy there is no cheap illusory inner peace. Instead, the fight between the opposites is internalized and expresses itself in the form of confrontation between individuals and groups. Battles are fought within legal and constitutional limits. That is one step on the road to the next goal: the discovery of the opponent *within ourselves*, in the insatiable power drive of our own shadow. Man's aggressive instincts cannot simply be turned off – human nature must be reckoned with as it is. Democracy, therefore, is a

---

[44] Cf. C.G. Jung, "The Fight with the Shadow", CW 10, § 452.

meaningful institution for it allows the necessary conflicts within certain national borders. Better still would be if we were to recognize that our worst enemy lives in our own heart.[45]

451   Jung took his obligations as a citizen of democratic Switzerland in all seriousness. Although there were many times when he would have liked to drive to his beloved Bollingen on a Sunday, he stayed at home whenever an important issue was to be voted on and discussed the question ahead of time with his gardener, Hermann Müller, who saved the available newspaper articles on controversial issues and gave them to Jung to read.[46] He even had a good word for the much maligned Swiss characteristics of obstinacy and mistrust, because, he said, these qualities have often served to ward off poisonous infections from abroad and fashionable and fantastic ideas. "In sober scepticism in regard to every passing wave of propaganda, in the sure instinctive contact with nature, and in the self-limitation grounded in self-recognition, I see far more health for our fatherland than in excited talk about renewal and hysterical attempts to seek out new directions. After a while, it will be discovered that nothing really 'new' has ever happened in world history. It would be possible to speak of something really *new* only in the inconceivable event that reasonableness, humanity and love should win a lasting victory."

452   That which in Jung's view constitutes our greatest danger today is the presence everywhere in the West of subversive minorities who hold the incendiary torches ready and rejoice in the protection of our sense of justice.[47] He often emphasized that one should not underestimate the danger inherent in this stratum, since it is not wise to be too optimistic about the "reasonableness" of the average citizen; among our respectable citizens there are too many criminals and personalities with latent pathology who, behind an appearance of normality, are undermined by unconscious illnesses and perverse tendencies. In the event of an upheaval, such individuals suddenly rise to the surface and strengthen the position of the public agents

[45] Ibid., § 456.
[46] Cf. A. Jaffé, *From the Life and Work of C.G. Jung,* p. 108.
[47] Cf. C.G. Jung, "The Undiscovered Self," CW 10, § 489.

of violence. They are ruled by infantile wish-fantasies and personal affects and resentments and infect the normal citizen with these, unless the latter already happens to be aware of these things in his own shadow.[48] Our habitual depreciation of the problem of evil has created a bad situation for us in this respect, and it is possible, in my opinion, that we may not mature into a more conscious evaluation of the situation until we have lived through any number of kinds of calamities. In any case, Jung was aware that he stood alone in a compensatory counter-position to the trends of the time and that his work and his ideas might be completely forgotten (as was the case with Meister Eckhart, for example) and not rediscovered for several centuries. This knowledge saddened him, but it did not change his conviction. He knew that, in spite of his aloneness, he had *one* secret but powerful ally on his side: the still unconscious spirit of the future.

---

[48] Ibid., § 490.

Chapter 14
Le Cri de Merlin

453 Through all the ages, poets and artists have often been prophets because their work, or the material for it, comes to them from the same depths of the collective unconscious in which the major transformations of a particular era are in process of creation. Thus, in the Middle Ages and on up to the 17th century, it was not only alchemy whose symbolism anticipated the problems of the new age; there was also a considerable number of poetical works, flowering largely at the same time as knighthood and chivalry, namely the legends and works of poetry which revolved around the vessel of the Holy Grail and the Grail stone.[1] The greatest poet to have dealt with this theme was Wolfram von Eschenbach, and in his *Parzival* there is a direct connection with alchemical symbolism. In this epic, the Grail vessel is replaced by a stone which has fallen from heaven. Wolfram calls it the *lapis exilis*, the term used by the alchemists for "their" stone. In other versions, the Grail was originally a leaden vessel in which Nicodemus caught the blood of the Crucified as it flowed from his heart. There is also a version in which Christ is supposed to have appeared to Joseph of Arimathea in prison and to have entrusted him with the vessel containing his blood. This is the reason Joseph was chosen as the first guardian of the Grail; he was then succeeded by a series of Grail kings.

454   In antiquity and in the Middle Ages blood was thought of as the seat, or home, of the soul, and the real-life principle of any creature. Seen from this point of view, the Grail vessel, which is also compared with Christ's tomb in some texts, contains the *living soul of Christ*, the mysterious essence of his being. Although his transfigured body

---

[1] For the following, cf. especially Emma Jung and M.-L. von Franz, *The Grail Legend*.

disappeared from the world, the living essence continues to work this side of eternity and gives forth the healing effect of his presence.

455   Certain versions of the history of the origins of the legend and of the symbolic meaning of the Grail motif point to connections with the Egyptian Osiris myth. The Egyptian pharaoh during his lifetime was an incarnation of the sun-god Ra; when he died, he became the god Osiris, who represented the passive, dark, feminine side of the godhead and of nature.[2] According to the legend, when Osiris was murdered by the demonic god Seth, the latter shut him into a lead coffin and threw it into the sea. The coffin was washed up onto the shore and hung suspended from a heath bush. The lead Grail vessel containing the blood of Christ was lost in a similar fashion, according to certain versions of the legend. It fell into the sea and was washed onto land in France, where it hung from a fig tree. It began to work miracles and was thereby discovered.

456   Osiris's lead coffin was identified with the alchemical retort as early as the third century of this era, and was described as the real "secret of alchemy."[3] It also played a part in the Isis mysteries of late antiquity. In the cultic ritual, Osiris was represented by a round vessel filled with water from the river Nile. The Roman author Apuleius describes it as "a symbol of the sublime and ineffable mysteries of the Goddess, which are never to be divulged."[4] A curved or curled-up snake was often engraved or carved on the handle. This snake is the numen who guards the tomb and protects the transformation of the god. Psychologically, it symbolizes the deepest levels of the collective unconscious, where the transformation of the god-image occurs. This mythological motif of the god who continues to live after his death in a vessel filled with a living substance (blood, water from the Nile) adds a new aspect to the previously discussed motif of the death of the god and the transformation of the aging king: when the accepted god-image ages and dies in collective unconsciousness, then the psychic substance,

---

[2] Cf. H. Jacobsohn, "Der altägyptische, der christliche und der modern Mythos," *Gesammelte Schriften*, p. 79- 116, especially, p. 99 ff; and H. Jacobsohn, "Das Gegensatzproblem im altagyptischen Mythos," ibid., p. 51 – 78.

[3] Cf. C.G. Jung, "The Visions of Zosimos," CW 13, § 96.

[4] *The Golden Ass*, translated by Robert Graves, p. 233.

or elements, which had in him become visible, sink back to the region whence all revealed god-images which command belief once originated, into the psychic background and into the hidden life of the unconscious psyche. During the first millennium of this era, the image of Christ was "the sun of righteousness" for our culture. It was kept alive in and by its participation in the inner psychic life of men and women – through the dreams and visions of the faithful and of martyrs[5] (one thinks of the visions of Paul) which were regarded as living witnesses to the reality of the Redeemer. With the in-stitutionalization of belief, however, the above-mentioned repression of individual symbol formation began to set in. Dreams and visions were censured and the king began to age and grow rigid. But the living continuity of psychic life preserved that which was lost to collective consciousness. Both poets and common people began to weave fantasies around the idea of the tomb of Christ[6] (one thinks at once of the Crusades) and the vessel which contained the living psychic mystery of Christ.

457   The image of the vessel is a *feminine* symbol, a maternal womb in which the figure of the god-man is transformed and reborn in a new form. This motif has historical connections with the gnostic religions as well as the Osiris myth. According to gnostic tradition, one of the highest gods, one who stood above the ambiguous creator of the world, sent down to mankind a mixing vessel (*krater*) in which those who sought a spiritual transformation and a higher conscious-ness must be immersed.[7] This gnostic teaching was taken over by one of the most important of the early alchemists, Zosimos of Panopolis, and from Zosimos onward the alchemists continued to work with the motif of the mysterious vessel of transformation. "One the procedure, one the vessel, one the stone" is unceasingly

---

[5] Cf. Von Franz, *Niklaus von Flüe and Saint Perpetua, A Psychological Interpretation of their Visions,* CW 6, Chiron, Asheville, 2022, p. 190ff.

[6] Cf. Helen Adolf, *Visio Pacis, Holy City and Grail.*

[7] Cf. C.G. Jung, *Memories, Dreams, Reflections,* p. 227 f. Jung writes: "The motif of the Gnostic Yahweh and Creator-God reappeared in the Freudian myth of the primal father and the gloomy superego deriving from that father. In Freud's myth he became a daemon who created a world of disappointments, illusions, and suffering. But the materialistic trend . . . had the effect of obscuring for Freud that other essential aspect of Gnosticism: the primordial image of the spirit as another, higher god who gave to mankind the *krater* (mixing vessel), the vessel of spiritual transformation. The *krater* is a feminine principle which could find no place in Freud's patriarchal world."

emphasized in the texts. Paradoxically, the vessel and its contents are identical: they are fire, water, Mercurius, and even the *lapis* itself.[8] In medieval mysticism the vessel became an image of the soul, which receives divine grace[9], and Caesarius of Heisterbach says that the soul is a spiritual substance and round like the sphere of the moon, "*like a glass vessel provided with eyes both in front and in back*," which can see the whole universe.[10] The Grail vessel also possesses a "seeing" quality since, according to the saga, the voice of an invisible presence issues from it, reveals what is hidden and foretells the future.

458   When Jung was in India early in 1938[11], he was overwhelmed by the "grandeur of India and its unutterable need, its beauty, and its darkness" and was once again concerned with the problem of evil.[12] While there, he had an unexpectedly impressive dream:[13]

459   "I found myself, with a large number of my Zurich friends and acquaintances, on an unknown island, presumably situated not far off the coast of Southern England. It was small and almost uninhabited. The island was narrow, a strip of land about twenty miles long. . . . On the rocky coast at the southern end of the island was a medieval castle. . . . Before us rose an imposing *belfroi*, through whose gate a wide stone staircase was visible. We could just manage to see that it terminated above in a columned hall. This hall was dimly illuminated by candlelight. I understood that this was the castle of the Grail, and that this evening there would be a 'celebration of the Grail' there. This information seemed to be of a secret character, for a German professor among us, who strikingly resembled old Mommsen, knew nothing

---

[8] Cf. C.G. Jung, "The Visions of Zosimos," CW 13, § 96 ff; C.G. Jung, *Psychology and Alchemy*, CW 12, §§ 116 and 338.
[9] Cf. Grete Lüers, *Die Sprache der deutschen Mystik des Mittelalters*.
[10] *Dialogus miraculorum* IV, 34. Cf. E. Jung and M.–L. von Franz, *The Grail Legend*, p. 138.
[11] On the invitation of the British Government of India to participate in the celebrations connected with the 25th anniversary of the Indian Science Congress; on this trip he received three honorary doctorates from the universities of Calcutta, Allahabad and Benares.
[12] Cf. *Memories*, p. 305.
[13] Ibid., p. 310 f.

about it. [There follows a discussion with this professor, whom Jung tries to convince that the Grail stories, which the professor thinks are simply the dead past, are psychically still the living present."

460 Jung continues:

461 "I looked around somewhat helplessly, and discovered that I was standing by the wall of a tall castle; the lower portion of the wall was covered by a kind of trellis, not made of the usual wood, but of black iron artfully formed into a grapevine complete with leaves, twining tendrils, and grapes. At intervals of six feet on the horizontal branches were tiny houses, likewise of iron, like birdhouses. Suddenly I saw a movement in the foliage; at first it seemed to be that of a mouse, but then I saw distinctly a tiny, hooded gnome, a *cucullatus*, scurrying from one little house to the next. 'Well', I exclaimed in astonishment to the professor, 'now look at that, will you. . . .'"

462 "At that moment a hiatus occurred, and the dream changed. We . . . were outside the castle, in a treeless, rocky landscape. I knew that something had to happen, for the Grail was not yet in the castle and still had to be celebrated that same evening. It was said to be in the northern part of the island, hidden in a small, uninhabited house, the only house there. I knew that it was our task to bring the Grail to the castle. [With six companions, Jung set out, but reached an arm of the sea which separated the island into two halves. His companions gave up and fell asleep.]

463 I considered what could be done, and came to the conclusion that I alone must swim across the channel and fetch the Grail. I took off my clothes. At that point I awoke."

464 Jung then explains that he had been impressed for a long time by the fact that the dream of the Grail seemed to be still alive in England. "This fact had impressed me all the more when I realized the concordance between this poetic myth and what alchemy had

to say about the *unum vas*, the *una medicine*, and the *unus lapis*. Myths which day has forgotten continue to be told by night, and powerful figures which consciousness has reduced to banality . . . are recognized again by poets and prophetically revived; therefore they can also be recognized 'in changed from' by the thoughtful person. The great ones of the past have not died, as we think; they have merely changed their names. 'Small and slight, but great in might', the veiled Kabir enters a new house."

465   The Grail story, as is well-known, does not revolve only around the vessel but also includes the motif of the "old, sick king"; Amfortas suffers from a wound which cannot be healed, and he cannot recover and hand over the authority to Parzival until the latter asks the question about the Grail. The ailing king is a symbol of the aging or senescent Christian attitude. His wound is in the thigh, or the genital region, undoubtedly an allusion to the problem of sexuality, unsolved in Christendom. The Christian hero Parzival is supposed to supersede him, but instead he keeps encountering dark Anthropos figures, with whom he must come to grips. But no union with this dark brother ever takes place, which delays the performance of his task.

466   Jung felt that the spiritual suffering of his own father, who wanted to "believe" and was no longer able to, and who was an image of the Amfortas fate. He writes[14], "My memory of my father is of a sufferer stricken with an Amfortas wound, a 'fisher' king whose wound would not heal – that Christian suffering for which the alchemists sought the panacea. I as a 'dumb' Parisfal was the witness of this sickness during the years of my boyhood, and, like Parsifal, speech failed me. I had only inklings."

467   Curiously enough, another saga motif of the highest importance was joined to the legend of the Grail vessel as early as the Middle Ages: *the figure of Merlin*. In several French versions of the Grail saga, Perceval, in his search for the Grail, keeps coming across the tracks of a mysterious being who is finally revealed as the real "secret of the Grail": it is *Merlin*, the great magician, medicine man and bard

---

[14] *Memories*, p.241 f.

of Celtic mythology. Perceval soon meets him as a man with a wooden leg, as an old man with two snakes wound around his throat, as a grey-haired hermit clad in white like a spirit, or he simply meets him suddenly as an *ombre* (shadow) across his path. The man gives Perceval advice or some commission, or his beautiful daughter appears, riding a mule, and tells the hero what he must do.

468   Merlin has a remarkable fate, according to the saga: begotten by the devil and born of an innocent virgin[15], he renounces – under the influence of his pious mother and his teacher, the priest Blaise – the evil inclinations inherited from the devil and becomes a seer and bringer of health and wholeness. Nevertheless, those primal opposites which the Christian teaching has torn apart into an unresolvable conflict exist together in his nature.

469   When Merlin is still a boy, the King Vertigier decides to have him killed so that his blood may be mixed with the mortar to be used in building an impregnable tower which is under construction but which keeps collapsing. If the blood of a fatherless boy is mixed with mortar, the building will proceed successfully. Merlin promises to reveal the reason for the troubles with the tower if he is allowed to live; thereupon he says that there are two dragons in the water under the tower, a red one and a white one, and that the tower keeps collapsing because the two dragons disturb it with their fighting. As soon as excavations are made and the dragons are uncovered, the white one kills the red one. Merlin then reveals that the red dragon stands for King Vertigier, the usurper of the throne, while the white one represents the rightful heirs, Uter and Pendragon. It shortly comes to pass that the rightful heirs conquer the evil usurper and Merlin is appointed permanent counsellor to Uter (Pendragon dies shortly after the victory). He stands by the king in word and deed, and has the gift of being able to see into all people and to foretell the future. On his advice, the monument at Stonehenge is erected. Merlin had already instructed his stepfather, Blaise, to write down what he would tell him: the story of the vessel of the Holy Grail and of Joseph of Arimathea and of his own birth. He says to Blaise: "The

---

[15] Cf. E. Jung and M.–L. von Franz, *The Grail Legend*, pp. 350 – 51.

Apostles write nothing concerning Our Lord that they have not seen or heard for themselves; thou too must write nothing about me except what thou hast heard from me. *And because I am dark and always will be, let the book also be dark and mysterious in those places where I will not show myself.*" Merlin then tells King Uter the story of the Holy Grail and says to him: "Thou must believe that Our Lord came down to earth to save mankind." Then he relates the story of the vessel and of Joseph of Arimathea and calls upon the King to set up the so-called third table of the Grail. The first table was that at which Christ celebrated the Last Supper with his disciples; the second, which is square, is a table Joseph of Arimathea set up and on which he kept the Grail in memory of the Last Supper. The third table, which the King must now provide, must be *round*. The King chooses Carduel, in Wales, as the site of the table, and summons 50 especially selected knights to the Round Table at Whitsuntide. This is the origin of the Brotherhood of the Knights of the Holy Grail. Merlin, however, declares that from then on, he will stay far away: "Those who are gathered together here must believe what they see happen and I would not that they should think that I had brought it about."

470   Merlin later plays a part in connection with the birth and coronation of King Arthur, but again he does not remain at court. He retires into the forest, for he has become mad with suffering over the war between the Britons and the Scots and is reluctant to be lured back into the company of men. A house is built for him in the forest, his *esplumoir*, in which he can devote himself to astronomical observations, "where he explores the stars and sings about future happenings." Outwardly his appearance is that of a hairy wild man or a friend and guardian of the forest animals.[16] A spring miraculously breaks through the ground near his tower, and when a madman wanders by and drinks from it, he is cured of his madness. (The same spring had previously cured Merlin's own despair over the warring among men.) To the cured madman Merlin

---

[16] For the connection with the Celtic Buile Suibne, cf. Brigitte cBenes, "Spuren von Shamanismus in der Sage des Buile Suibne," *Zeitschrift für keltische Philologie*, 1961.

speaks the significant words, "Now must thou go hesitantly forward to thy confrontation with God, *who gave thee back to thyself,* and now mayest thou remain with me, in order, again *in obedience to God (obsequio Domini),* to redeem the days of which madness robbed thee."

471   In the saga, Merlin's laugh is famous. He laughs aloud, for instance, when he sees a poor tattered man sit down, or when he meets a youth who is buying himself a pair of shoes. He laughs because he knows that the poor man, without being aware of it, is sitting on a buried treasure, and that the youth will die the next day and will not need the shoes. This kind of knowledge makes Merlin lonely because he has so much more of it than the people around him. When he becomes very old, with a reputation for great holiness and is surrounded by many pupils who have learned about the things of the spirit from him, he bids farewell to all this and "withdraws into eternal silence." He vanishes into his *esplumoir* or into a rock tomb, and with the passage of time, men speak only of "Merlin's stone," *perron de Merlin,* where time and again heroes meet together to set out upon some brave adventure. According to other versions, he becomes entangled in love for the fairy Viviane and disappears with her into the beyond, and now only his distant cry is heard, the famous "cri de Merlin."[17]

472   Merlin is an archetypal figure; he is one of the many figures of pagan anchorites and of Christian forest friars who carry on and keep alive the pattern of fate of the archaic shamans and medicine men.[18] As Ch.-A. Williams has shown, Merlin also possesses traits which link him with Elijah.[19] The saga relates that a cleric named Helyas wrote down Merlin's prophecies; this Helyas is none other than Elijah, the same who appears in alchemistic tradition as *Helyas artista.*[20]

473   But Elijah, it will be remembered, is the figure who first appeared in Jung's active imagination as the personification of the wisdom of

---

[17] Cf. Heinrich Zimmer, 'Merlin', *Corona* 9, Part 2.
[18] Cf. Benes, *op cit.* All these forms are interrelated inasmuch as they seek the primordial inner experience through introversion.
[19] *Oriental Affinities of the Legends of the Hairy Anchorite,* 2 (May 1925).
[20] Cf. P. Zumthor, *Merlin le Prophète,* p. 198.

the unconscious (later superseded by the figure of Philemon). Elijah appears, as has been mentioned, in legends of late antiquity and the Middle Ages, as a prophetic personality with some roguish or mischievous traits; he loves to wander about the world, disguised and unrecognized, testing people.[21] He was also identified with the Metatron, God's first angel, who was called, among other things, "the little Yahweh." His image, therefore, is that of one aspect of God, inasmuch as the individuation process, when seen from the unconscious side, does in fact amount to a process of incarnation of the godhead. The Metatron was equated, in late antiquity, with Elijah, Enoch, and John the Baptist, and in the work called *Pistis Sophia* it is written of him, "The power of the little Yahweh, that of the man, and the soul of the prophet Elijah, they are bound to the body of John the Baptist."[22] Both Elijah and John are pictured as being unusually hairy hermits; this characteristic was also transferred to Merlin. The latter had a close connection with the symbol of the stag, which brings him closer to the Celtic god Kerunnus and to the figure of the alchemistic Mercurius, and the alchemists actually recognized him in their Mercurius (the *cervus fugitivus*). But Mercurius is a personification of the alchemical transformation substance *par excellence*, and these connections make it plain that Merlin is therefore *himself the secret of the Grail vessel*. That is why Jung's dream was saying to him, in short, "Seek the Self within, and then you will find both the secret of the Grail and the answer to the spiritual problem of our cultural tradition." This secret, however, is contained nowhere save in the symbolism of alchemy. On returning home from India, Jung therefore began anew to work with alchemy, this time more deeply than ever.

474   When, almost 20 years after the Grail dream related above, Jung became acquainted with details of the Merlin saga[23], he was shaken. Without in the least being aware of the fact, he had done and experienced so much which is reminiscent of Merlin: he had built himself a stone tower, in order to get away from the bustle of

---

[21] Cf. C.G. Jung, Letter to Père Bruno O.C.D, CW 18/II, §§ 1518 – 1531.
[22] Cf. H. Bietenhard, *Die himmlische Welt im Urchristentum und Spätjudentum*, p. 157.
[23] He had known only Heinrich Zimmer's work, "Merlin," in *Corona* 9, Part 2.

everyday life, a refuge like Merlin's *esplumoir*[24] (the word *esplumoir* has never been explained, but it probably refers to the cage in which falcons moulted, hence a place for "moulting," or transformation). Jung's tower was where he lived in No. 2, his larger form, or Self. He writes[25], "From the beginning I felt the Tower as in some way a place of maturation – a maternal womb or a maternal figure in which I could become what I was, what I am and will be. It gave me a feeling as if I were being reborn in stone. . . .

475   At Bollingen I am in the midst of my true life, I am most deeply myself. Here I am, as it were, the "age-old son of the mother." That is how alchemy puts it, very wisely, for the 'old man,' the 'ancient,' whom I had already experienced as a child, is personality Number 2, who has always been and always will be. . . . In my fantasies, he took the form of Philemon, and he comes to life again at Bollingen.

476   There I live in my second personality and see life in the round, as something forever coming into being and passing on."[26]

477 Jung's tower, like Merlin's, had at first no spring. Jung had to take his water from the lake. After a few years, however, a spring was discovered quite nearby; he had it captured and used it. It is true that it heals no form of madness, but the spring that Jung discovered in his psyche assuredly does. Like Merlin, too, Jung was known for his laugh. If there was humour in a situation, he always saw it and rejoiced in it. Once a driver stopped his car in the street above the "Casa Eranos" and went to ask who down there had laughed so heartily and infectiously. Laurens van der Post once said to Jung, "You are really the only honorary Bushman, because you are the only European I know who laughs like the first man on earth!"[27]

[24] Cf. Jessie Weston, "The Esplumoir Merlin," *Speculum*, 1946, p. 173.
[25] *Memories*, p. 252.
[26] Ibid., p. 265,
[27] *Bulletin Supplement of the Analyt. Psychol. Club of New York* 24:1 (January 1962).

478   When Jung had finished hewing out the cubic stone mentioned earlier, it occurred to him to chisel "Le Cri de Merlin" on the backside of it.[28] "For what the stone expressed reminded me of Merlin's life in the forest, after he had vanished from the world. Men still hear his cries, so the legend runs, but they cannot understand or interpret them.

479   Merlin represents an attempt by the medieval unconscious to create a parallel figure to Parsifal. Parsifal is a Christian hero, and Merlin . . . is his dark brother. In the twelfth century, when the legend arose, there were as yet no premises by which his intrinsic meaning could be understood. Hence he ended in exile, and hence "le cri de Merlin" which still sounded from the forest after his death. . . . His story is not yet finished, and he still walks abroad. It might be said that the secret of Merlin was carried on by alchemy, primarily in the figure of Mercurius. Then Merlin was taken up again in my psychology of the unconscious and – remains uncomprehended to this day!

480   Just as Merlin once said, "Je voel mieus m'ame sauver que la terre,"[29] and then renounced all worldly power, so Jung, too, rejected the temptation to make any bid for spiritual power. He would say to his pupils when they asked him to make certain decisions for them, "I refuse to turn into an old power devil like Freud. Make your own decisions. When I am no longer here, you will still have to know what to do." He always tried to help other people to be free and self-reliant.

481   The poet and bard Taliesin, so the legend goes, later joined Merlin in his forest observatory. Beautiful shamanic poetry has been ascribed to him, for example in the *Book of Ballymote*:[30]

482   I am the wind that blows upon the sea;
     I am the ocean wave;
     I am the murmur of the surges;

---

[28] *Memories*, p. 255. He did not carry out this idea.
[29] "I would sooner save my soul than (have) the earth." From the *Huth-Merlin*. Cf. also E. Jung and M.–L. von Franz, *The Grail Legend*, p. 393.
[30] Cf. C. Squire, *Celtic Myths and Legends*; cf. also *The Grail Legend*, p. 309. There is a similar beautiful poem in the *Book of Cecan*; cf. E. Jung and M.–L. von Franz, *The Grail Legend*, p. 370.

I am seven battalions;
I am a strong bull;
I am an eagle on a rock;
I am a ray of the sun;
I am the most beautiful of herbs;
I am a courageous wild boar;
I am a salmon in the water;
I am a lake upon the plain;
I am a cunning artist;
I am a gigantic, sword-wielding champion;
I can shift my shape like a god. . . .

483 Each of these statements by Taliesin about himself would also fit the alchemistic Mercurius, for *he* is also extolled in the texts as wind, as sea-water, as hero, as eagle, as the sun's rays and as a shape-changing god – as a spirit pervading all of nature.

484 Does it not sound rather like Taliesin's poem, when Jung says of his life in the tower at Bollingen[31], "At times I feel as if I am spread out over the landscape and inside things, and am myself living in every tree, in the splashing of the waves, in the clouds and the animals that come and go, in the procession of the seasons. . . . Here . . . is space for the spaceless kingdom of . . . the psyche's hinterland."

485 The art of poetry meant much to Jung, who was even, one might say without distortion, a hidden poet. He was especially fascinated by those works of art which he referred to as the "visionary" type[32], because in them the poet gives voice to things from the collective unconscious, like a seer and prophet. He viewed the curious estrangement from reality which is typical of modern art in this light. Periods of this kind mean a time of incubation, when unconscious transformations occur. Thus, the barbaric infantilism of early Christian art simply represents the shift from the Roman Empire to the city of God. Modern art is "an accumulation of the shards of our culture." But its rage to destroy shatters all our false

---

[31] *Memories*, p. 252.
[32] Cf. "Psychology and Literature," CW 15, §§ 133 ff. Cf. also Jung's analysis of Joyce's *Ulysses* (§§ 163 ff.) and his essay on Picasso (11 204 ff.) in the same volume.

sentimentality and also the brutality it covers. In all the mud and all the nonsense, though, one senses the painful birth of a new world-consciousness.[33]

486   When Jung looked at paintings, his eye would involuntarily sweep past all the signs of disintegration in search of whatever content there might be which would reveal the new and the psychologically creative. In "Flying Saucers" he discusses paintings by two artists, Erhard Jacoby and Peter Birkhäuser, in this light, because in both paintings the artists are feeling their way toward new symbols of totality[34], toward the motif of the circle or mandala, which "bid each of us remember his own soul and his own wholeness, because this is the answer the West should give to the danger of mass-mindedness."[35] Peter Birkhäuser once showed him a new picture that he had painted of a black, four-armed youth riding a grey-white boar-like horse.[36] The rider stretches out his hand, and a beautiful flower appears out of the void. He is, so to speak, a new god of creation who promises a new spring of the spirit, riding on the white horse, the Paranatellon constellation of the Aquarian Age.[37] Shortly afterward, Jung wrote the following to Birkhäuser[38], "I want to tell you that your horse-boar-monster has had its after-effects in me. As a prelude to my latest illness, I had the following dream:

487   In an unknown place and at an unknown time, as though standing in the air, I am with a primitive chieftain who might just as well have lived 50,000 years ago. We both know that now at last *the* great event has occurred: the primeval boar, a gigantic mythological beast, has finally been hunted down and killed. It has been skinned, its head cut off, the body is divided lengthwise like a slaughtered pig, the two halves only just hanging together at the neck.

---

[33] Cf. also A. Jaffé, "Symbolism in the Visual Arts," *Man and His Symbols*, pp. 230 ff.
[34] C.G. Jung, "Flying Saucers: A Modern Myth," §§ 589 – 824, here §§ 725 – 747.
[35] Ibid., § 723.
[36] Reproduced in *Man and His Symbols*, p. 199.
[37] The blackness of his figure points to its nocturnal origin.
[38] Cf. C.G. Jung, *Letters*, Vol. 2, p. 606.

488 We are occupied with the task of bringing the huge mass of meat to our tribe. The task is difficult. Once the meat fell into a roaring torrent that swept it into the sea. We had to fetch it back again. Finally, we reach our tribe.

489 The camp, or settlement, is laid out in a rectangle, either in the middle of a primeval forest or on an island in the sea. A great ritual feast is going to be celebrated.

490 The background of this dream is as follows: At the beginning of our *Kalpa* (cosmic age) Vishnu created the new world in the form of a beautiful maiden lying on the waters. But the great serpent succeeded in dragging the new creation down into the sea, from which Vishnu retrieved it, diving down in the shape of a boar. . . .

491 At the end of this cosmic age, Vishnu will change into a white horse and create a new world. This refers to Pegasus, who ushers in the Aquarian Age.

492 Jung also portrayed this Pegasus on his tower, in the last bas-relief he chiselled, together with an anima-mother figure who is about to drink of his milk, his spiritual essence. He writes, "The sea in which the unconscious fish are swimming is now past, now the water is in the jug of Aquarius, that is, in the vessel of consciousness. We are cut off from instinct, from the unconscious. Therefore, we have to nourish instinct, or otherwise we shall dry up. That is why Aquarius is giving the fish water to drink."

493 Music, as well as poetry and the pictorial and plastic arts, meant a great deal to Jung. Among composers, he valued Johann Sebastian Bach more than most. He said once that Bach, like Shakespeare, was one of the very few geniuses who lived from the creative depths in a wholly unreflecting way. The art of Bach and Shakespeare were for him expressions of the unconscious unclouded by ego elements. Jung was in general extremely sensitive to beauty. He reacted to the finest nuances, but he took care not to get lost in the byways of aestheticism, where beauty becomes an end in itself and is morally

indifferent or neutral and no longer an integral part of the *total* human being. Not long before his death he played with the notion of making an "Aeolian harp" in Bollingen: a stringed instrument hung in a tree which produces curious sounds as the wind strokes it. A truly Merlinesque idea! What he had in mind is actually a primordial image or primordial musical phenomenon of the kind so beautifully described by Chuang Tzu, who calls it the earth's organ harmonies[39]: "Great Nature exhales, one calls it wind. Just now it is not blowing; but when it blows then all the hollows of the earth are filled with sound. Have you never heard the blowing of this wind? The hanging steeps of the mountain woods, the hollows and holes of age-old trees; they are like noses, mouths, ears, like choir-stalls, like rings, mortars, pools, like laughing water. Now it hisses, now it buzzes, now it scolds and now it snorts; now it calls, now it whines, hums, cracks. At first it sounds strident, but afterwards panting sounds follow it. When the wind blows softly, there are gentle harmonies, when a cyclone blows up, there are violent harmonies. When the cruel storm calms down, all the stops are out. Have you never noticed how everything stirs and trembles then? And the harmonies of heaven's organ: They resound in a thousand different ways. But behind them is a driving force which causes those sounds to cease and causes them to come to life again. This driving force – who is it?"

494   In certain versions of the saga, Merlin disappears, bewitched by a fairy – Vivane, Niniane, la Dame du Lac or Morgane (probably the Celtic water goddess Muirgen). She entangles him in a hawthorn patch or lowers him into a grave in which lie two embalmed lovers (the alchemical partners of the *coniunctio* in the retort!) Heinrich Zimmer has described Merlin's withdrawal incomparably[40]: "The unconscious, having given a hint of the mystery to the world, sinks back into stillness. Inasmuch as Merlin consciously yields to Niniane's enchantment . . . he rises to the imperturbable height of

---

[39] Chuang Tzu, *Das Wahre Buch vom Südlichen Blütenland*, translated by R. Wilhelm, p. 11. On Jung's relation to music, cf. Aniela Jaffé, *From the Life and Work of C.G. Jung*, p. 116.
[40] "Merlin," *Corona* 9, Part 2, pp. 15 f., 154.

an Indian god, unconcernedly withdrawing from the world into the stillness of his own self. . . . The world is for Round Table knights, for expeditions and adventures. But the hawthorn patch blooms everlastingly and Merlin is at home in it. He, the "magician" is at home in the timeless, looking at the future, like the changing images within a crystal, while he hovers above the follow of time. .."

495   As Jung drew near the end of his earthly life[41], those images of a "sacred marriage," which he had seen once before when near to death, returned to him. When Miguel Serrano visited him, on May 5, 1959, they spoke of the problem of the *coniunctio*. Jung, Serrano reports, seemed as if lost in a dream, and said[42], "Somewhere there was once a Flower, a Stone, a Crystal, a Queen, a King, a Palace, a Lover and his Beloved, and this was long ago, on an Island somewhere in the ocean five thousand years ago. . . . Such is Love, the Mystic Flower of the Soul. This is the Centre, the Self. . . . Nobody understands what I mean . . . only a poet could begin to understand."

496   Death is the last great union of the inner world-opposites, the sacred marriage of resurrection, which the ancient Chinese have called the "dark union at the yellow sources." According to them, man at death breaks up into his two psychic parts: a dark one, belonging to the Yin principle, the feminine part "p'o" which sinks down to earth; and a bright "hun," belonging to the Yang principle, which ascends to heaven. Both then continue their journey, the feminine part to the feminine divinity of the West, the other eastward to the "dark city" or to the "yellow source." As "Mistress of the West" and "Lord of the East" they then celebrate the "dark union" and in this union the dead man arises as a new being, "weightless and invisible," who can "soar like the sun and sail with the clouds."[43]

497   Merlin's disappearance into the union of love with Niniane suggests the same death-and-marriage motif. At the same time, he becomes again what he was from the beginning, a "spirit in the stone." He is *entombé*, or *enserré* in a stone grave, and from there his

---

[41] He died on 6th June, 1961.
[42] Cf. M. Serrano, *C.G. Jung and Hermann Hesse*, p. 60.
[43] For further details, cf. M.–L. von Franz, *Number and Time*, p. 290 and the literature cited there.

voice can be heard.[44] From time to time certain heroes meet at this stone before setting out upon great adventures.[45] This stone grave is at the same time also a nuptial couch and the vessel of the *unio mystica* with the godhead.[46]

498　　　A few days before his death, Jung told of a dream he had had, the last one he was able to communicate. He saw a great round stone in a high place, a barren square, and on it were engraved the words, "And this shall be a sign unto you of Wholeness and Oneness."[47] Then he saw many vessels to the right in an open square and a quadrangle of trees whose roots reached around the earth and enveloped him and among the roots golden threads were glittering.

499　　　When the Tao, the meaning of the world, and eternal life are attained, the Chinese say, "Your longevity will blossom with the essence of stone and the radiance of gold."[48]

500　　　How many heroes will meet at this stone, now, to set out upon the great adventure of individuation, the journey to the interior? The fate of our Western culture depends, if I am right, on the answer to this question.

---

[44] Thus, Gawain and his men 'si viennant à une pierre, qui a nom li Perons Merlin.' Cf. P. Zumthor, *Merlin le Prophète*, pp. 218-19. In Boiardo, this grave is called *Petron di Merlino*, in Girard d'Amiens, *Perron Merlin*.

[45] Cf. E. Jung and M.-L. von Franz, *The Grail Legend*, p. 390.

[46] Cf. ibid.

[47] Cf. Serrano, p. 104 (from a letter to Serrano from Ruth Bailey).

[48] Cf. K.M. Shipper, *L'empereur Wou des Han dans la légende Taoiste*, p. 16: "Par la volonté supreme le Tao est attaint . . . mais en maintenant en paix l'essence, ta longévité fleurira, avec l'essence de la pierre et l'éclat d'or. . . . Tu pourras traverser le vide et dissimuler la forme: Longue Vie et Jeunesse Eternelle. Ton éclat sera semblable à celui du Ciel."

Bibliography

Adler, Gerhard. "C.G. Jung." *Middlesex Hospital Journal* 63, no. 4. London, 1963.

–. *The Living Symbol: A Case Study in the Process of Individuation.* Princeton, NJ: Princeton University Press, 1961.

–. *Studies in Analytical Psychology.* Abingdon, Oxon: Routledge, 1999.

Adolf, Helen. *Visio Pacis, Holy City and Grail: An Attempt at an inner History of the Grail Legend.* Pennsylvania: Pennsylvania State University Press, 1960.

Affemann, Rudolf. "Die Frage der Tiefenpsychologie nach der Echtheit des Glaubens." *Evangelische Theologie* 24, no. 6 (1964): 311–23.

Agrawal, Padma. *Symbolism: A Psychological Study.* Benares: Manovigyan Prakashan, 1955.

Allenby, A. I. "A Tribute to C. G. Jung." In *Contact with Jung: Essays on Influence of His Work and Personality,* edited by Michael Fordham, 67–69. London: Tavistock Publications, 1963.

Agrippa von Nettesheim. *De occulta philosophia.* Cologne: Soter, 1533.

Alm, Ivar. "C.G. Jungs Erfahrungen in theologischer Sicht." *Theologische Zeitschrift der Theologischen Fakultät der Universität Basel* 19, no. 15. Basel: Reinhardt, 1963.

Alphandéry, cf. Dupront.

Altizer, Thomas J. *The Gospel of Christian Atheism.* London: Collins, 1967.

Ammann, Adolf N. *Tannhäuser im Venusberg: Der Mythos im Volkslied.* Zurich: Origo-Verlag, 1964.

Andrews, F. M., cf. Pelz.

Apuleius von Madaura. *The Golden Ass.* Translated by Robert Graves. New York: Farrar Straus & Giroux, 2009.

Banerjee, Samiran. "Prof. Dr. C.G. Jung." *The Psychotherapy* 1, no. 14 (Kalkutta 1956).

Baudouin, Charles. "Jung, Homme concrêt." *Le Disque vert.* Paris: Editions de l'Arche, 1955.

Beit, Hedwig von. *Gegensatz und Erneuerung im Märchen.* 4th ed. 2 vols. Bern: Francke, 1977.

–. *Das Märchen: Sein Ort in der geistigen Entwicklung.* Bern: Francke, 1965.

–. *Symbolik des Märchens: Versuch einer Deutung.* 4th ed. Bern: Francke, 1971.

Bender, Hans, und John Mischo. "Praekognition in Traumserien." *Zeitschrift für Parapsychologie und Grenzgebiete der Psychologie* 4, no. 43 (1960/61); 5, no. 1 (1961); and cf. 4, no. 1 (1960).

Beneš, Brigit. "Spuren von Schamanismus in der Sage des 'Buile Suibne'." *Zeitschrift für celtische Philologie* 28, no. 1. Edited by Jürgen Uhlich, Torsten Meißner, and Alderik H. Blom (1960–1961): 309–34.

Bennet, Edward Armstrong. *C.G. Jung.* Wilmette, Ill: Chiron Publications, 2006.

–. *What Jung Really Said.* London: Abacus, 2001.

Benz, Ernst. *Adam: Der Mythos vom Urmenschen.* Munichh: Barth, 1955.

Bernet, Walter. *Inhalt und Grenze der religiösen Erfahrung: Eine Untersuchung der Probleme der religiösen Erfahrung in Auseinandersetzung mit der Psychologie Carl Gustav Jungs.* Bern: Haupt, 1955.

Berthelot, Marcelin. *Collection des anciens Alchimistes Grecs.* 2 vols. Paris: Steinheil, 1887/88.

Bertine, Eleanor. *Human Relationships: In the Family, in Friendship, in Love.* New York: D. Mckay, 1958.

–. *Jung's Contribution to Our Time.* New York: Putman, 1967.

Beyer, Wilhelm Raimund. *Das Sinnbild des Kreises im Denken Hegels und Lenins.* Meisenheim am Glan: Hain, 1971.

Bietenhard, H. *Die himmlische Welt im Urchristentum und Spätjudentum.* Tübingen: Mohr, 1951.

Biran, Sigmund. *Die ausserpsychologischen Voraussetzungen der Tiefenpsychologie.* Munich: Reinhardt, 1966.

Bloch, Ernst. *The Principle of Hope.* Translated by Neville Plaice. Cambridge, MA: MIT Press, 1986.

Böhler, Eugen. *Der Mythus in Wirtschaft und Wissenschaft.* Freiburg i. Br.: Rombach, 1955.

. "Ideologie und Ideal." *Industrielle Organisation* 10 (1958).

. *Zukunft als Problem des modernen Menschen.* Freiburg i. Br.: Rombach, 1966.

Boehm, Walter. „Versuch einer Metaphysischen Gesamtschau." In *Die metaphysischen Grundlagen der Naturwissenschaft und Mathematik,* 159–85. Wien: Herder, 1966.

Böhme, Jakob. *XL Questions Concerning the Soule.* Propounded by Dr. Balthasar Walter and answered by Jacob Behmen. London, 1647.

Bousset, Wilhelm. *Die Himmelsreise der Seele.* Darmstadt: Wissenschaftliche Buchgesellschaft, 1960.

Boye, Hedwig. *Menschen mit grossem Schatten.* Zurich: Büchergilde Gutenberg, 1945.

Braden, William. *The Age of Aquarius: Technology and the Cultural Revolution.* 2nd print. Chicago, IL: Quadrangle Books, 1970.

Brodeur, Arthur Gilchrist, trans. *The Prose Edda: Tales from Norse Mythology.* Mineola, NY: Dover Publications, 2006.

Brügge, Peter. "Über die apolitische Jugendbewegung in der Bundesrepublik." *Der Spiegel* 25, no. 33, August 1971.

Bruneton, J.-L. "Jung, l'homme, sa vie, son caractère." *Revue d'Allemagne* 7, no. 70 (August 1933): 673–89.

Brunner, Cornelia. *Anima as Fate.* Translated by Julius Heuscher. Edited by David Scott May. Dallas, TX: Spring Publications, 1986.

Buddruss, G., cf. Friedrich, A.

Byers, Sarah. „The Psychology of Compassion: Stoicism in City of God 9.5." In *Augustine's City of God: A Critical Guide.* Edited by

James Wetzel, 130–48. Cambridge: Cambridge University Press, 2012.

Campbell, Joseph. *The Hero with a Thousand Faces.* 3rd ed. Novato, CA: New World Library, 2008.

Carol, Hans. "Man and his Environment [1950]." In *C.G. Jung Speaking: Interviews and Encounters,* edited by William McGuire and R. F. C. Hull, 201–204. Princeton, NJ: Thames and Hudson, 1978.

Chardin, Pierre Teilhard de. *The Phenomenon of Man.* Foreword by Julian Huxley. New York: Harper and Row, 1961.

Chuang Tzu. *Das wahre Buch vom südlichen Blütenland.* Translated by Richard Wilhelm. Jena: Diederichs, 1923.

Corbin, Henry. *L'imagination créatrice dans le Soufisme d'Ibn 'Arabi.* Paris: Flammarion, 1958.

–. "La Sophia Éternelle." *Revue de culture Européenne* 5 (1953): 11–44.

Corti, Walter Robert. "Vingt ans d'Eranos." *C.G. Jung,* edited by C.G. Jung, Gerhard Adler, Walter Robert Corti et al. Paris: Le Disque vert, 1955.

Cox, David. *Jung and St. Paul: A Study of the Doctrine of Justification by Faith and its Relation to the Concept of Individuation.* New York: Association Press, 1959.

Davis, cf. Lu-Ch'iang Wu.

Dement, William. "Die Wirkungen des Traumentzuges." In *Bedeutung und Deutung des Traumes in der Psychotherapie,* edited by Jutta von Graevenitz, 321–30. Darmstadt: Wissen-schaftliche Buchgesellschaft, 1968.

De Vries, Jan. *Forschungsgeschichte der Mythologie.* Freiburg i. Br.: Verlag Karl Alber, 1961.

Dieckmann, Hans. *Märchen und Träume als Helfer des Menschen.* Psychologisch gesehen 4. Stuttgart: Bonz, 1966.

Diels, Hermann. *Die Fragmente der Vorsokratiker.* Berlin: Weid-mann, 1951.

Dieterich, Albrecht. *Eine Mithrasliturgie,* edited by Otto Weinreich. 3rd ed. Leipzig: Teubner, 1923.

Dorn, Gerhard. "De Transmutatione metallorum." *Theatrum Chemicum* I, edited by Lazarus Zetzner. Strassburg, 1602.

Dupront, Alphonse. "Introduction à l'étude d'un archetype." *La Table Ronde* 120 (Decembre 1957): 11–28.

–, and Paul Alphandéry. *La Chrétienté et l'idée de la Croisade*. 2 vols. Paris: Michel, 1959.

Durand, Gilbert. *Les structures anthropologiques de l'imaginaire: Introduction à l'archétypologie générale*. Grenoble: Presses Universitaires de France, 1960.

Edinger, Edward F., ed. *Carl Gustav Jung, 1875–1961: A Memorial Meeting, New York, December 1, 1961*. The Analytical Psychology Club of New York. New York: 1962.

Eibl-Eibesfeldt, Irenäus. *Love and Hate: The Natural History of Behavior Patterns*. Translated by Geoffrey Strachan. London: Methuen, 1973.

Eiseley, Loren. *The Immense Journey*. New York: The Library of America, 2016.

Eliade, Mircea. *C.G. Jung*. Edited by C.G. Jung, Gerhard Adler, Walter Robert Corti et al. Paris: Le Disque vert, 1955.

–. *The Forge and the Crucible*. 2nd ed. Chicago: University of Chicago Press, 1978.

–. *The Myth of the Eternal Return*. Translated by Willard R. Trask. New York: Pantheon Books, 1954.

–. *Shamanism: Archaic Techniques of Ecstasy*. Translated by Willard R. Trask. Princeton, NJ: Princeton University Press, 1970.

Evans, Richard I. *Conversations with Carl Jung: And Reactions from Ernest Jones*. Akron, OH: The University of Akron Press, 2020.

Evans-Wentz, W. Y. *The Tibetan Book of the Great Liberation*. London: Oxford University Press, 1972.

–. *The Tibetan Book of the Dead*. London: Oxford University Press, 1960.

Evola, Julius. *The Hermetic Tradition: Symbols and Teachings of the Royal Art*. Translated by E. E. Rehmus. Rochester, VT: Inner Traditions International, 1955.

Fierz-David, Linda. *The Dream of Poliphilo: The Soul in Love.* Translated by Mary Hottinger. Dallas, TX: Spring Publications, 1987.

–. *Dreaming in Red: The Women's Dionysian Initiation Chamber in Pompeii.* New York: Putnam, 2005.

Fordham, Michael. *Children as Individuals.* London: Free Association Books, 1994.

–. *The Life of Childhood: A Contribution to Analytical Psychology.* London: Kegan Paul, 1944.

–. *The Theory of Archetypes as Applied to Child Development.* Basel: Karger, 1964.

–. "Individuation in Childhood." *The Reality of the Psyche,* edited by J. Wheelwright. New York: Putnam, 1965.

–. *New Developments in Analytical Psychology.* London: Routledge & Kegan Paul, 1957.

Franz, Marie-Louise von. "Active Imagination in the Psychology of C.G. Jung." In *Psychotherapy,* 146–62. Boston, MA: Shambhala, 1993. New edition in preparation by Chiron Publications, Asheville. Vol. 26, CW.

   –. *Archetypal Dimensions of the Soul.* Boston, MA: Shambala Publications, 1997.

–. *Aurora Consurgens.* Vol. 7, CW. Asheville: Chiron Publications, 2022.

–. "A Contribution to the Discussion of C.G. Jung's Synchronicity Hypothesis." In *Psyche and Matter.* Boston: Shambhala, 1992. New edition in preparation by Chiron Publications, Asheville. Vol. 27, CW.

–. "C.G. Jung's Library." *Spring Journal.* New York: Spring Publications, 1970.

–. "The Dream of Descartes." In *Dreams: A Study of the Dreams of Jung, Descartes, Socrates, and other Historical Figures.* Translated by Andrea Dykes and Elizabeth Welsh, 107–92. Boston, MA: Shambhala Publications, 1991. New edition in preparation by Chiron Publications, Asheville. Vol. 26, CW.

–. "The Cosmic Man as Image of the Goal of the Individuation Process and Human Development." In *Archetypal Dimensions of the Psyche*, 133–57. Boston, MA: Shambhala, 1997. New edition in preparation by Chiron Publications, Asheville. Vol. 27, CW.

–. "The Idea of the Macro- and Microcosmos in the Light of Jungian Psychology." In *Psyche and Matter*, 169–84. Boston: Shambhala, 1992. New edition in preparation by Chiron Publications, Asheville. Vol. 27, CW.

–. "The Individuation Process." In *Archetypal Dimensions of the Psyche*, 292–363. Boston, MA: Shambhala, 1999. New edition in preparation by Chiron Publications, Asheville. Vol. 27, CW.

–. *Niklaus von Flüe and Saint Perpetua: A Psychological Interpretation of their Visions*. Vol. 6, CW. Asheville: Chiron Publications, 2022.

–. *Number and Time: Reflections Leading toward a Unification of Depth Psychology and Physics*. Evanston, IL: Northwestern University Press, 1974. New edition in preparation by Chiron Publications, Asheville. Vol. 19, CW.

–. *The Problem of the Puer Aeternus*. Toronto: Inner City Books, 2000. New edition in preparation by Chiron Publications, Asheville. Vol. 14, CW.

–. *A Psychological Interpretation of "The Golden Ass" of Apuleius*. Irving: Spring Publications, 1980. New edition in preparation by Chiron Publications, Asheville. Vol. 12, CW.

–. *Psychotherapy*. Boston, MA: Shambhala Publications, 1993. New edition in preparation by Chiron Publications, Asheville. Vol. 26, CW.

–. *Projection and Re-collection in Jungian Psychology Reflections of the Soul*. La Salle: London Open Court Publishing, 1980.

–. *On Dreams and Death: A Jungian Interpretation. Translated by Emmanuel Kennedy-Xipolitas and Vernon Brooks*. Chicago, IL: Open Court, 1998. New edition in preparation by Chiron Publications, Asheville. Vol. 23, CW.

–. "On Group Psychology." In *Psychotherapy*. Boston: Shambhala, 1993. New edition in preparation by Chiron Publications, Asheville. Vol. 26, CW.

–. "On the Religious Background of the Puer Aeternus Problem." In *Psychotherapy*, 306–23. Boston, MA: Shambhala, 1993. New edition in preparation by Chiron Publications, Asheville. Vol. 26, CW.

–. "Symbols of the *Unus Mundus*." In *Psyche and Matter*, 39–62. Foreword by Robert Hinshaw. Boston, MA: Shambhala Publications, 1992. New edition in preparation by Chiron Publications, Asheville. Vol. 27, CW.

–. "The Synchronicity Principle of C.G. Jung." In *Psyche and Matter*, 203–28. Boston, MA: Shambhala, 1992. New edition in preparation by Chiron Publications, Asheville. Vol. 27, CW.

Fordham, Michael. *Children as Individuals*. London: Free Association Books, 1994.

–. *The Life of Childhood: A Contribution to Analytical Psychology*. London: Kegan Paul, 1944.

Frazer, James George. *The Golden Bough*. Cambridge: Cambridge University Press, 2012.

Frei, Gebhard, OSB. *Imago mundi*, edited by A. Resch. Paderborn: Schöningh, 1969.

–. "C.G. Jung zum 70. Geburtstag." *Schweizer Rundschau* 45 (July 1945).

–. "Zur Psychologie des Unterbewussten." *Gloria Dei: Zeitschrift für Theologie und Geistesleben* 2, Part 3 (1947/48).

Freud, Sigmund. *The Interpretation of Dreams and on Dreams*. Translated by James Strachey. Vol. 4 and 5 of the Standard Edition of the Complete Psychological Works of Sigmund Freud. London: Hogarth Press, 1978.

–, and Ralph Manheim, and C.G. Jung. *The Freud/Jung Letters: The Correspondence between Sigmund Freud and C.G. Jung*, edited by William McGuire. Translated by Ralph Manheim and R. F. C. Hull. London: Penguin Books, 1991.

Frey-Rohn, Liliane. *From Freud to Jung: A Comparative Study of the Psychology of the Unconscious*. Translated by Fred E. Engreen and Evelyn K. Engreen. Boston, MA: Shambhala, 1990.

Friedrich, Adolf, and Georg Buddruss, eds. *Schamanengeschichten aus Sibirien*. Berlin: Barth, 1987.

Friklin, Hans Jürgen. *Was weiss man von der Seele?: Erforschung und Erfahrung*. Stuttgart: Kreuz-Verlag, 1967.

Frischknecht, Max. *Die Religion in der Psychologie von C.G. Jung*. Bern, 1945.

Fritsch, Vilma. *Links und Rechts in Wissenschaft und Leben*. Stuttgart: Kohlhammer, 1964.

Froböse, Felicia. *Träume – eine Quelle religiöser Erfahrung?* Darmstadt: Wissenschaftliche Buchgesellschaft, 1972.

Furrer, Walter L. *Objektivierung des Unbewussten*. Bern: Huber, 1969.

Ge, Hong. *Alchemy, Medicine and Religion in the China of A. D. 320 the Nei p'ein of Ko Hong (Pao-p'u tzu)*, edited by James R. Ware. New York: Dover, 1981.

Gebser, Jean. *Abendländische Wandlung. Abriss der Ereignisse moderner Forschung in Physik, Biologie und Psychologie Ihre Bedeutung für Gegenwart und Zukunft*. 3rd ed. Constance: Europa Verlag, 1950.

–. *Der unsichtbare Ursprung: Evolution als Nachvollzug*. Olten: Walter, 1970.

Giehrl, Hans Eberhard. "Volksmärchen und Tiefenpsychologie." PhD diss., Munich: Ehrenwirth, 1970.

Goetz, Bruno. *Das Reich ohne Raum: Eine Vision der Archetypen, eine Chronik wunderlicher Begebenheiten*. 4rd. ed. Preface Walter R. Corti. With a commentary by Marie-Louise von Franz. Bern: Origo-Verlag, 1995.

Goldbrunner, Josef, SJ. *Cure of Mind and Cure of Soul*. Notre Dame, IN: University of Notre Dame Press, 1963.

–. "Dialog zwischen Tiefenpsychologie und katholischer Theologie." *Festschrift für W. Bitter*. Stuttgart: Klett, 1968.

–. *Individuation: A Study of the Depth Psychology of Carl Gustav Jung*. South Bend: University of Notre Dame, 1966.

–. *Realization: The Anthropology of Pastoral Care*. South Bend: University of Notre Dame, 1966.

Graevenitz, Jutta von, ed. *Bedeutung und Deutung des Traumes in der Psychotherapie*. Darmstadt: Wissenschaftliche Buchgesellschaft, 1968.

Granet, Marcel. *Das chinesische Denken: Inhalt, Form, Charakter*. 2nd ed. Munich: Piper, 1980.

Gray, Ronald Douglas. *Goethe, the Alchemist: A Study of Alchemical Symbolism in Goethe's Literary and Scientific Works*. Cambridge: Cambridge University Press, 1932.

–. *A Study of Alchemical Symbolism in Goethe's Literary and Scientific Works*. Cambridge: Cambridge University Press, 2010.

Grimm, Jacob, and Wilhelm Grimm. *Grimm's Fairy Tales: Complete Edition*, edited by James Stern. Translated by Margaret Hunt. London: Routledge & Kegan, 1948.

Grobel, Kendrick, trans. *The Gospel of Truth: A Valentinian Meditation on the Gospel*. London: Black, 1960.

Gynz-Rekowski, Georg von. *Symbole des Weiblichen im Gottesbild und Kult des Alten Testamentes*. Zurich: Rascher, 1963.

Haas, Aloys M. *Nim din selbes war: Studien zur Lehre der Selbsterkenntnis bei Meister Eckhart, Johannes Tauler und Heinrich Seuse*. Freiburg, CH: Universitätsverlag Freiburg Schweiz, 1971.

Händler, Otto. *Das Leib-Seele-Problem in theologischer Sicht*. Berlin: Renner, 1954.

–. *Tiefenpsychologie, Theologie und Seelsorge*, edited by Joachim Scharfenberg and Klaus Winkler. Göttingen: Vandenhoech & Ruprecht, 1971.

Hannah, Barbara. "The Problem of Contact with the Animus." *Jungiana*. Series A, Vol. 3. Kusnacht: Verlag Stiftung für Jung'sche Psychologie, 1991.

–. "Some Glimpses of the Individuation Process in Jung Himself." *Quadrant: Journal of the C.G. Jung Foundation for Analytical Psychology* (New York) 16 (Spring 1974): 26–33.

–. "The Beyond." *Quadrant: Notes on Analytical Psychology* (New York) 3 (Winter 1969): 12–23.

–. *Encounters with the Soul: Active Imagination as Developed by C.G.* Boston, MA: Sigo Press, 1981.

–. *C.G. Jung, his Life and Work: A Biographical Memoir.* Wilmette, IL: Chiron Publications, 1997.

–. "The Healing Influence of Active Imagination in a Specific Case of Neurosis." *Encounters with the Soul: Active Imagination as Developed by C.G. Jung.* Boston, MA: Sigo Press, 1981.

–. *Striving towards Wholeness.* Boston, MA: Sigo Press, 1988.

Harding, Esther. *The Way of All Women.* Boston, MA: Shambhala, 2001.

–. *Journey into Self.* Boston, MA: Sigo Press, 1991.

–. "Jung's Influence on Contemporary Thought." *Journal of Religion and Mental Health* 1, no. 3 (April 1961): 249–61.

–. *Psychic Energy: Its Source and its Transformation.* 2nd ed. Bollingen Series 10. New York: Pantheon Books, 1963.

–. *The 'I' and the 'Not-I': A study in the Development of Consciousness.* Bollingen Series 79. Princeton, NJ: Princeton University Press, 1973.

–. *Woman's Mysteries: Ancient & Modern.* Boston, MA: Shambhala, 2001.

–. *The Parental Image: Its Injury and Reconstruction: A Study in Analytical Psychology.* 3rd ed. Toronto: Inner City Books, 2003.

Harms, Ernest. "Carl Gustav Jung, Defender of Freud and the Jews." *Psychiatric Quarterly* 20, no. 2 (April 1946): 199–230.

Hartmann, Sven S. *Gayômart.* Uppsala: Almquist, 1933.

Heiler, Friedrich. "Das neue Mariendogma im Lichte der Geschichte und im Urteil der Ökumene." *'Ökumenische Einheit': Archiv für ökumenisches und soziales Christentum (Munich)* 2, no. 2 (1951): 161–286.

Heisenberg, Werner. *Der Teil und das Ganze: Gespräch im Umkreis der Atomphysik.* Munich: Piper, 1969.

Heisterbach, Caesarius von. *Libri VIII Miraculorum,* edited by Ferdinand Schöningh. Paderborn, 1962.

Henderson, Joseph. *Thresholds of Initiation.* Connecticut: Wesleyan University Press, 1967.

Henel, Heinrich. *R. D. Gray, Goethe the Alchemist.* Cambridge: University Press, 1952.

Herrmann, Paul. "Das altgermanische Priesterwesen." *Deutsche Volksheit* 64. Jena, 1929.

Hillman, James. "Senex and Puer: An Aspect of the Historical and Psychological Present." *Polarität des Lebens*, 301–60. Eranos-Jahrbuch 1967, vol. 21. Zurich: Rhein-Verlag, 1968.

. *Psychology, Monotheistic or Polytheistic.* New York: Spring Publications, 1971.

Hochheimer, Wolfgang. *The Psychotherapy of C.G. Jung.* Translated by Hildegard Nagel. New York: C.G. Jung Foundation for Analytical Psychology, 1969.

Hof, Hans. „Scintilla animae: Eine Studie zu einem Grundbegriff in Meister Eckharts Philosophie mit besonderer Berücksichtigung des Verhältnisses der Eckhartschen Philosophie zur neuplatonischen und thomistischen Anschauung." PhD diss., Lund: C. W. K. Gleerup, 1952.

Hofstaetter, Peter R. *Gruppendynamik: Kritik der Massenpsychologie.* Rowohlts deutsche Enzyklopädie. Vol. 38. Hamburg: Reinbek, 1957.

–. *Einführung in die Sozialpsychologie.* Hamburg: Kröner, 1957.

Hooft, W. A. Visser't. *Kein anderer Name: Synkretismus oder christlicher Universalismus?* Basel: Basileia, 1965.

Hostie, Raymond, SJ. *Religion and the Psychology of Jung.* New York: Sheed & Ward, 1957.

Hume, Robert Ernest, trans. "Brihad-aranyaka Upanishad." In *The Thirteen Principal Upanishads.* 2nd ed. Delhi: Oxford University Press, 1995.

Hurwitz, Siegmund. *Die Gestalt des sterbenden Messias: Religionspsychologische Aspekte der jüdischen Apokalyptik.* Forword by Alexander Altmann. Zurich: Rascher, 1958.

Imboden, Max. *Die Staatsformen: Versuch einer psychologischen Deutung staatsrechtlicher Dogmen.* Basel: Helbing & Lichenhahn, 1959.

Isler, Gotthilf. *Die Sennenpuppe: Eine Untersuchung über die religiöse Funktion einiger Alpensagen.* Schriften der Schweizerischen Gesellschaft für Volkskunde 52. Basel: Krebs, 1971.

Jacobi, Jolande. *The Psychology of C.G. Jung: An Introduction with Illustations*. London: Kegan Paul, 1975.

–. *Complex/Archetype/Symbol in the Psychology of C.G. Jung*. Princeton, NJ: Princeton University Press, 1971.

–. *The Way of Individuation*. Translated by R. F. C. Hall. New York: New American Library, 1983.

Jacobs, Hans. *Indische Weisheit und westliche Psychotherapie: Ein Beitrag zu vergleichenden Studien in Psychologie und Metaphysik*. Munich: Lehmanns, 1965.

Jacobsohn, Helmuth. "Das Gegensatzproblem im altägyptischen Mythos" In *Gesammelte Schriften*, 51–78. Hildesheim: Georg Olms, 1992.

–. "Der altägyptische, der christliche und der moderne Mythos." In *Gesammelte Schriften*, 79–116. Hildesheim: Georg Olms, 1992.

Jacobsohn, Helmuth, Marie-Louise von Franz, and Siegmund Hurwitz. *Timeless Documents of the Soul*. An Arbor, MI: UMI Books on Demand, 1998.

Jaffé, Aniela. *C.G. Jung, Bild und Wort*. Zurich: Ex Libris, 1979.

–. *Erinnerungen, Träume, Gedanken von C.G. Jung*. 10th ed. Zurich: Walter, 1997.

–. "Symbolism in the Visual Arts." In *Man and His Symbols*, edited by C.G. Jung. New York: Doubleday, 1968.

–. *From the Life and Work of C.G. Jung*. Translated by R. F. C. Hull and Murray Stein. Expanded Edition. Einsiedeln: Daimon Verlag, 1989.

–. *The Myth of Meaning in the Work of C.G. Jung*. Translated by R. F. C. Hull. Zurich: Daimon Verlag, 1984.

–. *Der Mythus vom Sinn im Werk von C.G. Jung*. Zurich: Daimon-Verlag, 1993.

Joël, Karl. *Der Ursprung der Naturphilosophie aus dem Geiste der Mystik*. Jena: Diederichs, 1906.

Jones, Ernest. *Life and Work of Sigmund Freud*, edited by Lionel Trilling and Steven Marcus. 3 vols. London: Penguin Books, 1993.

Jordan, Pascual. *Verdrängung und Komplementarität*. Hamburg: Strom-Verlag, 1947.

Jung, Carl Gustav. *Bollingen Series XX: The Collected Works of C.G. Jung*, edited by Herbert Read, Michael Fordham, Gerhard Adler and William McGuire. Translated by R. F. C. Hull. 20 vols.

–. "A Psychological Approach to the Dogma of the Trinity." In *Psychology and Religion: West and East*, §§ 169 ff. Vol. 11. Princeton, NJ: Princeton University Press, 1989.

–. "A Psychological View of Conscience." In *Civilization and Transition*, §§ 825–57. 2nd ed. Vol. 10. Princeton, NJ: Princeton University Press, 1970.

–. "A Study in the Process of Individuation." In *Archetypes and the Collective Unconscious*, §§ 525–626. 2nd ed. Vol. 9/I. Princeton, NJ: Princeton University Press, 1980.

–. "An Astrological Experiment." In *The Symbolic Life: Miscellaneous Writings*, §§ 1174 ff. Vol. 18. Princeton, NJ: Princeton University Press, 1977.

–. "Analytical Psychology and Education." In *The Development of Personality*, § 159. Vol. 17. Princeton, NJ: Princeton University Press, 1955.

–. "Answer to Job." In *Psychology and Religion: West and East*, §§ 553–758. 2nd ed. Vol. 11. Princeton, NJ: Princeton University Press, 1989.

–. "Archaic Man." In *Civilization and Transition*, § 141. 2nd ed. Vol. 10. Princeton, NJ: Princeton University Press, 1970.

–. "Commentary on ‚The Secret of the Golden Flower.'" In *Alchemical Studies*, §§ 1–84. Vol. 13. Princeton, NJ: Princeton University Press, 1968.

–. "Concerning Mandala Symbolism." In *Archetypes and the Collective Unconscious*, §§ 627–712. 2nd ed. Vol. 9/I. Princeton, NJ: Princeton University Press, 1980.

–. "Flying Saucers: A Modern Myth of Things Seen in the Skies." In *Civilization and Transition*, §§ 589–824. 2nd ed. Vol. 10. Princeton, NJ: Princeton University Press, 1970.

–. "Foreword to Suzuki's "Introduction to Zen Buddhism"." In *Psychology and Religion: West and East*, §§ 877 ff. 2nd ed. Vol. 11. Princeton, NJ: Princeton University Press, 1989.

–. "Foreword to the I Ching." In *Psychology and Religion: West and East*, §§ 964 ff. Vol. 11. Princeton, NJ: Princeton University Press, 1989.

–. "Freud's Theory of Hysteria: A Reply to Aschaffenburg." In *Freud and Psychoanalysis*, §§ 1–26. Vol. 4. Princeton, NJ: Princeton University Press, 1962.

–. "General Aspects of Dream Psychology." In *The Structure and Dynamics of the Psyche*, §§ 443–529. 2nd ed. Vol. 8. Princeton, NJ: Princeton University Press, 1981.

–. "Instinct and the Unconscious." In *The Structure and Dynamics of the Psyche*, § 280. 2nd ed. Vol. 8. Princeton, NJ: Princeton University Press, 1981.

–. "On Psychic Energy." In *The Structure and Dynamics of the Psyche*, §§ 6 ff. 2nd ed. Vol. 8. Princeton, NJ: Princeton University Press, 1981.

–. "On the Nature of Dreams." In *The Structure and Dynamics of the Psyche*, §§ 91-92. 2nd ed. Vol. 8. Princeton, NJ: Princeton University Press, 1981.

–. "On the Nature of the Psyche." In *The Structure and Dynamics of the Psyche*, § 397. 2nd ed. Vol. 8. Princeton, NJ: Princeton University Press, 1981.

–. "On the Psychological Diagnosis of Facts." In *Psychiatric Studies*, §§ 478 ff. Vol. 1. Princeton, NJ: Princeton University Press, 1970.

–. "On the Psychology and Pathology of So-called Occult Phenomena." In *Psychiatric Studies*, §§ 1–150. Vol. 1. Princeton, NJ: Princeton University Press, 1970.

–. "On the Psychology of the Unconscious." In *Two Essays on Analytical Psychology*, §§ 36 – 41. Vol. 7. Princeton, NJ: Princeton University Press, 1967.

–. "Paracelsus as a Spiritual Phenomenon." In *Alchemical Studies*, §§ 148 ff. Vol. 13. Princeton, NJ: Princeton University Press, 1983.

–. "Paracelsus the Physician." In *The Spirit in Man, Art, and Literature*, §§ 18–43. Vol. 15. Princeton, NJ: Princeton University Press, 1967.

–. "Picasso." In *The Spirit in Man, Art, and Literature*, §§ 204 ff. Vol. 15. Princeton, NJ: Princeton University Press, 1967.

–. "Psychological Commentary on W. J. Evans-Wentz "The Tibetan Book of the Dead"." In *Psychology and Religion: West and East*, §§ 831 ff. Vol. 11. Princeton, NJ: Princeton University Press, 1989.

–. "Psychological Commentary on W. J. Evans-Wentz "The Tibetan Book of the Great Liberation"." In *Psychology and Religion: West and East*, §§ 759 ff. Vol. 11. Princeton, NJ: Princeton University Press, 1989.

–. "Psychology and Literature." In *The Spirit in Man, Art, and Literature*, §§ 133 ff. Vol. 15. Princeton, NJ: Princeton University Press, 1967.

–. "Psychology and Religion: A Reply to Martin Buber." In *The Symbolic Life: Miscellaneous Writings*, §§ 1499–513. Vol. 18. Princeton, NJ: Princeton University Press, 1977.

–. "Psychology of the Transference." In *The Practice of Psychotherapy*, § 392. 2nd ed. Vol. 16. Princeton, NJ: Princeton University Press, 1985.

–. "Psychophysical Researches." *Experimental Researches*, §§ 1015–311. Vol. 2. Princeton: Princeton University Press, 1973.

–. "Richard Wilhelm: In Memoriam." In *The Spirit in Man, Art, and Literature*, §§ 74–96. Vol. 15. Princeton, NJ: Princeton University Press, 1967.

–. "Studies in Word Association." *Experimental Researches*. Vol. 2. Princeton: Princeton University Press, 1973.

–. "Symbols and the Interpretation of Dreams." In *The Symbolic Life: Miscellaneous Writings*, §§ 416–607. Vol. 18. Princeton, NJ: Princeton University Press, 1977.

–. "Synchronicity: An Acausal Connecting Principle." In *Structure and Dynamics of the Psyche*, §§ 816–958. 2nd ed. Vol. 8. Princeton, NJ: Princeton University Press, 1981.

–. "The Concept of the Libido." In *Symbols of Transformation: An Analysis oft he Prelude to a Case of Schizophrenia*, §§ 190–203. 2nd ed. Vol. 5. Princeton, NJ: Princeton University Press, 1990.

–. "The Fight with the Shadow." In *Civilization and Transition*, § 452. 2nd ed. Vol. 10. Princeton, NJ: Princeton University Press, 1970.

–. "The Phenomenology of the Spirit in Fairytales." In *Archetypes and the Collective Unconscious*, § 385. 2nd ed. Vol. 9/I. Princeton, NJ: Princeton University Press, 1980.

–. "The Philosophical Tree." In *Alchemical Studies*, § 384. Vol. 13. Princeton, NJ: Princeton University Press, 1983.

–. "The Problems of Psychotherapy." In *The Practice of Psychotherapy*, §§ 114–74. 2nd ed. Vol. 16. Princeton, NJ: Princeton University Press, 1985.

–. "The Psychological Foundation of Belief in Spirits." In *The Structure and Dynamics of the Psyche*, §§ 570–600. 2nd ed. Vol. 8. Princeton, NJ: Princeton University Press, 1981.

–. "The Psychology of Dementia Praecox." In *The Psychogenesis of Mental Disease*, §§ 1–316. Vol. 3. Princeton, NJ: Princeton University Press, 1960.

–. "The Psychology of Eastern Meditation." In *Psychology and Religion: West and East*, § 935. 2nd ed. Vol. 11. Princeton, NJ: Princeton University Press, 1989.

–. "The Relations between the Ego and the Unconscious." In *Two Essays on Analytical Psychology*, §§ 202–406. Vol. 7. Princeton, NJ: Princeton University Press, 1967.

–. "The Soul and Death." In *The Structure and Dynamics of the Psyche*, § 800. 2nd ed. Vol. 8. Princeton, NJ: Princeton University Press, 1981.

–. "The Spirit Mercurius." In *Alchemical Studies*, §§ 239–303. Vol. 13. Princeton, NJ: Princeton University Press, 1983.

–. "The Stages of Life." In *The Structure and Dynamics of the Psyche*, § 772 f. 2nd ed. Vol. 8. Princeton, NJ: Princeton University Press, 1981.

–. "The Transcendent Function." In *The Structure and Dynamics of the Psyche*, §§ 131 ff. 2nd ed. Vol. 8. Princeton, NJ: Princeton University Press, 1981.

–. "The Undiscovered Self." In *Civilization and Transition*, §§ 488–588. 2nd ed. Vol. 10. Princeton, NJ: Princeton University Press, 1970.

–. "The Visions of Zosimos." In *Alchemical Studies*. Vol. 13. Princeton, NJ: Princeton University Press, 1983.

–. "Transformation Symbolism in the Mass." In *Psychology and Religion: West and East*, §§ 296–448. 2n ed. Vol. 11. Princeton, NJ: Princeton University Press, 1989.

–. "Ulysses: A Monologue." In *The Spirit in Man, Art, and Literature*, §§ 163 ff. Vol. 15. Princeton, NJ: Princeton University Press, 1967.

–. *Aion: Researches into the Phenomenology of the Self*. 2nd. ed. Vol. 9/II. Princeton, NJ: Princeton University Press, 1978.

–. *Archetypes of the Collective Unconscious*. 2nd ed. Vol. 9/I. Princeton, NJ: Princeton University Press, 1980.

–. *Mysterium Coniunctionis: An Inquiry into the Separation and Synthesis of Psychic Opposites in Alchemy*. 2nd ed. Vol. 14. Princeton, NJ: Princeton University Press, 1989.

–. *Psychological Types*. Vol. 6. Princeton, NJ: Princeton University Press, 1990.

–. *Psychology and Alchemy*. 2nd ed. Vol. 12. Princeton, NJ: Princeton University Press, 1968.

–. *Psychology and Religion: West and East*. 2n ed. Vol. 11. Princeton, NJ: Princeton University Press, 1989.

–. *The Development of Personality*. Vol. 17. Princeton, NJ: Princeton University Press, 1955.

–. *The Symbolic Life: Miscellaneous Writings*. Vol. 18. Princeton, NJ: Princeton University Press, 1977.

Jung, C.G. *Children's Dreams: Notes from the Seminar Given in 1936-1940*, edited by Lorenz Jung und Maria Meyer-Grass. Princeton, NJ: Princeton University Press, 2010.

–. "Ein Brief zur Frage der Synchronizität." *Zeitschrift für Parapsychologie und Grenzgebiete der Psychologie* 5, no. 1 (1961).

–. *Exercitia Spiritualia of Ignatius Loyola.* Lectures given at the Federal Institute of Technology (ETH) in Zurich (Winter 1940/41, privately printed).

–. *Letters.* Vol. 2. Selected and edited by Gerhard Adler. Princeton, NJ: Princeton University Press, 1973–1975.

–. *Man and His Symbols.* New York: Doubleday, 1968.

–. *Memories, Dreams, Reflections.* Recorded and edited by Aniela Jaffé. Translated by Richard Winston and Clara Winston. London: Fontana Paperbacks, 1983.

   –. *Nietzsche's Zarathustra: Notes of the Seminar given in 1934–1939,* edited by James L. Jarret. Vol. 1 and 2. Princeton, NJ: Princeton University Press, 1988.

   –. *Seminar in Polzeath.* Cornwall, 1923 (unpublished notes taken by Dr. Esther Harding).

–. *The Red Book,* edited and with an Introduction by Sonu Shamdasani. New York: W. W. Norton & Company, 2012.

–, and W. Pauli. *The Interpretation of Nature and the Psyche.* New York: Pantheon Books, 1955.

Jung, Emma. *Animus and Anima.* Translated by Cary F. Baynes and Hildegard Bagel. Zurich: Spring Publications, 1974.

, and Marie-Louise von Franz. *The Grail Legend.* Translated by Andrea Dykes. Princeton, NJ: Princeton University Press, 1998.

Kaune, Jürgen. *Selbstverwirklichung: Eine Konfrontation der Psychologie C.G. Jungs mit der Ethik.* Munich: Reinhardt, 1967.

King, L. C. "Archetypische Symbolik und Synchronizitäten im aktuellen Weltgeschehen." *Verborgene Welt* (1965/66).

Klopfer, Bruno. "Jungian Analysis and Professional Psychology." *The Reality of the Psyche.* Edited by J. Wheelwright. New York: Putnam, 1968.

–, and Marvin Spiegelmann. "Some Dimensions of Psychotherapy." *Spectrum Psychologiae.* Festschrift für C. A. Meier. Zurich: Rascher, 1965.

-, et al. *Developments in the Rorschach Technique.* 2 vols. New York: Harcourt, 1954.

Schärf Kluger, Rivkah. *Satan in the Old Testament.* Translated by Hildegard Nagel. Evaston, IL: Northwestern University Press, 1967.

-. *The Archetypal Significance of Gilgamesh: A Modern Ancient Hero.* Edited by H. Yehezkel Kluger. Einsiedeln: Daimon Verlag, 1991.

Knorr von Rosenroth. *Kabbala Denudata.* 2 vols. Frankfurt a. M.: Sulzbach, Lichtentaler und Zunner, 1677.

Köberle, Adolf. "Das Evangelium und das Geheimnis der Seele." *Zeitschrift für systematische Theologie* 21 (1950): 419.

Kraft-Ebing, R. von. *Lehrbuch der Psychiatrie: Auf Klinischer Grundlage für praktische Ärzte und Studierende.* 6th ed. Stuttgart: Verlag von Ferdinand Enke, 1897.

Kreitler, Shulamith. "Symbolschöpfung und Symbolerfahrung: Eine experimentalpsychologische Untersuchung." PhD diss., University of Bern. Munich: Reinhardt, 1965.

Kretschmer, Ernst. *Physique and Character: An Investigation of the Nature of Constitution and of the Theory of Temperament.* 2nd ed. London: Routledge, 2001.

Kretschmer, Wolfgang. "Die meditativen Methoden in der Psychotherapie." *Zeitschrift für Psychotherapie und Medizinische Psychologie* 1, no. 3 (May 1951).

Laiblin, Wilhelm, ed. *Märchenforschung und Tiefenpsychologie.* 5 th ed. Darmstadt: Primus, 1997.

Lauterborn, Eleonore. *Swami Omkarananda und C.G. Jung: Der psychologische Schatten und das überpsychologische Selbst.* Zurich: ABC-Verlag, 1970.

Leisegang, Hans. *Die Gnosis.* 4th ed. Stuttgart: Kröner, 1955.

Lindsay, Jack. *The Origins of Alchemy in Graeco-Roman Egypt.* London: Muller, 1970.

Lorenz, Konrad. "The Role of Gestalt Perception in Animal and Human Behaviour." In *Aspects of Form,* edited by L. L. Whyte. Bloomington: Indiana University Press, 1951.

-. *On Aggression.* Translated by Marjorie Kerr Wilson. Foreword by Julian Huxley. London: Routledge, 2002.

–. and P. Leyhausen. *Antriebe tierischen und menschlichen Verhaltens.* 4rd ed. Munich: Piper, 1973.

Lindsay, Jack. *The Origins of Alchemy in Graeco-Roman Egypt.* London: Muller, 1970.

Lu, K'uan Yü. *Taoist Yoga: Alchemy and Immortality.* London: Rider, 1970.

–. "The Story of Ch'an Master Han Shan." *World Buddhism* 11, no. 7. Translated by Lu K'uan Yü (February 1963).

–. *The Secrets of Chinese Meditation: Self-cultivation by Mind Control as Taught in the Chan, Mahayana and Taoist Schools in China.* York Beach, ME: Samuel Weiser, 1999.

–. *Practical Buddhism: The Application of Ch'an Teaching to Daily Life.* London: Rider, 1988.

Lüers, Grete. *Die Sprache der deutschen Mystik des Mittelalters im Werke der Mechthild von Magdeburg.* Munich: Reinhardt, 1926.

Mahnke, Dietrich. *Unendliche Sphäre und Allmittelpunkt.* Stuttgart: Frommann, 1966.

Malinine, Michel, Henri-Charles Puech, and Gilles Quispel, eds. *De resurrectione (Epistula ad Rheginum): Codex Jung,* 43–50. Zurich: Rascher, 1963.

–. *Evangelium veritatis: Codex Jung.* Zurich: Rascher, 1956–61.

Mann, Ulrich. "Quaternität bei C.G. Jung." *Theologisch-lutherische Zeitschrift* 92. 1967.

. "Hermeneutische Entsagung." *Seelsorge als Lebenshilfe.* Festschrift für W. Uhsadel. Heidelberg, 1965.

. "Symbole und tiefenpsychologische Gestaltungsfaktoren der Religion." *Grenzfragen des Glaubens.* Einsiedeln, 1967.

. "Tiefenpsychologie und Theologie." *Lutherische Monatshefte* 4. 1965.

. *Theogonische Tage: Die Entwicklung des Gottesbewusstseins in der altorientalischen und biblischen Religion.* Stuttgart: Klett, 1970.

Mao Tse-tung. *Worte des Vorsitzenden Mao Tse-tung.* Essen: Verlag Neuer Weg, 1993.

Marti, Hans. *Urbild und Verfassung: Eine Studie zum hintergründigen Gehalt einer Verfassung.* Bern: Huber, 1958.

Maupoil, Bernhard. *La Géomancie à l'Ancienne Côte des Esclaves*. Paris: Institut Ethnologique, 1943.

McCormick, Fowler. *Carl Gustav Jung: A Memorial Meeting*. New York: Analytical Psychology Club of New York, 1961.

Meier, C. A. *The Unconscious in its Empirical Manifestations: With Special Reference to the Association Experiment of C.G. Jung*. Boston, MA: Sigo Press, 1985.

–. *Ancient Incubation and Modern Psychotherapy*. Translated by Monica Curtis. Evanston, Ill.: Northwestern University Press, 1967.

Moltmann, Jürgen. *Theory of Hope: On the Ground and the Implications of a Christian Eschatology*. London: SCM classics, 1967.

Neihardt, John G. *Black Elk Speaks: Being the Life Story of a Holy Man of the Oglala Sioux*. Albany, NY: Excelsior Editions, State University of New York Press, 2008.

Neumann, Erich. *Depth Psychology and a New Ethic*. Translated by Eugene Rolfe. Preface by C.G. Jung, Gerhard Adler and James Yandell. Boston, MA: Shambhala, 1990.

–. "Die Psyche und die Wandlung der Wirklichkeitsebenen." *Mensch und Energie*, 169–216. Eranos Jahrbuch 1952, vol. 21. Zurich: Rhein-Verlag, 1953.

–. *Amor and Psyche: The psychic development of the feminine*. Princeton, NJ: Princeton University Press, 1973.

–. *Art and the Creative Unconscious. Four Essays*. Translated by Ralph Manheim. London: Routledge, 1959.

–. *Origins and History of Consciousness*. Abingdon, OX: Routledge, 2015.

–. *The Archetypal World of Henry Moore*. New York: Pantheon Books, 1959.

–. *The Child: Structure and Dynamics of the Nascent Personality*. London: Taylor and Francis, 2018.

–. *The Great Mother*. Princeton, NJ: Princeton University Press, 2015.

Nioradze, Georg. *Der Schamanismus bei den sibirischen Völkern*. Stuttgart: Schröder-Strecker, 1925.

Pauli, Wolfgang. "The Influence of Archetypal Ideas on the Scientific Theories of Kepler." In C.G. Jung und W. Pauli, *The Interpretation of Nature and the Psyche*. New York: Pantheon Books, 1955.

–. "Naturwissenschaftliche und erkenntnistheoretische Aspekte der Idee vom Unbewussten." In *Aufsätze und Vorträge über Physik und Erkenntnistheorie*, 113–28. Braunschweig: Vieweg, 1961.

Pelz, Donald C., and Frank M. Andrews. "Autonomy, Coordination and Stimulation in Relation to Scientific Achievement." *Behavioral Science* 11, no. 2. (March 1966): 89–97.

Perry, John Weir. *Self in the Psychotic Process: Its Symbolization in Schizophrenia*. 2nd ed. Foreword by C.G. Jung. Dallas, TX: Spring Publications, 1987.

Philp, Howard Littleton *Jung and the Problem of Evil*. London: Rockliff, 1958.

Plutarch. "Über den Schutzgeist des Sokrates." In *Über Gott und Vorsehung, Dämonen und Weissagung*. Zurich: Artemis, 1952.

Porkert, Manfred. „Wissenschaftliches Denken im alten China." *Antaios* 2, no. 6 (1961).

Priestley, John Boynton. *Man and Time*. London: Bloomsbury Books, 1989.

Quispel, Gilles. *Gnosis als Weltreligion: Die Bedeutung der Gnosis in der Antike*. 3rd ed. Bern: Origo Verlag, 1955.

Rahner, Hugo. *Greek Myths and Christian Mystery*. New York: Biblo and Tannen, 1971.

Read, Sir Herbert. *C.G. Jung zum 85. Geburtstag*. Rede vom 26. Juli 1960. Zurich: Rascher, 1960.

Remplein, Heinz. *Psychologie der Persönlichkeit: Die Lehre von der individuellen und typischen Eigenart des Menschen*. Munich: Reinhardt, 1975.

Riklin, Franz. "C.G. Jung – ein Porträt." In *Was weiss man von der Seele?* Stuttgart: Kreuz Verlag, 1969.

Röösli, J. "Der Gottes- und Religionsbegriff bei C.G. Jung." *Schweizerische Kirchenzeitung* 112 (1944): 302–304.

Rudin, Joseph, SJ. *Psychotherapie und Religion: Seele, Person, Gott*. Olten: Walter, 1964.

. "C.G. Jung und die Religion." In *Psychotherapie und religiöse Erfahrung: Ein Tagungsbericht*, edited by Wilhelm Bitter, 73–86. Stuttgart: Klett, 1965.

. *Neurose und Religion*. Olten: Walter, 1964.

Rump, Ariane. "Die Verwundung des Hellen als Aspekt des Bösen im I-Ging." PhD diss., University of Zurich, 1967.

Sanford, John A. *Dreams: God's Forgotten Language*. San Francisco: Harper & Row, 1989.

Schär, Hans. *Seelsorge und Psychotherapie*. Zurich: Rascher, 1961.

–. *Religion and the Cure of Couls in Jung's Psychology*. Translated by R. F. C. Hull. New York: Pantheon, 1950.

Schmaltz, Gustav. *Komplexe Psychologie und körperliches Symptom*. Stuttgart: Hippokrates, 1955.

. "Das Machen der Wahrheit im eigenen Herzen." In *Östliche Weisheit und westliche Psychotherapie*, edited by W. Bitter. Stuttgart: Klett, 1951.

Schmidbauer, Wolfgang. *Mythos und Psychologie*. Munich: Reinhardt, 1970.

Scholem, Gershom. *On the Kabbalah and Its Symbolism*. Translated by Ralph Manheim. London: Routledge and Kegan Paul, 1965.

Schwartz, Nathan. "Entropy, Negentropy and the Psyche." Unpublished Phd diss., C.G. Jung-Institut. Zurich, 1969.

Seidmann, Peter. *Der Weg der Tiefenpsychologie in geistesgeschichtlicher Perspektive*. Zurich: Rascher, 1959.

Seltmann, Charles. *The Twelve Olympians and their Guests*. London: Pan Books, 1952.

Serrano, Miguel. *C.G. Jung and Hermann Hesse: A Record of two Friendships*. Einsiedeln: Daimon Verlag, 1997.

Shan, Han. "The Story of Ch'an Master Han Shan." *World Buddhism* 11, no. 7 (February 1963).

Schipper, Kristofer Marinus. *L'empereur Wou des Han dans la légende Taoiste*. Paris: Adrien-Maisonneuve, 1965.

Silberer, Herbert. *Problems of Mysticism and Its Symbolism*. Whitefish: Kessinger Publishing, 2006.

Silveira, Nise da. *Jung, Vida e obra*. Rio de Janeiro: Alvaro, 1968.

. "Sir Herbert Read, in Memoria." *Quaternio.* Rivista da Grupo de Estudo C.G. Jung. Rio de Janeiro, 1970 (privately printed).

. "Expérience d'art spontané chez des Schizophrènes dans un Service thérapeutique occupationel." Unpublished Phd diss. C.G. Jung-Institute, Zurich, 1957.

Solié, Pierre. "Psychologie analytique et Imagerie Mentale." *Action et Pensée* 44, no. 1 and 2, edited by Ch. Baudouin (March–June, 1968).

Snorri Sturluson. *The Prose Edda: Tales from Norse Mythology.* Translated by Arthur Gilchrist Brodeur. Mineola, NY: Dover Publications, 2006.

Speck, Frank. *Naskapi: The Lonely Hunter of the Labrador-Peninsula.* Norman: University of Oklahoma Press, 1935 (New editions 1963, 1977).

Spiegel, Der, cf. Brügge.

Squire, Charles. *Celtic Myths and Legends, Poetry & Romance.* London: Gresham, [191-].

Suzuki, D. T. *Introduction to Zen Buddhism.* Kyoto: The Eastern Buddhist Society, 1934.

Tillich, Paul. *C.G. Jung: A Memorial Meeting,* edited by Club for Analytical Psychology. New York, 1961 (privately printed).

Toynbee, Arnold J. "Rise and Fall of Cultures." In *A Study of History,* 1–50. Vol. 1. New York: Oxford University Press, 1987.

Trinick, John. *The Fire-tried Stone.* London: Vincent Stuart and Watkins, 1967.

Trüb, Hans. *Heilung aus der Begegnung: Überlegung zu einer dialogischen Psychotherapie,* edited by Milan Sreckovic. Bergisch Gladbach: EHP – Verlag Andreas Kohlhage, 2015.

Tucker, Robert. *Philosophy and Myth in Karl Marx.* Cambridge: Cambridge University Press, 1961.

Ueberweg, Friedrich. *Grundriss der Geschichte der Philosophie.* Basel: Schwabe, 1983.

Uhsadel, Walter. *Der Mensch und die Mächte des Unbewussten: Studie zur Begegnung von Psychotherapie und Seelsorge.* Kassel: Stauda, 1952.

. "Tiefenpsychologie als Hilfswissenschaft der praktischen Theologie." *Wege zum Menschen* 21, no. 4 (1969).

Urban, Peter. "Philosophische und empirische Aspekte der Synchronizitätstheorie." *Grenzgebiete der Wissenschaft* 17, no. 4 (1968).

Uslar, Detlev von. *Der Traum als Welt: Untersuchungen zur Ontologie und Phänomenologie des Traums.* Pfullingen: Neske, 1964.

Van der Post, Laurens. "C.G. Jung." *Bulletin of Analytical Club of New York* 33, no. 3. New York, 1971.

Vasavada, Arvind V. "The Place of Psychology in Philosophy." *Indian Philosophical Congress* 38, (1964).

Vlaikovič, Stefan. "Biologie des Träumens in tiefenpsychologischer Sicht." Unpublished PhD diss., C.G. Jung-Institut. Zurich, 1971.

Vries, Jan de. *Forschungsgeschichte der Mythologie.* Freiburg i. Br.: Verlag Karl Alber, 1961.

Walder, Peter. *Mensch und Welt bei C.G. Jung.* Zurich: Origo-Verlag, 1951.

Waley, Arthur. "Notes on Chinese Alchemy." *Bulletin of Oriental School of London* 6 (1930): 1–24.

Ware, James R., trans. *Alchemy, Medicine and Religion in the China of A. D. 320: The Nei P'ien of Ko Hung (Pao-p'u-tzu).* Cambridge, MA: MIT Press, 1966.

Wehr, Gerhard. *An Illustrated Biography of C.G. Jung.* Boston, MA: Shambhala, 1989.

Wei Po-Yang, cf. Lu-Ch'iang Wu, cf. Waley.

Weiss, Victor. *Die Gnosis Jakob Böhmes.* Zurich: Origo-Verlag, 1955.

Werblowsky, Zwi. *Lucifer and Prometheus: A Study of Miltons Satan.* London: Routledge, 1952.

Weston, Jessie. "The Esplumoir Merlin: A Study in Its Cabalistic Sources." *Speculum* 21, no. 2 (April 1946): 173–93.

White, Victor, OP. *Gott und das Unbewusste.* Zurich: Rascher, 1957.

–. *Seele und Psyche.* Salzburg: Müller, 1964.

Whitrow, Gerhard James. *The Natural Philosophy of Time.* London: Nelson, 1961.

Whyte, Lancelot Law. *The Unconscious before Freud*. London: J. Friedmann, 1979.

Wickes, Frances Gillespy. *The Inner World of Childhood*. New York: Appleton-Century, 1927.

–. *The Creative Process*. New York: Spring Publications, 1948.

–. *The Inner World of Choice*. New York: Harper & Row, 1963.

–. *The Inner World of Man: With Psychological Drawings and Paintings*. London: Methuen, 1950.

Wilhelm, Helmut. "The Concept of Time in the Book of Changes." *Eranos Yearbooks* 3. Princeton, NJ: Princeton University Press, 2015.

Wilhelm, Richard, trans. *I Ching: The Book of Changes*. Translated from Chinese into German by Richard Wilhelm, rendered into English by C. Baynes. Princeton, NJ: Princeton University Press, 1955.

, and C.G. Jung. *The Secret of the Golden Flower*. Abingdon: Routledge, 2001.

Williams, Charles Allyn. *Oriental Affinities of the Legends of the Hairy Anchorite*. Vol. 2. University Urbana, OH: University of Illinios Press, 1925.

Wittcut, William Purcell. *Catholic Thought and Modern Psychology*. London: Burns Oates and Washbourne, 1943.

Wolf, Karl Lothar. "Symmetrie und Polarität." *Studium Generale* 2, no. 4–5 (1949): 213–24.

Wolff, Toni Anna. *Studies in Jungian Psychology*. Translated by Eugene M. E. Rolfe. New York, in press?

Wu, Lu-Chiang, Tenney L. Davis and Wei Po-Yang. „An Ancient Chinese Treatise on Alchemy Entitled Ts'an T'ung Ch'i." *Isis* 18, no. 2 (October 1932): 210–89.

Wünsche, August. *Schöpfung und Sündenfall des ersten Menschenpaares. im jüdischen und moslemischen Sagenkreise, mit Rücksicht auf die Überlieferungen in der Keilschrift-Literatur*. Ex Oriente Lux 2, no. 4. Leipzig: Pfeiffer, 1906.

Wymann, Leland C. "Origin Legends of Navaho Divinatory Rites." *The Journal of American Folklore* 49, no. 191/192 (Jan.–Jun. 1936): 134–42.

Yates, Frances. *Giordano Bruno and the Hermetic Tradition*. London: Routledge, 2002.

Zacharias, Gerhard P. *Psyche und Mysterium: Die Bedeutung der Psychologie C.G. Jungs für die christliche Theologie und Liturgie*. Zurich: Rascher, 1954.

Zetzner, Lazarus, ed. "Dialogus Mercurii Alchemistae et Naturae." In *Theatrum Chemicum*, 448–56. Vol. 4. Strasbourg: 1659–60.

Zimmer, Heinrich. "Merlin: Knowledge and Power through the Ages." *Corona* 9, no. 2 (1939): 133–55.

Zimmermann, Rolf Christian. *Das Weltbild des jungen Goethe: Studien zur hermetischen Tradition des deutschen 18. Jahrhunderts*. Munich: Finke, 1969.

Zumthor, Paul. *Merlin le Prophète: Un thème de la littérature polémique de l'historiographie et des romans*. Genève: Slatkine, 2000.

Index

M

S

www.ingramcontent.com/pod-product-compliance
Lightning Source LLC
Chambersburg PA
CBHW021125270326
41929CB00009B/1053